universalism vs.
communitarianism

universalism vs. communitarianism

contemporary debates in ethics

edited by david rasmussen

The MIT Press
Cambridge, Massachusetts
London, England

First MIT Press edition, 1990

This work originally appeared as volume 14, numbers 3/4, of the journal *Philosophy and Social Criticism*. The essays by Chantal Mouffe and by Stuart and Hubert Dreyfus have been added for this edition.

©1990 *Philosophy and Social Criticism*

Printed and bound in the United States of America.

Library of Congress Cataloging-in-Publication Data

Universalism vs. communitarianism : contemporary debates in ethics / edited by David Rasmussen. — 1st MIT Press ed.
    p.   cm.
  "Originally published as volume 14, numbers 3/4, of the journal Philosophy and social criticism. The essays by Chantal Mouffe and by Stuart and Hubert Dreyfus have been added for this edition"—T.p. verso.
  ISBN 0-262-18140-1. — ISBN 0-262-68063-7 (pbk.)
  1. Ethics. 2. Social ethics. 3. Ethics, Modern—20th century. I. Rasmussen, David M.
  BJ1012.U52 1990
  170—dc20   90-32967
                                                 CIP

table of contents

DAVID M. RASMUSSEN
universalism v. communitarianism:
an introduction   1

I. UNIVERSALISM VS. COMMUNITARIANISM

ALESSANDRO FERRARA
universalisms: procedural, contextualist
and prudential   11

GERALD DOPPELT
beyond liberalism and communitarianism:
towards a critical theory of social justice   39

KENNETH BAYNES
the liberal/communitarian controversy
and communicative ethics   61

JEAN COHEN
discourse ethics and civil society   83

II. ETHICS IN HISTORICAL PERSPECTIVE

ROLF ZIMMERMANN
equality, political order and ethics:
hobbes and the systematics of
democratic rationality   109

AXEL HONNETH
atomism and ethical life: on hegel's
critique of the french revolution   129

MICHAEL KELLY
the gadamer-habermas debate revisited:
the question of ethics   139

III. PRACTICAL REASON AND ETHICAL RESPONSIBILITY

AGNES HELLER
what is and what is not practical reason?   163

HAUKE BRUNKHORST
adorno, heidegger and postmodernity   183

IV. JUSTIFICATION, APPLICATION AND HISTORY

KLAUS GÜNTHER
impartial application of moral and legal
norms: a contribution to discourse ethics   199

JÜRGEN HABERMAS
an interview on ethics, politics and history
by jean-marc ferry   207

V. COMMUNITARIAN ALTERNATIVES

CHANTAL MOUFFE
rawls: political philosophy without politics   217

HUBERT L. DREYFUS
STUART E. DREYFUS
what is morality? a phenomenological account
of the development of ethical expertise   **237**

VI. BIBLIOGRAPHY

MICHAEL ZILLES
universalism and communitarianism:
a bibliography   **267**

david m. rasmussen
universalism v. communitarianism: an introduction

Ethics is once again at the center of current philosophical discussion. Ethico-moral perspectives abound in a post-positivistic world where reflection continues unabated by images of the end of philosophy. The re-evaluation of the ethical dimension, or lack thereof, in Heidegger's philosophy, the recent ethical turn of post-modernism led by Derrida's discovery of the moral dimension of *différance*, the reconstruction of arguments for moral universalism, Rorty's discovery of his own pragmatic ethical commitment, the relatively new development of ethics under the umbrella term, communitarianism, Rawls's re-evaluation of the place of origins in his theory of justice, the emergence of the feminist critique of philosophy, new developments in analytic ethics—all these movements point to the moral or ethical transformation of philosophy. Not only in philosophy in particular, but also in the public sphere in general, ethical issues dominate. Whether the issue is ethics in government, the role of the courts as adjudicators of contemporary morality, new considerations of law and morality, the abortion question, medicine and morality, one has the feeling that the *Zeitgeist* bears the mark of ethics.

I.

The debate between the relative merits of communitarianism vs. universalism, in our judgment the two principal orientations in contemporary ethics, dominates this volume. The first section, **Universalism vs. Communitarianism**, introduces the debate. Alessandro Ferrara's essay, *"Universalisms: Procedural, Contextualist and Prudential,"* begins with an argument which locates universalism not as the exclusive property of a single group but as underlying modern ethical debates per se. Hence, he contrasts the "procedural universalism" in Habermas with the "communitarian universalism" of Walzer and MacIntyre. Although he argues that the great advantage of Habermas is the distinction between structure and content, the distinction is not without its difficulties, particularly, argues Ferrara, with regard to pluralism and the question of competing conceptual schemes. While communitarians are willing to face this issue without recourse to *a priori* standards, Ferrara claims that they are unable to deal with the derivation of ethical norms from a bad society. In the end, Ferrara attempts to go beyond both procedural and communitarian universalism by opting for a third, "prudential" universalism.

Gerald Doppelt, in his essay *"Beyond Liberalism and Communitarianism: Towards a Critical Theory of Social Justice,"* joins Ferrara in attempting to move beyond the debate between communitarianism and liberalism. He locates his argument in the context of Sandel's critique of Rawls, arguing that Sandel misses the Kantian motivation for the difference principle, i.e., the liberal democratic argument from human dignity. Because, in Doppelt's view, Rawls backs out of the philosophical argumentation, opting to accept aspects of the communitarian critique, he is unable to "found an adequate theory of justice for our time and place." In a telling argument, Doppelt suggests that Rawls gives the state the right to restore inequality among persons. In other words, Rawls legitimates capitalist economic practice. Doppelt concludes by arguing that in order to establish a critical theory of social justice, it is necessary to deal with the rival theories at the heart of modern political society.

Kenneth Baynes, in *"The Liberal/Communitarian Controversy and Communicative Ethics,"* takes Doppelt's argument a step further, transforming the problem into one of justification. Baynes argues that while liberals have not considered sufficiently the source and justification of individual rights, communitarians have not addressed the nature and condition of a citizen's autonomy. In his judgment there are three issues to be considered in this debate, particularly from the perspective of the kind of critiques made of liberalism by communitarians, namely, the priority of right over good, conceptions of the self as moral agency, and justification of political ideals and institutions. Baynes reformulates these issues through a constructive appeal to Habermas's communicative ethics. The critical argument, using

Rawls's liberalism as a basis, shifts to the question of justification. Following Habermas on the first issue, Baynes wants to separate questions of justice from those of the good life. Second, Baynes argues that the self is not atomist, as communitarians suggest, but comes from post-conventional moral reasoning. Finally, he suggests that the justification of rights fundamental to the liberal position depends upon having dealt with prior questions of justification.

Jean Cohen, in *"Discourse Ethics and Civil Society,"* advances the discussion a step further by turning from a theoretical argument regarding the foundations of moral theory to a practical argument regarding potential democratization beyond the liberal democratic model. Her essay addresses the current controversy in political theory over whether liberalism is antithetical to democracy. Cohen wants to articulate a view of democratic civil society through the presentation of a discourse ethics that will create a new orientation to both democratic legitimacy and basic rights within civil society. In essence she sees in discourse ethics, with its orientation toward communication, a basic potential for democratization beyond the liberal democratic understanding of political society.

Taken as a group, the four essays just cited constitute an introduction to the issues in the debate between universalism and communitarianism in ethics with, to be sure, a particular orientation toward the universalist critique of communitarianism. Whether or not one finds solace in the prudential option offered by Ferrara, in the moves beyond the limitations of communitarian liberalism in Doppelt or Baynes, or in the applied universalism of Cohen, the essays taken as a whole lead to a certain practical universalism which seems to be the direction in which the more recent form of universalism in ethics is moving.

II.

In the second section, **Ethics in Historical Perspective**, three essays address the universalist-communitarian debate from the perspectives of Hobbesian political philosophy, Hegelian ethical philosophy, and the Gadamer-Habermas debate of the 60s and early 70s. Rolf Zimmermann, in *"Equality, Political Order and Ethics: Hobbes and the Systematics of Democratic Rationality,"* argues that Hobbes's political theory requires a concept of equality different from natural equality. In other words, Hobbes's theory assumes that even if humans were by nature unequal, it would be in their interest to assume equality. Zimmermann labels this notion "voluntative equality," which can be taken as both an empirically existing attitude and a normative requirement existing at a theoretical level. Zimmermann argues that such a discursive notion is necessary in order for Hobbes's argument to work, even though this notion is only implicit in Hobbes's theory. Accordingly, the notion of "sovereignty" given so much credence in Hobbesian interpretation is essentially a procedure for conflict resolution. Zimmermann concludes that voluntative equality can be thought of either on the basis of a Kantian model or as historically situated; he chooses the second possibility. In so doing, he juxtaposes his discursive interpretation against the more idealized (Kantian) view of Habermas and Apel.

In his essay *"Atomism and Ethical Life: On Hegel's Critique of the French Revolution,"* Axel Honneth provides an illuminating interpretation of Hegel's attempt to derive from the major political event of his life, the French Revolution, a principle which could be integrated into the ethical life of the community. For Hegel, the French Revolution represented the principle of abstract freedom which was said to be won through political struggle. The negative consequence of this freedom, however, was the potential for atomization it unleashed. Hence, Hegel became concerned with how abstract freedom achieved through revolution could become a positive political force which would make a fundamental contribution to the life of the ethical community. In the end, the "early" Hegel "wishes to instruct the revolution as to the political path that needs to be taken if the process of social atomization, which has already factually commenced, is to be transformed in a new form of ethical unity." Eventually, Hegel opted for a "substantialist" model of ethical life which, in Honneth's view, led to the subordination of the individual will to the authority of the state. The attempt of the early Hegel to make a concrete event, the French Revolution, into a communitarian principle is instructive for the contemporary debate which is at issue in this volume.

Michael Kelly, in an essay on a problematic of more recent vintage, *"The Gadamer-Habermas Debate Revisited: The Question of Ethics,"* reconstructs the earlier debate between Gadamer and Habermas as if it were conducted on the issue of ethics. Accordingly, Gadamer's more communitarian neo-Aristotelian approach, which emphasizes categories like "solidarity," the orientation toward "die Sache" and phenomenological "doubt," is confronted with Habermas's "critical," "procedural," universalist approach, which concentrates upon finding a procedure for justification. Kelly's thesis is that Habermas can only sustain the "possibility" of universality and hence must turn to a form of historical argumentation more like that of Gadamer. Kelly acknowledges that critics would call such a turn relativistic. He concludes by arguing that Gadamer's principal ethical notions are universal and could, as a consequence, be appropriated by Habermas's attempt at rational reconstruction.

III.

In the section **Practical Reason and Ethical Responsibility**, the two essays begin respectively with considerations of the debate regarding Heidegger and political philosophy. That point of departure is significant inasmuch as it provides a kind of test of the respective theses of communitarian and universalist positions. To what extent do the contextualist elements in Heidegger's philosophy support the universalist claim that, without a critical (transcendental) perspective, ethical reflection in a bad society will bear the traits of that society? In an essay entitled *"What Is and What Is Not Practical Reason?,"* Agnes Heller uses the Heidegger discussion to raise a fundamental moral question: "The new upsurge of the Heidegger-debate re-opened the question of whether certain philosophies or philosophers can be held morally or politically accountable for the gravest collective crimes of modern history." In order to answer that question, Heller seeks to distinguish between the practical and the theoretical role of the philosopher. Beginning with the Heidegger discussion, she develops a distinction between the philosopher per se and the philosopher as practical, committed and engaged moral agent.

Hauke Brunkhorst, in *"Adorno, Heidegger and Postmodernity,"* uses the Heidegger debate in a slightly different manner to juxtapose Adorno's postmodernism to that of Heidegger and others, including Rorty. In contrast to Heidegger, Brunkhorst finds Adorno's postmodernity to be more informed by Enlightenment categories. Fascinated by Adorno's suggestion that "ratio" must "transcend" the self-preserving tendency of instrumental thought, Brunkhorst interprets Adorno as moving in a somewhat univer-salist direction. According to this interpretation, although Adorno would agree with Heidegger's critique of "identifying thought," he would find in the category of "rational identity" to be much more positive than did Heidegger. Brunkhorst suggests that rational identity for Adorno is "consciousness of the non-identical," which includes "anamnestic solidarity with those who have suffered." Hence, in contrast to Heidegger, Adorno's critique of instrumentality has a strong ethical component.

IV.

In the section, **Justification, Application and History**, we are given a brief summary of the most recent contribution to discourse ethics and an application of the concept of universalization to current debates on the nature of historical interpretation. Klaus Günther, in *"Impartial Application of Moral and Legal Norms: A*

5

Contribution to Discourse Ethics," argues that it is necessary to make a distinction between universalization which is said to provide a critique of existing life forms. Against the objection that universalization is insensitive to particular life situations, Günther develops a theory of application which draws on the appropriateness of argumentation. This argumentation is based on all normative viewpoints in order to sustain the universalization of a validity claim. As such, Günther's argument counters the one advanced by neo-Aristotelians and communitarians which claims that universalism loses its force when confronted with problems of application.

In an interview with Jürgen Habermas conducted by Jean-Marc Ferry, entitled *"Ethics, Politics and History"* Habermas constructs a practical argument for moral universalism in historical perspective against a political theory of national identity. The interview addresses the link between universalism and contemporary history and thus constitutes an extension of Habermas's ethical theory. Speaking in terms of post-conventional identity in the context of a discussion of German history, Habermas defines moral universalism. "What then does universalism mean? Relativizing one's own form of existence to the legitimate claims of other forms of life, according equal rights to aliens and others with all their idiosyncrasies and unintelligibility, not sticking doggedly to the universalization of one's own identity, not marginalizing that which deviates from one's own identity, allowing the sphere of tolerance to become ceaselessly larger than it is today—all this is what moral universalism means today."

V.

In the final section, entitled **Communitarian Alternatives**, the essays turn to Rawls and Habermas from a perspective informed by the communitarian critique of liberalism and universalism. Chantal Mouffe, in an essay entitled *"Rawls: Political Philosophy Without Politics,"* argues that, "Once it is recognized that the existence of rights and a conception of justice cannot exist previously and independently of specific forms of political association which by definition imply a conception of the good-- it becomes obvious that there can never be a priority of right over good." In other words, if Rawls opts for a new more contextualist theory of right, as he has done in the later post-**Theory of Justice** writings, he cannot sustain the priority of right over good implicit in the earlier work. Mouffe argues that what is lacking in Rawls is a notion of the political which includes conflict, power, interaction, and, one might add, pluralism. Mouffe's "foundationless" approach to justice, insofar as it it is communitarian and contextualist, is distinctly "modern" in contrast to the nostalgia of

Sandel and others for a "unified moral order." Following Walzer's **Spheres of Justice** she argues that there can never be a final agreement regarding the principles of justice. Instead, a theory of justice which includes the political would highlight the different discourses about justice characteristic of modern society.

In an essay addressed to Habermas rather than Rawls, Hubert and Stuart Dreyfus construct "*A Phenomenology of Ethical Expertise*" which questions the universalist tendency to ground moral discussion in "judgment" independent of "ethical comportment." Using a model based on the acquisition of skill, a phenomenology of skill acquisition, the Dreyfus brothers argue that an ethic based on the model of skill acquisition as opposed to cognitive deliberation conceives ethical comportment to be derived from an almost intuitive application of acquired abilities. On the basis of the construction of a five-stage model of skill acquisition, the essay attempts to draw the implications for ethical experience. The claim is that moral decision making is more a matter of pragmatic "know-how" than it is a matter of cognitive deliberation. As a contextualist or communitarian argument, the essay seeks to show that it is in the mastery of the cultural value sphere that ethical comportment is manifest rather than in advancing to a post-conventional level of cognitive deliberation as is the case with Habermas and Kohlberg. Using a phenomenological version of Carol Gilligan's critique of Kohlberg which locates the "different voice" in the context of concrete ethical behavior the essay seeks to show that a post-conventional level of moral judgment and acting would be one where a certain "authentic care" is manifested in the turn from the formal to the existential.

VI.

The bibliography, prepared by Michael Zilles, will provide a comprehensive guide to both the communitarian and the universalist side of the debate.

Boston College

7

I.
universalism v.
communitarianism

alessandro ferrara
universalisms: procedural, contextualist and prudential

More than likely, our century will go down in history as a skeptical one. Among the targets of its critical focus is the conception of rationality and validity associated with the Enlightenment. Among the tasks that it will leave for future accomplishment is the re-establishment of a credible form of universalism in philosophy and in social theory.

The new universalism will have to come to terms with one important aspect of the transformation undergone by philosophy during the last hundred years, namely, the discovery of the contextuality of knowledge and normativity. Such discovery can be described as the realization that the truth of propositions or the rightness of norms can be assessed only against the background of a shared conceptual scheme and, moreover, that there exists **an irreducible plurality** of conceptual schemes.[1] Among the forerunners of this idea is Dilthey with his critique of Hegel's philosophy of history. For Dilthey, it was the different historical epochs that provided the self-contained "contexts" within which alone one could speak of valid propositions and norms. A similar view, centered on the notion of culture, was formulated by Evans-Pritchard, Malinowski, and others in their anthropological studies. Within the phenomenological tradition, Husserl's notion of the "life-world" provided the means for similar reflections on the contextuality of knowledge and normativity. Within the philosophy

alessandro
ferrara

of language of analytic descent, an analogous role is played by Searle's notion of the "background" and within hermeneutics by Gadamer's idea of tradition. The most influential formulation of this insight, however, comes from Wittgenstein's later works. His picture of a multiplicity of **language games** which are structured as sets of rules, contain their own criteria for validity, and allow no transfer of validity across one another, is reproduced in countless disciplines under one terminology or other. Equivalents can be found in post-empiricist philosophy of science (Kuhn's paradigms), in Foucault's early works *(episteme)*, in Berger and Luckmann's notion of symbolic universes, in the socio-linguistic notion of a speech community, and in many other fields.

The awareness of the contextuality of truth and justice throws into question the idea of an Archimedean point on which claims valid in all places and times rest, no matter whether such idea makes reference to the rationality of an abstract subject (the Cartesian ego or the Kantian "I think") or to a collective subject (Spirit, the species) which unfolds its potentials within history. The new universalism, if there will be one, will have to dispense with **all** *a priori* standards of justice and truth, and will have to accept powerful limitations. Just as the proponents of early-modern universalism had to renounce the ontological anchoring of truth in the essence of things and the grounding of morality on ultimate ends dictated by human nature, so today a universalistic solution to the "objectivism versus relativism" deadlock[2] will have to dispense with that methodical demonstrability of the validity of propositions and norms which was the pride of modern universalism from Kant to logical positivism. The Cartesian fascination with the cogency of method will have to give way to a sort of "exemplary" universalism, which also raises its claims as **singular** claims, after the model of aesthetic judgment, when it deals with truth and justice. The subjectivization of reason, initiated in early modernity with the replacement of ontological objectivity by a weaker, but still overly strong, notion of objectivity as "impartial" subjectivity—impartial insofar as it is based on a rational method—will have to take another step. The only imperatives which in our time are acknowledged as unconditional, and thus as a possible basis for universally valid claims, are the requirements of the well-being of a concrete identity, individual or collective. To paraphrase Kant, the only thing which for us is unconditionally good is a good identity. This is the basis on which to build a universalistic position that does not sacrifice individuality to universality, and yet retains the possibility of criticizing the existent in the name of its own unfulfilled potentials.

In this paper I will examine two promising attempts to reconcile universalism with a genuine acceptance of the pluralism of life universalisms forms: critical theory and communitarianism. They are the only approaches that offer a way to overcome the opposition of a context-insensitive, "objectivistic" universalism, still in search of ultimate frameworks, methods, and the like on the one hand, and a sophisticated relativism aware of the "local" cogency of rules, norms and standards, but incapable of overcoming a particularist perspective or even of questioning it on the other hand. The means employed by critical theory and communitarianism are different, however, and so is their distribution of strong points and weaknesses. I will contrast Habermas's "procedural" universalism with the "contextualist" universalism developed by two thinkers whom I take as exemplars of a communitarian orientation, Michael Walzer and Alasdair MacIntyre.

Within the scope of this paper I will not be able to examine the whole range of reflections that these authors provide on the state of modernity, on the erosion of all-encompassing world-views, on the remedies against modern anomie, and on the modern prevalence of rule-oriented over virtue-oriented ethics and of ethics which assign priority to the right over ethics assuming a primacy of the good. Interesting contrasts could be observed here: while Habermas defends a deontological primacy of the right, MacIntyre sees such hierarchy as one of the main roots of the contemporary predicament; while MacIntyre tries to formulate a telic framework within which descriptive and evaluative aspects would no longer be separated, for Habermas the unity of reason is to be conceived only in procedural terms as the unity of a set of presuppositions of argumentation which underlie all kinds of discourse. At the risk of constraining the wealth of their thought into a somewhat narrow framework, I will concentrate only on the way in which these authors ground their positions and on the implications that their way of arguing has for the articulation of a concrete universalism.

Critical theory and communitarianism have a common adversary in the strong objectivism exemplified by Kantian transcendentalism, logical positivism, and the Hegelian-Marxist tradition. They also share a common aversion to the notion of the individual as constituted prior to all social interaction which is implicit in contract theories of society, in natural right theories, and within the methodological individualistic epistemology. In most other respects, however, they present antagonistic solutions to the problem of reconciling universalism and pluralism. Habermas subscribes to many of the liberal views which the communitarians criticize. Like the liberals, he tries, through his procedural approach, to ground norms without prejudging questions of values. Unlike the liberals, however, he abandons natural right theory and the contractarian perspective, and elaborates a communicative theory of justification based on the notion of

13

alessandro
ferrara

rational consensus. His approach leads him to transpose into the theoretical realm the "art of separation" which the liberals practice in the sphere of politics.[3] Not only the "is" and "ought," but also the form and the content of moral cultures, world-views, identities, and forms of social integration, are rigidly separated. So are spheres of rationality, modes of argument, and, in ethics, questions about justice, the good, the grounding of norms, and the application of such norms. The gain, for which such a heavy price is paid, is the possibility of rescuing some notion of progress in the normative sphere, i.e., the possibility of grounding the superiority of a post-conventional moral consciousness, a differentiated world-view, a rationalized modern life-world and ego-identity over their pre-modern counterparts.

The communitarians, conversely, wish to bridge or minimize the gap between descriptive and evaluative expressions, between the right and the good, between the grounding of norms and their application. Their attacks are directed, within each of their fields of inquiry, against the "formalistic" bias typical of "liberal" theories, by which they generally mean the pretense to generate norms, rules, institutions and principles that are "neutral" with respect to values, culture or historical situation—i.e., ones that any actor, no matter how situated, must accept as valid. The formalistic view of society is that it is held together only by shared "rules of the game" which can be agreed to by individuals and groups who hold diverse ideas as to what the game is about. The exact nature of the communitarians' positive proposal is not easy to specify. According to some, a revitalization of the feeling for tradition and community is needed in the face of the erosion of tradition and the fragmentation of our value horizon after three centuries of liberal hegemony; others emphasize a participatory politics. On a theoretical level, the common denominator is the affirmation of the context-specific quality of the validity of norms and principles of justice, as well as an emphasis on the role of judgment and the need to mediate what modern thought has differentiated: facts and values, rules and application, the right and the good, the individual and the community, form and content, methodological and substantive problems.4

Both positions are fraught with problems. Neither finally provides a fully convincing reconciliation of universalism and pluralism, for reasons that I will examine below, but the difficulties into which they run are instructive. Taken together, they constitute the best starting point for developing a concrete universalism capable of meeting the challenge of post-modernist skepticism.

* * *

14

Let me begin with critical theory. I focus on Habermas because his communicative approach to questions of justice and, more generally, of validity is the only one within the tradition of critical theory that truly addresses the problems raised by contextuality. Habermas's thesis is that it is possible to think of validity in a universalistic but not an objectivist way if we see truth and justice in "procedural" terms, i.e., as resting on the rational consensus emerging from a discussion, under ideal conditions, among all those concerned with a given issue or affected by a given norm. The only defensible universalism after the discovery of contextuality, argues Habermas, is one that renounces its ability to ground **substantive claims** and redefines its task as the grounding of the universal cogency of certain **rules of argument**. The validity of propositions and norms is then defined with reference to the fulfillment of these rules rather than with reference to content. This view of validity expresses what we presuppose when we state the truth of a proposition or the rightness of a norm. But Habermas assigns a relevance broader than merely methodological to the argumentative conditions of rational consensus. They also constitute the common core of rationality which underlies the various moments of modern decentered reason, as well as a procedural solution to the problems of integration that affect modern society after the fragmentation of the medieval and ancient world-views. The unity of reason and the integration of pluralistic societies rest on these argumentative conditions.

The problems raised by this position fall into two main categories. One series of problems concerns the conditions under which an instance of consensus is really qualified in establishing the validity of a proposition or a norm. The second host of problems stems from the necessity for Habermas to make a case for his consensus approach on grounds other than consensus. Ironically, Habermas shares with his skeptical adversaries the unfortunate predicament of having to grant his own position the status of an exception. He must show what justifies his consensus theory of validity, short of a general consensus not yet in sight. I will neglect here the problems linked with abstractness and ambiguity of the concept of rational consensus and will focus only on the second set of questions.[5]

We can reconstruct Habermas's case for a consensus approach to truth and justice in five steps.[6] First, he grounds the consensus conception of validity on a formal-pragmatic analysis of the presuppositions of argumentation. When we enter discourse, Habermas points out, we cannot avoid assuming that the only legitimate criterion for agreeing or disagreeing on the validity of a proposition or norm is the cogency of the reasons adduced to support it. If we admitted that authority, power, prestige or positive

alessandro
ferrara

incentives were influencing our stance on the matter, we would also have to concede that we are not taking part in a discursive event, but in some other kind, or we would run into a performative contradiction. It has been objected that such criterion is binding only to the extent that we are engaged in argumentation and that, since no prescription to enter discourse can be derived from the presuppositions of argumentation, Habermas's account remains vitiated by a residue of decisionism.[7] In response to this objection, to which the pragmatic transcendentalism of Apel remains vulnerable, Habermas tries to steer a middle course between the equally undesirable alternatives of treating the discursive way of handling controversial validity claims as a matter of subjective preference and of claiming for it the transcendental status of a condition of the possibility of social action. The difficulty of this middle course, centered on a fallibilistic reconstruction of the structures and genealogy of communicative action, is testified by the bulkiness and intricacy of the **Theory of Communicative Action**.

Habermas contends that the discursive assessment of the validity claims associated with statements and norms is but a special case of what takes place in everyday communicative action when, by performing speech acts, we implicitly raise three validity claims (those concerning the truth and presuppositons of the propositional content, the legitimacy of the social relation presupposed or generated by the illocutionary force, and the sincerity of the internal state expressed by the speaker) which are accepted or rejected by the hearer on the basis of actual reasons or on the supposition that adequate reasons could be provided.

Communicative action in turn—here we move on to Habermas's third step—is constitutive of social interaction. On one hand it is impossible to think of a society which does not somehow include what Habermas calls communicative action and, on the other hand, communicative action is crucial for the reproduction of the symbolic aspects of the life-world. No tradition can be renewed and handed down, no solidarity can be maintained, and no identity can be stabilized in the medium of purely strategic relations.[8] Thus, within the concept of a social order and the requirements for the reproduction of a life form, the idea of relations free of coercion is somehow implicit.[9] The problem is, however, that the conception of rationality as openness to critique and of validity as consensus free of coercion presupposes a **modern** frame of reference. It would make no sense to speak of rational agreement on the soundness of a validity-claim within a tradition-oriented culture. Furthermore, the distinction of three kinds of validity-claims presupposes the differentiation of objective, social, and subjective world—a differentiation which takes place only with modernity. The question then arises as to the sense in which the consensual theory of truth and rightness can be considered anything more than a generalization of the parochialism of modernity. Furthermore, the normative significance attributed by Habermas to the functional requisites of a **modern** life-world presupposes the intrinsic desirability of a modern form of life.[10] What allows this supposition?

These two questions are addressed by Habermas in his reconstruction of Weber's theory of Western rationalism and modernity and in his discussion of Winch's theses[11]—the last step of his argument. Along with the thesis that processes of cultural modernization are irreversible except at the cost of massive repression, self-deception and suffering—a thesis which Habermas supports by applying Piaget's and Kohlberg's theories to cultural evolution—he advances the thesis of the primacy of modernity as the form of life which realizes, more than any other, the presuppositions of discourse and the attitude of unrestrained openness to critique which form the kernel of rationality. The question "What grounds the validity of the consensus approach to validity?" is thus answered. The consensus theory of validity captures argumentative presuppositions which are constitutive not only of discourse but also of a kind of *praxis* which is important for all social life and crucial to the reproduction of the life-form located at the highest point in cultural evolution.

Let me now mention a few weaknesses in Habermas's argument. The universality of the complexes of rationality brought about by modernity is questionable, the superiority of modern rationality over that of pre-modern and primitive societies is questionable, and the factual irreversibility of modernization cannot lend normative force to the modern conception of validity. Habermas's claim that only six pragmatic relations to the world—institutionalized in the modern West in the form of an objectivating relation to the natural and social world (science, social technology), of a conformatory relation to the social (law) and subjective world (morality), and an expressive relation to the subjective (eroticism) and natural world (art)—are suited to the accumulation of knowledge and contain a distinct form of argumentation, is not convincing. The idea of cumulative progress is dubious even in the domain of science, not to mention art and morality, and it is hard to see why the possibility of specialized kinds of argumentation concerning non-instrumental attitudes towards nature or expressive attitudes towards the social world is ruled out altogether.[12]

In addition, Habermas concedes, in his discussion of Winch, that a primitive culture cannot be evaluated in terms of its technological potential, but suggests that the relative indifference of the Azande to the inconsistencies of their world-view be read

alessandro
ferrara

as an indicator of a "more irrational conduct of life." Underlying this suggestion is the idea that cultures can be placed on a continuum of openness/closure based on the extent to which they (a) favor learning processes in the cognitive sphere and (b) allow a critique of their basic assumptions as well as the development of a *praxis* where cognitive, moral and expressive moments find adequate expression. It is hard to avoid the impression that Habermas here begs the question. His criterion for evaluating the rationality of cultures does not appear sufficiently independent from a restatement of the salient features of modern Western culture: a potential for cognitive learning, an unlimited criticizability and the differentiation of *praxis* and discourse into a cognitive, moral, and expressive point of view. All that can be found in support of the thesis is the contention that a differentiation of spheres of *praxis* and discourse represents a better realization of the rationality inherent in the structures of communicative action. Should we accept this contention as an independent criterion, and should we accept the functional argument about the indispensability of a modicum of communicative action, we would still need to know why the modern realization of a level of rationality which far exceeds that modicum is to be preferred—a question made all the more pressing by Habermas's own admission that the gain in rationality brought about by the modern decentering of rationality entails crucial losses on other planes.[13]

Occasionally Habermas advances the weaker argument that the modern form of differentiated rationality and the modern differentiation of validity claims, kinds of worlds, and attitudes towards the world constitute an **inescapable standpoint** for us. While the plausibility of this claim cannot be denied, this move leads Habermas's argument into the same difficulty that it was supposed to eliminate. If the consensus theory of justice and truth is but a reconstruction of what we Western moderns cannot but mean by those terms, then we have no case for universalism, but simply a description, compatible with the Wittgensteinian picture, of one language game alongside others. Such description, furthermore, is no refutation of the thesis that the very preoccupation with universalism and functions, being part of a modern language game, can be superseded by a new post-modern perspective, no longer affected by the universalistic itch.[14] Conversely, if Habermas makes the stronger claim that the modern meaning of truth and justice is a better account of those notions than any other account, then the structure of his argument commits him to the desirability of a full realization of communicative rationality over the partial realization characteristic of pre-modernity. Regardless of the difficulty of establishing this claim, it must be noted that Habermas's argument would thereby leave the formal level at which it was supposedly formulated and would endorse a substantive vision of the good.

18

universalisms One of the reasons why Habermas's procedural universalism leads to such a dead end is its insufficient detachment from the rationalistic conception of rationality typical of modern thought. To put it in Kantian parlance, Habermas shares with his epistemological adversaries (neo-positivists, critical rationalists and system-theorists) the tendency to reduce judgment of the moral to determinant judgment and to make of reflective judgment an irrelevant psychological dimension or, in the context of moral theory, a mere moment of "application" of principles. There is no adequate role for reflective judgment understood as a capacity to mediate the universal and the particular without eliminating the specificity of the particular. Aside from the lack of context-sensitivity in his universalism, Habermas is led by this general orientation to other implausible claims. For example, on the one hand he conceives any argument concerning values or the equilibrium of an identity to be second rate, because no guarantee of consensus exists even under ideal conditions,[15] and, on the other hand, he maintains that in **discourse** proper it is possible to decide on the validity of cognitive claims or norms without taking a stance in matters of values. Furthermore, his decision to eliminate questions of value from scientific or ethical discourse leads Habermas to a conception of scientific truth and normative rightness in which universalistic decidability is purchased at the cost of limiting its scope to intra-paradigmatic questions in science and to a shared life-world in ethics.[16] The Wittgensteinian picture of a plurality of incommensurable language games and life-forms is thus not really overcome.

The originality and the limits of Habermas's procedural universalism are strictly linked and difficult to disentangle. The originality consists in his introduction of a distinction between the **structure** of a symbolic complex (a world-view, an ethic, a personal identity) and its **content**. The distinction allows Habermas to argue in evolutionary terms for the superiority of certain kinds of symbolic structures (e.g., of a decentered world-view over a mythical one, of a post-conventional ethic over a conventional one, of an ego-identity over a role-identity) while accepting a pluralistic equivalence of the concrete cultural contents. This strategy for reconciling universalism with "value pluralism" does not succeed for the reasons mentioned above, but also because its central presupposition—the possibility of sharply distinguishing form and content—can rarely be satisfied. Simply, the most interesting questions in ethics and in science are those which transcend the boundaries of a conceptual scheme and force us to choose between alternative schemes, cultures, or paradigms. Furthermore, in a case common in our complex societies, where the alternatives in a moral or scientific dilemma share the same structure (e.g., two post-conventional ethics, two scientific paradigms), the Habermasian approach fails to provide any orientation.

19

alessandro ferrara

The lesson drawn from these difficulties is, in my opinion, that no real reconciliation of universalism with pluralism can be effected unless one indicates, without invoking ontological hierarchies or *geschichtphilosophisch* teleologies, some way of assessing the validity of a choice between competing conceptual schemes and, since these have conflicting value stances embedded within them, between values. As will be shown, communitarianism has the merit of facing the problem of distinguishing a good value-stance from a bad one without recourse to *a priori* standards.

* * *

In his book, **Spheres of Justice**, Walzer offers a theory of justice that embodies all the main aspects of communitarianism. Two assumptions in particular make it a good example of contextualist universalism. One is the idea that no unique distributive principle can accommodate the plurality of goods which form the object of distributive practices in all times and cultures. Rather, justice demands that different social goods be distributed according to different reasons and through different procedures.[17] The other is the idea that while there is no abstract standard of justice, nonetheless one can pass judgment on the fairness of concrete societies and institutions. Let me try to briefly reconstruct how Walzer makes his case before addressing the problems that arise from his theory.

Walzer's theory of distributive pluralism can be summed up in four points. First, the goods that form the object of distributive practices are always socially constituted; their meaning, value, affinities and dissimilarities are not matters for individual choice but are socially created and change historically. Furthermore, such socially constituted goods contribute to the formation of the identities of their recipients. Second, there is no such thing as a set of primary goods crucial for all societies and historical times. Perhaps such a set could be reconstructed analytically, but in order to encompass the actual variance inherent in its object domain it would have to be so abstract that it would be useless. Third, there is nothing inherent in a certain kind of goods that makes one or another way of distributing them just or unjust. Rather, the fairness of a distributive practice depends on the prevailing conception of the relevant social goods in a given society. For example, in our society public offices cannot be bought or sold, while in certain pre-modern societies this was legally and morally possible. Fourth, every social good constitutes a distributive sphere with a logic of its own, in which only certain specific distributive principles are appropriate.[18]

Two distinctions are also important for Walzer's theory. The first contrasts **reductionist** theories of justice, which account for the just distribution of all sorts of goods on the basis of one principle, be it merit, free exchange or need, with **pluralist** theories of justice (e.g. Walzer's) which operate with the principle "different goods to different associations of men and women for different reasons and through different procedures."[19] This conception of justice does not exclude the existence of inequality within single spheres.

The second distribution contrasts **simple** and **complex** equality. In a regime of simple equality everybody is to receive the same amount of the same goods. In complex equality the unequal possession of certain goods is allowed, but the possession of one good will not give the owner a privileged access to other goods. While the conflation of equality with simple equality has led most egalitarian theorists to call for cumbersome political apparatuses in order to repress the spontaneous restoration of inequalities, equality, for Walzer, is no longer at odds with freedom. Not only is the suppression of the market or a massive politicization of civil society unnecessary, but even the monopoly of certain groups over certain goods becomes compatible with justice if it does not result in an unfair advantage in other distributive spheres. Underlying Walzer's view of an egalitarian yet pluralist conception of justice is the principle "No social good **x** ought to be distributed to men and women who possess another good **y** just because they possess **y** and without considering the meaning of **x**."[20]

From a substantive point of view, Walzer distinguishes 11 distributive spheres, governed by such diverse principles as distribution according to merit, need, or out of free exchange. The spheres identified are those (1) of membership and citizenship, two goods to be distributed only on the basis of the consensus of the possessors; (2) of social security and health care, where the relevant criterion is need; (3) of public office, governed by the principle of merit; (4) of money, where free exchange should remain the rule; (5) of hard work, regulated through strict equality; (6) of leisure, regulated through a mix of free exchange and need; (7) of education, where a minimal provision is ensured through strict equality and where additional educational opportunities are distributed through a mix of market and merit; (8) of family and love, governed by "prescriptive altruism"; (9) of religious grace, refractory to all distributive principles other than a free pursuit; (10) of recognition, ruled by free exchange; and (11) of the sphere of political power proper. Consistent with the premises outlined above, justice is to be achieved, according to Walzer, through a system of blocked exchanges between these spheres. Some blocks are already operating: political offices, jury verdicts, policy decisions or exemption from the draft cannot be sold. New blockages could be envisaged: education should no longer procure wealth and status, money should no longer exempt one

21

from hard work. Among other proposals that Walzer draws from his principles are workers' control over investments and company policy, citizenship for immigrants, the disestablishment and divestment of corporate powers, and the expansion of the welfare state.[21]

Walzer breaks with the old objectivist universalism when he denies that there could be an inherently just conception of the social good or a distributive scheme. The upshot of his theory is that while criteria for justice cannot be specified independently of an account of the society where they are supposed to work, nevertheless for every existing society, no matter how pervaded by injustice, arrangements exist that could be recognized as arrangements of that society **and** be just. Basically, justice is understood by Walzer as congruence of all conceptions of the relevant social goods with one another. For a society to be unjust means that what takes place in one distributive sphere violates conceptions that exist in some other sphere of the collective representation of the goods in question.[22] The originality of Walzer's theory consists in the fact that justice is conceived reflexively; the predicate "just" is understood as "just in its own terms." There is a sense, in other words, in which a capitalist society and a society based on caste can both be just "in their own way."[23] On the other hand, claims regarding the injustice of some specific provision always rest on the conception of other social goods whose distribution is undesirably affected by the institution or arrangement criticized. This conception of justice is certainly contextualist, but in what sense is it a universalistic one?

It is universalist insofar as (1) it challenges to the self-understanding of a given society and passes a critical judgment on its institutions, and (2) such judgment does not just express the arbitrary preferences of the observer, but lays a claim to a consensus that goes beyond the boundaries of the here and now. As in the case of aesthetic judgment, however, such universal consensus cannot be won out through demonstration or deductive inference, nor even through the *zwanglosen zwang* of the best argument. But then on what basis can it be invoked? Walzer's answer points to the coherence of the distributive views of a society. He assumes that the removal, or at least the reduction, of cultural contradictions commands both a normative force and a motivational impact.[24] More generally, the compelling quality of social criticism rests on the fact that good criticism keeps a foothold in what it criticizes. The connected critic—a contextualist equivalent to Gramsci's organic intellectual—as opposed to the detached philosopher, criticizes society in the name of something which his or her addressees share.[25] In the relation of the **object** to the **recipient** of critique lies the universalistic moment of social criticism. Although we renounce designing the ideal city for everybody and only wish to design the best city **for us**, implicit in our judgment concerning the kind of city that is best for us is the anticipation that **all** those who know enough about who we are would agree.

Is coherence enough for justice?

Let me now turn to some of the problems raised by Walzer's theory. To begin with, the "coherence postulate" at the center of the theory is problematic. While Walzer suggests that the culture shared by all social groups and communities carries some, if not the same, potential for distributive justice, it remains unclear how he would deal with the case of wicked communities. If a capitalist society or a caste society can be just in its own terms, what are we to make of the idea of a just Nazi society? A parallel with personality perhaps clarifies the point. A theory of personality à la Walzer would emphasize the pointlessness of looking for a unique standard of the healthy personality; different kinds of persons can all be healthy in their own terms. The way of being healthy for an individual with strong anal tendencies will differ in its structure, and not just in a few details, from that for an individual with oral tendencies or for someone with narcissistic traits, and there is no way of saying what **the** fulfilled individual would necessarily look like. Yet there are limits to the kind of diversity that can be reconciled with a meaningful notion of mental health: it would be odd to say that a psychotic can be healthy on his or her own terms, since to become healthy that person would have to become another.

What if the people themselves fail to note that good and principle are in conflict?

Second, how do we establish that these discrepancies between actual distributive practices and conceptions of the goods being distributed are real contradictions, capable of throwing into question the claim to justice raised by an institutional order, given that those who inhabit that order often explain them away as false problems? Take, for example, Walzer's claim that in the United States the provisions offered by the welfare state fall below the level required by the sphere of social security and health care, and below the level that the citizens would favor.[26] How can this claim be vindicated in the face of the large consensus that, over the last ten years, has supported not the expansion but the curtailment of the welfare state? It would have to be shown that the consensus of the majority who voted for the legislators responsible for the present situation was an ideological or somehow warped consensus. But it is hard to see how Walzer could legitimately draw a line between ideological and non-ideological views. A similar problem arises with MacIntyre. It is surprising to note that a set of questions pre-empted by Habermas's proceduralism,[27] unexpectedly re-emerges within the contextualist area.

Diversity within society.

23

Third, in complex societies, different groups defend different traditions and often hold conflicting views of a given social good.

Take the case of the abolition of slavery in the United States. In the South, abolition was fought by many on the ground that it would sentence to death a whole way of life. Abolition, for these Southerners, far from rectifying social arrangements that clashed with important convictions, introduced inconsistencies into an otherwise consistent tradition. Furthermore they considered the lot of the slaves not worse than that of the industrial workers of the North. In this case it seems that Walzer would have to either measure the fairness of the institutions of **the whole society**, including the South, on the basis of the conception of membership and citizenship held by **a section** of the society, i.e., the northern states, or fall back on a kind of "one community, one justice" postulate, which would lead his theory back into the Wittgensteinian picture. A theory of justice that equates justice with coherence between distributive practices and shared conceptions of the good is bound to generate difficulties when applied to a complex society in which issues of distributive justice arise precisely because there is no such shared understanding.[28]

Perhaps we could understand Walzer's position as requiring a **weaker** kind of coherence. According to this view, a just solution to distributive controversies would not have to completely reconcile institutions and shared conceptions of the good, but could simply be the solution which, while failing to remove all inconsistencies, nonetheless "makes the most"—to borrow the phrase used by R. Dworkin in his hermeneutical approach to law—of **the complex of traditions** underlying the life of a community or, in a terminology I prefer, the solution which most favors the flourishing of the identity of the community.[29] The abolition of slavery conforms to justice in that, despite its failure to reconcile the conflicting views of important segments of American society, and despite the restructuring that it imposed on the life-form of one of those segments, offered a better chance for a more complete unfolding of the American identity. The argument would have to be substantiated in historical terms, with reference to the contents of an overarching American identity and to what its fulfillment might mean. Yet, this version of Walzer's position would also raise problems. The flourishing of a collective identity cannot, any more than the flourishing of an individual one, be reduced to the sole dimension of coherence, even broadly understood. Rather, we need to spell out the other conditions that define, and the evaluative dimensions that help us to assess, the fulfillment of an identity. Walzer indirectly adumbrates one of these dimensions of the fulfillment of identities in his discussion of political power.[30] In that context, self-respect emerges as a kind of ultimate value whose status is ambiguous. The worth and significance of the democratic institutions and of the struggle to realize justice are related to their capacity to preserve, and possibly increase, self-respect in the citizens. As in the case of coherence, the status of self-respect in a contextualist theory of justice is best understood as one of those requisites to the well-being of an identity, on which Walzer would have to say more. I will return to this point in my discussion of MacIntyre's notions of the good for a human life and of the rationality of a tradition.

* * *

A similar pattern of strong points and weaknesses is found in MacIntyre's attempt to develop a moral theory centered on the notions of virtue and the rationality of tradition. **After Virtue** begins with a critical assessment of contemporary moral culture: "There seems to be no rational way of securing moral agreement in our culture."[31] This predicament, which MacIntyre purports to remedy, originates in the fragmentation, during the transition to the modern age, of the teleological framework embedded in Aristotle's ethics and in the contemporary presence of several major traditions which advance incompatible claims concerning justice, action, and rationality. These traditions are the Aristotelian, especially in its Thomistic version, the Augustinian, the Scottish, liberalism, and also Judaism, German idealism and some non-Western traditions. Liberalism and the Enlightenment are held responsible for the subjectivization of the ends of morality, for the shift from a virtue-oriented to a rule-oriented moral theory, and for the rise of an emotivist conception of the self. In **After Virtue**, MacIntyre accuses the Enlightenment of inconsistently conflating a renunciation of the teleological framework with the pretense of maintaining the notion of an "objective," in the sense of "undisputable," validity of practical claims.[32] This critique leads him to single out Nietzsche as the only true antagonist of Aristotle. Only the complete renunciation of all universalistic foundations and the disenchanted recognition that underlying the normative pretense of scientific statements or ethical prescriptions is a "will to power" has as much coherence as the Ancients' ontological view of humans and cosmos. A partially different picture emerges from **Whose Justice? Which Rationality?** Even if ahistorical and anti-traditional liberal views had not arisen and gained a hegemonic position, we still would not have an integrated moral view, for at least three major traditions, which raise different and sometimes incompatible claims, would be vying for supremacy.

For all his contempt for the Enlightenment, however, MacIntyre retains so many elements of the modern approach to validity that it is not inappropriate to view him as a "modernist *malgré lui*."[33] First, his proposal is not meant as an account of essential structures of Being but as an argument which enjoins our acceptance by virtue of its holding the most rational remedy to our predicament, where "most rational" should not be construed in transcendental or foundational terms, but in a pragmatist-historicist way as the quality of being the "best theory in town."[34] Second, his reference to the Aristotelian notion of *eudaimonia* must not blind us to the fact that what MacIntyre offers is a fully individuated, and thus modernized, version of this concept. Aware of the risk of flattening his position on a Burkean traditionalism, MacIntyre repeatedly stresses that having one's identity embedded in a larger tradition by no means prevents one from taking a critical stance toward that tradition or from transcending its limitations.[35] Also, MacIntyre subscribes to the modern notion that no one citizen should be excluded from deliberations concerning the common good and that no discrimination among citizens should exist in that respect.[36] Third, MacIntyre acknowledges the possibility of insoluble moral conflicts and embraces the same pluralism of ultimate value orientations which he sees at the heart of the modern conception of morality. His definition of the good life as "The life spent in seeking for the good life" is as "formal" and modern as any in that it is intended to be compatible with a variety of substantive conceptions of the good.

In order to overcome the fragmentation of our moral vocabulary, MacIntyre attempts a reconstruction of the telic framework, centered around the notion of virtue, along modern, pluralist lines. The concept of virtue is supposed to bridge the gap between the particularities of different cultures and to heal the split between factual and evaluative judgments without invoking the strong claims of Aristotelian metaphysics. To understand how this can be done requires that we briefly recapitulate MacIntyre's account of the virtues. We can divide it into a **formal** specification of the concept of virtue with reference to the notions of a practice, of the unity of a human life and of a tradition, and in a **substantive** outline of some fundamental virtues.

The formal specification of the concept of virtue includes a three-fold elucidation of the relevance of such a concept to the understanding of (a) the notion of a practice, (b) the notion of the good life, and (c) the notion of a tradition.

The aspect of practice that bears a special significance for moral discourse is its embedding of internal, as opposed to external, goods.[37] Internal goods are those standards of excellence and non-material rewards of excellence that command the allegiance of every accomplished participant in a practice. Excellence in practices such as medicine, law, architecture, or painting often procures wealth, status, power and other external goods, but also internal goods. The difference between the two kinds of goods consists in the fact that while internal goods cannot be obtained in any other way than by following the canons of the practice in question, external goods may be acquired also through other means and are not the exclusive form of reward for any practice. Furthermore, while external goods often are a sort of zero-sum reward, the achievement of internal goods does not hinder another's chances to attain them, and also represents a good for the whole community engaged in the practice. The virtues are relevant to practices in two senses: on the one hand, they are acquired human qualities which enable us to receive the goods internal to practices (whereas they are irrelevant, and in some cases even a hindrance, to the acquisition of external goods);[38] on the other hand, the maintenance and reproduction of practices requires institutions. Yet, because institutions, among other things, also fulfill the function of distributing external goods, they may be a source of corruption, especially through their tendency to lend importance to external goods at the expense of internal ones. The virtues, then, constitute a factor of resistance on the part of practice.[39] From a substantive point of view, MacIntyre identifies the basic virtues of **justice, truthfulness** and **courage**. They are basic or fundamental in that without these specific virtues no internal goods, but only external ones, could be obtained and no resistance could be opposed to the colonization of a practice by its sustaining institutions.[40] For this reason, while there certainly exist other virtues, and while different cultures and epochs exhibit different codes of truthfulness, justice and courage, every society where practices with internal goods are pursued must acknowledge the three basic virtues in one form or another.

The nature of the virtues, however, cannot be clarified solely with reference to the concept of a practice. This is for two reasons. First, we could not answer the question of why I should be concerned with acquiring the virtues. To simply say that if I did not I would miss the internal goods does not help. For I might not care about those goods, as in fact millions of other people do. Second, if the virtues were characterized solely in terms of practice, we would have no way of understanding the sense in which an individual can make better or worse decisions whenever the requirements of one practice, e.g., painting, collide with those of another, e.g., caring for one's family, as in the case of Gauguin. Thus, without an account of the good life, contends MacIntyre, our understanding of the basic virtues (e.g., integrity or constancy of purpose) could not be understood at all. What is needed is an account of the good human life that does not depend on Aristotle's assumptions about nature. MacIntyre centers his account on the notion of a narration. A human being is essentially "a story-telling animal. [One] is not essentially, but becomes through [his/her] history, a teller of stories that aspire to truth."[41] From this perspective the unity of an individual life consists in the unity of a "narrative quest" which encompasses it. "To ask 'What is good for me?' is to ask how best I might live out that unity and bring it to completion."[42] But a quest for what? According to MacIntyre we all search for our good, but we do not search for it in the way a geologist looks for oil. Rather, we start out with a vague vision of what the good for us might be and we grow more and more aware of what we are looking for as we proceed in our quest. In the meantime we also learn more about ourselves, about the things we value, and about the kind of balance of goods which really satisfies us. From this vantage point we can gain insight into the nature of the good for humans in general, which consists in spending one's life in seeking the good. The virtues, from this perspective, are "those dispositions which sustain us in the relevant kind of quest for the good."[43]

Our clarification of the nature of the virtues remains incomplete, however, until we characterize them with reference to the concept of a tradition. The reason for this is that we are never able to seek or exercise the virtues *qua* individuals alone. A tradition, understood as an "historically extended, socially embodied argument, and an argument precisely in part about the goods which constitute the tradition" provides the necessary context within which the individual can make sense of his or her life. Now the virtues can also help sustain and reproduce traditions. "Lack of justice, lack of truthfulness, lack of courage, lack of the relevant intellectual virtues—these corrupt traditions."[44]

MacIntyre's position certainly falls under the category of "contextualist" universalism. He wants to overcome the fragmentation of moral discourse, but at the same time he does not wish to fall into some form of generalizing universalism, least of all into one based on ontological assumptions. His position is universalist in the softer sense that he maintains that there are better or worse ways of dealing with value conflict, and his theory purports to render explicit the basis on which we formulate such judgments. I will raise four objections against the argument outlined in **After Virtue**. Then I will briefly discuss the modifications introduced in MacIntyre's later book **Whose Justice? Which Rationality?**

First, as Walzer's theory of justice is faced with the problem of wicked communities, so MacIntyre's moral theory must be confronted with the question of wicked traditions. MacIntyre admits the existence of wicked practices, such as torture, but suggests that the qualities which **seem** to be virtues in those practices really are not, because while they may be of some help within the practices in question, they are not conducive to the good for a human life and do not contribute to the reproduction of a tradition. But we can also imagine, along with wicked practices, wicked life courses and wicked traditions, the sustaining of which necessitates negative virtues, such as mercilessness, duplicity, or cynicism. While Habermas has at least some argument, hinging on the requirements of the reproduction of the life-world, on why an entirely wicked tradition could not reproduce itself successfully, I do not see any argument on the point in MacIntyre. The same holds for wicked life-plans. Again, MacIntyre's failure to convincingly rule out their possibility has adverse consequences for his account of the virtues. It can be seen both that the "positive" virtues turn out not to be necessary conditions for the good life after all, or for the maintenance of practices and traditions, and that therefore the universal relevance of truthfulness, justice and courage is thrown into question.

Second, MacIntyre argues that "if in a particular society the pursuit of external goods were to become dominant, the concept of the virtues might suffer first attrition and then perhaps something near total effacement, although simulacra might abound."[45] Here, a comparison with Walzer may be useful. As Walzer's contextual universalism burdens him with the necessity of drawing a line between beliefs that should be taken into account and ideological or *ad hoc* constructs, so MacIntyre is committed to distinguishing a real virtue from the semblance of one. Given the propensity of all societies to consider as virtues the qualities functional to their reproduction, with which yardstick, compatible with his contextualism, can MacIntyre discount, as a "simulacrum of virtue," conduct considered virtuous by some tradition or society? For all its formalism, Habermas's consensus approach to truth and justice has the merit, over Walzer's theory of justice and MacIntyre's moral theory, of bypassing the thorny question of ideology altogether.

Third, the relation of MacIntyre's formal characterization of virtue to his substantive argument concerning the basic virtues is unclear. He contends that the cultivation and exercise of truthfulness, justice and courage is a condition of the reproduction of practices and traditions. While such claim *prima facie* does not seem implausible, different specifications of the basic virtues also seem possible. At one point MacIntyre introduces virtues like patience and integrity without clarifying their status, and one wonders why self-reliance or altruism or humility could not also be understood as necessary for the reproducing traditions and practices. Furthermore, while MacIntyre contends that his three basic virtues are acknowledged by all cultures at all times, the exact meaning of such acknowledgement is hard to understand from his examples. It is hard to see how the fact that Bantu parents teach their children not to tell the truth to unknown strangers in order not to expose themselves to witchcraft, or the fact that Westerners are told to lie to elderly great-aunts who invite them to admire their new hats,[46] can be construed as

alessandro
ferrara

acknowledgements of the virtue of truthfulness. All that follows from these prescriptions is the propensity of both cultures to subordinate truthfulness, respectively, to cautiousness and to a kind of charitable compassion. If that counts as an endorsement of truthfulness, then the Nazi practice in extermination camps, of telling Jews on their way to the gas chambers that a warm shower was awaiting them, should also count.

Fourth, while being on the whole sympathetic to MacIntyre's treatment of validity in terms of the good for a human life or in terms of the requirements for the well-being of an identity, I find his conception somewhat reductive. The point of MacIntyre's moral theory is that, by referring to the virtues of truthfulness, justice and courage, we can, if not solve the problem of the "warring gods," at least recognize better and worse solutions to the tragic confrontation of "good with good." In **After Virtue**, better and worse are spelled out as more or less conducive to (a) the attainment of the good life for the individuals involved, and (b) the reproduction of the traditions within which those lives are embedded. Let us leave aside, for the time being, the risk of a relativist acceptance of the reproduction of **any** tradition as a good in itself—a risk partially corrected by MacIntyre's later discussion of the rationality of traditions in **Whose Justice? Which Rationality?**—and let us focus on the notion of the good for a human life. The problem is that MacIntyre understands the good for a human life almost exclusively as synonymous with the coherence of an identity or a life-narrative. Such conception captures only one dimension of the fulfillment of an identity and overlooks other plausible dimensions such as a sense of vitality, a capacity for self-reflection, and maturity in the choice of goals and ideals. Furthermore, reducing the good life to coherence leads to counter-intuitive consequences. Take the case of MacIntyre's virtuous chess player.[47] Imagine a person who dedicates her entire life to playing chess, achieves an unequalled mastery of the game, but because of the compensatory quality of her search for excellence feels empty and meaningless, has no insight into the reasons that motivate her or into why excellence fails to deliver joy and fulfillment, and at the same time harbors wild fantasies about her capacities. The life of such a person could not really be called an instantiation of the good life, yet her life-course would exhibit as high a degree of coherence and unity as can be wished. On the other hand, a person who radiates a sense of lively self-presence and a readiness to enjoy the self and the diversity of others, who is aware of her basic needs and is able to feel enthusiastic about her goals while maintaining a realistic sense of the intrinsic limitations of all human ideals, but who does not excel at any one practice and has undergone so many changes that her life-narrative is fraught with gaps and inexplicable turns, seems then to come closer to the good life, or at least as close to it as MacIntyre's chess player.

In **Whose Justice? Which Rationality?**, MacIntyre addresses the problem of the relative superiority of conceptions of justice rooted in different and rival traditions. Equally critical of the Enlightenment's quest for a "tradition-independent standard of judgment" and of the relativist denial "that rational debate between and rational choice among rival traditions is possible," MacIntyre grounds his contextualist universalism on the notion, which both the Enlightenment and its relativist adversaries fail to understand, of the "rationality of a tradition." Accusing Burke of having done a positive harm to the cause of an historically minded conception of rationality,[48] MacIntyre, with a kind of historicist equivalent of Lakatos's rescue of critical rationalism, links the rationality of a tradition with the progress made by that tradition through a number of developmental stages and in particular with the quality of its response to epistemological crisis. An epistemological crisis occurs when a tradition "by its own standards of progress ... ceases to make progress," when "hitherto trusted methods of enquiry have become sterile," "conflicts over rival answers to key questions can no longer be settled rationally" and the use of the methods thus far developed "begins to have the effect of increasingly disclosing new inadequacies, hitherto unrecognized incoherences, and new problems for the solution of which there seem to be insufficient or no resources within the established fabric of belief."[49] In these circumstances a tradition is rational which, by means of inventing new concepts and theories, is able to generate a **progressive** solution. By "progressive" MacIntyre means that the new conceptual scheme (1) provides a "solution to the problems which had previously proved intractable in a systematic and coherent way" and (2) provides "an explanation of just what it was which rendered the tradition, before it had acquired these new resources, sterile or incoherent or both." At the same time there must exist (3) some fundamental continuity of the new conceptual scheme with the beliefs that had been constitutive for the identity of the tradition up to the time of the crisis.[50] In radical dilemmas, then, our preference for the solution propounded by the most rational tradition expresses our intuition that the viewpoint is most trustworthy that has proven able to overcome the most serious crises in the most creative way. An example of such a creative solution is Thomas Aquinas's reconciliation of Aristotelian and Augustinian themes, a reconciliation "without which anyone whose allegiance was given to both the Aristotelian and Augustinian traditions would necessarily have lapsed either into incoherence or, by rejecting one of them, into a sterile one-sidedness."[51]

alessandro
ferrara

This conception of the rationality of traditions has implications for the problem of determining what justice requires of an individual **After Virtue**, within the larger context of the advancement of a tradition. The teleological framework designed to lend a factual status to statements such as "doing **x** would be better for my own or my own group's self,"[52] required a standpoint, beyond the formal definition of the good life, which MacIntyre had not specified. In fact, the expression "the good for **X**" picks out a unique referent only if we share the same view on life in the first place. Different traditions would assign different referents to the expression. Therefore only now that MacIntyre has developed an account of validity across traditions can his reconstruction of the telic framework fulfill the task of orienting our conduct in a world with a plurality of goodness.

The impression remains, however, that MacIntyre's position would require a theory of individual and collective identity.[53] The idea that the superior tradition is that which solves its crises in the most creative way presupposes a notion of the flourishing of an identity which again, although it is related to coherence, cannot be reduced to it and remains vague in MacIntyre's account. Allegiance to a tradition seems not so much to be a mere function of past record but to presuppose a confidence (based on, but not reducible to, past record) in its future ability to overcome difficulties and offer meaning-resources to those who inhabit it. It also seems plausible to say that we value most the tradition which carries the best promise of bringing the collective identity embedded in it to a fulfillment that must include, beyond an enhanced coherence, a moment of increased vitality, of deepened self-reflection, and of mature awareness.

* * *

To summarize, Habermas's proceduralism and the communitarians' contextualism are affected by complementary shortcomings. While the former suffers from a lack of context-sensitivity rooted (a) in the understanding of validity as consensus under idealized conditions, (b) in the corresponding inability to articulate a meaningful sense of validity in the here and now, under non-ideal conditions, and (c) in an inadequate conceptualization of the role of judgment in matters of science and morality, the communitarians' contextualism is affected by a foundational deficit. Walzer's reformulation of the question "Which distributive arrangements are just?" into the question "Which social arrangements are just for us, given who we are?" sets for him the task of specifying the minimal endowment which must be shared by us and those who live differently, in order for them to be able, despite their diversity, to agree on what is best for us. But all that Walzer provides are general statements to the universalisms   effect that we are all "culture producing creatures."[54] MacIntyre posits the universal significance of the three virtues of justice, truthfulness and courage. Supposedly what we all share, underneath the diversity of culture, and what allows us to evaluate alternatives cross-culturally in terms of the "good for x," is a sense of the relevance of these virtues for the attainment of the good life and for the reproduction of any tradition within which a human life is embedded. MacIntyre fails, however, to provide a convincing argument about why only these virtues play this singular role and about their universal diffusion. Ironically, a better case for their universal significance could be made in terms of Habermas's presuppositions of communication.

The lesson to be drawn from these reflections is, in my opinion, that an adequate version of a non-objectivist and non-formalist universalism must conceive truth and justice as radically situated but, unlike contextualism, must complement this view with a reconstruction of the common basis which allows differently situated actors to assess, and recognize as binding, trans-schematic or transcultural judgments. Besides the presuppositions of communication investigated by Habermas, one of the crucial components of this common basis is the competence possessed by all human beings to various degrees to assign priorities, in the absence of established criteria, to conflicting values in the service of the flourishing of an identity. This ability can be called *phronesis* or judgment and the kind of concrete universalism based on it *prudential* universalism.

At the center of prudential universalism is the assumption that choices between rival conceptual schemes can be assimilated as the assignment of priorities to values, and that the ranking of values, in turn, bears important similarities with the assessment of the saliency of needs for the well-being of an identity. The object of a theory of *phronesis* or judgment is to spell out the concept of the well-being of an identity, individual or collective, into a set of basic dimensions (e.g., coherence, vitality, depth, maturity) that guide, though do not determine, our intuitions as to what it means for an identity to be fulfilled. These dimensions, as the convergence of a number of psychoanalytic schools and theorists suggests, are rooted in the constancy of certain stages and passages of the development of the human personality. They are not the traits of a tradition, though their description is couched in the language of one, but rather capture a core of subjectivity which all traditions express in different ways. In this sense, the reconstruction of these dimensions is a key to a universalistic approach to truth and justice which, while remaining true to the discovery of contextuality and avoiding formalism, does not end in contextualism.

33

alessandro ferrara

ENDNOTES

1. The term conceptual scheme, borrowed from Davidson, is used here in a different sense, as a generic term to designate all the equivalents of the Wittgensteinian notion of a self-contained language-game. Cf. D. Davidson, "On the Very Notion of a Conceptual Scheme," **Inquiries into Truth and Interpretation**, Oxford, Clarendon Press, 1984, pp. 183-198.

2. Cf. R. Bernstein, **Beyond Objectivism and Relativism: Science, Hermeneutics, and Praxis**, Oxford, Blackwell, 1983.

3. Cf. M. Walzer, "Liberalism and the Art of Separation," **Political Theory** 12:3, 1984, pp. 315-30.

4. For a representative selection of communitarian positions, see M. Walzer, **Sphere of Justice: A Defense of Pluralism and Equality**, New York, Basic Books, 1983, and **Interpretation and Social Criticism**, Cambridge, Harvard University Press, 1987; A. MacIntyre, **After Virtue**, Notre Dame, University of Notre Dame Press, 1981, and **Whose Justice? Which Rationality?**, Notre Dame, University of Notre Dame Press, 1988; M. Sandel, **Liberalism and the Limits of Justice**, Cambridge, Cambridge University Press, 1982; Ch. Taylor, **Philosophy and the Human Sciences: Philosophical Papers**, Vol. 2, Cambridge, Cambridge University Press, 1985; R.M. Unger, **Knowledge and Politics**, New York, Free Press, 1975, and **Passion. An Essay on Personality**, New York, Free Press, 1975, and **Politics. A Work in Constructive Social Theory**, 3 Vol., Cambridge, Cambridge University Press, 1988; R. Bellah, *et al.*, **Habits of the Heart. Individualism and Commitment in American Life**, Berkeley, University of California Press, 1985; R. Beiner, **Political Judgment**, Chicago, University of Chicago Press, 1981; B. Williams, **Moral Luck**, Cambridge, Cambridge University Press, 1981, and **Ethics and the Limits of Philosophy**, London, Fontana Press, 1985. On the distinction between an "integrationist" and a "participationist" strand of communitarian politics, cf. S. Benhabib, "Autonomy, Modernity and Community. An Exchange Between Communitariansm and Critical Social Theory," paper read at the 1987 Annual Meeting of the American Political Science Association.

5. With regard to Habermas's unrealistic assumptions about the relation between language and thought, see A. Ferrara, "A Critique of Habermas's Consensus Theory of Truth," **Philosophy and Social Criticism**, 1987, 13:1, pp. 51-2. On the ambiguity of the notion of rational consensus, see A. Ferrara, "A Critique of Habermas's **Diskursethik**," in **Telos** 64, 1985, pp. 62-3.

6. The following reconstruction is based on Habermas's **Theory of Communicative Action**, 2 vols., Boston, Beacon Press, 1984-88; **Moral Bewußtsein und kommunikatives Handeln**, Frankfurt, Suhrkamp, 1983; **Vorstudien und Ergänzungen zur Theorie des kommunikativen Handelns**, Frankfurt, Suhrkamp, 1984; "A Reply to My Critics," J.B. Thompson and D. Held eds., **Habermas: Critical Debates**, London, MacMillan, 1982, pp. 219-83; "Questions and

Counterquestions," **Praxis International** 4, 1984, pp. 229-249; and "Entgegnung," A. Honneth and H. Joas eds., **Kommunikatives Handeln**, Frankfurt, Surhkamp, 1986.

7. Cf. A. Wellmer, **Ethik und Dialog**, Frankfurt, Suhrkamp, 1986, pp. 104-105.

8. Cf. Habermas, **The Theory of Communicative Action**, op. cit., Vol. 2, Chapter VI, p. 1.

9. Ibid., Vol. 1, Chapter IV, p. 2.

10. Only in a modern life-world, in fact, does communicative action exist in a differentiated form. The instrumental, strategic and communicative moments of action are still fused in the praxis of primitive societies.

11. Ibid., Vol. 1, Chapter II, and Vol. 1, Chapter I, p. 2.

12. For an excellent critique of Habermas on this point, see T. McCarthy, "Reflections on Rationalization in the Theory of Communicative Action," **Praxis International** 4, 1984, pp. 177-91.

13. Cf. Ibid., Vol. 2, Chapter VIII, p. 1. Cf. also "Life-forms, Morality and the Task of the Philosopher," in Habermas, **Autonomy and Solidarity. Interviews**, ed. and intro. P. Dews, London, New Left Books, 1987, p. 210.

14. Cf. J.F. Lyotard, **The Post-Modern Condition**, Minneapolis, University of Minnesota Press, 1984, and R. Rorty, **Philosophy and the Mirror of Nature**, Princeton, Princeton University Press, 1979.

15. Cf. Habermas, **The Theory of Communicative Action**, op. cit., Vol. 1, Chapter I, p. 1.

16. I cannot argue this point here. For the case of scientific claims, cf. my "Critique of Habermas's Consensus Theory of Truth," op. cit., pp. 55-57. As regards normative rightness, Habermas maintains that questions of rightness arise, and presumably can be solved, only within a horizon of shared assumptions about the good life. Cf. **Moralbewußtsein und kommunikatives Handeln**, op. cit., p. 117.

17. Cf. M. Walzer, **Spheres of Justice. A Defense of Pluralism and Equality**, op. cit., p. 6.

18. Cf. ibid., Ch. 1.

19. Ibid., Ch. 1.

20. Ibid., Ch. 1.

21. Cf. ibid., Ch. 12, Ch. 2, and Ch. 3.

22. Walzer admits that certain principles or conceptions of the social

goods may be a constant of human society but, consistent with his distrust of *a priori* universalism, wishes to maintain for such claims the status of empirical statements which cannot be vindicated by philosophical argument. Cf. *ibid.*, Ch. 13.

23. Cf. *ibid.*, Ch. 13.

24. Two examples of arguments of this sort are Walzer's discussion of the Pullman experiment and his critique of the American Welfare State. Cf. *ibid.*, Ch. 3 and 12.

25. Cf. the chapter on "The Practice of Social Criticism," in M. Walzer, **Interpretation and Social Criticism**, *op. cit.*, pp. 36-66, and "Philosophy and Democracy," **Political Theory** 9:3, 1981, pp. 379-99.

26. *Ibid.*, Ch. 3.

27. For Habermas, the attempt to identify ideological contents should give way to the attempt to identify distorted communication, i.e., unrecognized violations of the presuppositions of argumentation. Cf. "A Reply to my Critics," *op. cit.*, p. 254, and also S.K. White's discussion of this point, in his **The Recent Work of Jürgen Habermas. Reason, Justice and Modernity**, Cambridge, Cambridge University Press, 1988, pp. 117-118.

28. Cf. S. Benhabib, "Autonomy, Modernity and Community. An Exchange Between Communitarianism and Critical Social Theory," paper read at the 1987 Annual Meeting of the American Political Science Association, p. 18.

29. For a statement of his views that comes close to this interpretation, cf. M. Walzer, **Interpretation and Social Criticism**, *op. cit.*, pp. 28-30.

30. Cf. M. Walzer, **Spheres of Justice**, *op. cit.*, Ch. 12.

31. A. MacIntyre, **After Virtue**, *op. cit.*, p. 6.

32. For a critique of MacIntyre's interpretation of the Enlightenment attitude towards Aristotle, cf. D.M. Rasmussen, "The Enlightenment Project: After Virtue," **Philosophy and Social Criticism** 1982, 3/4. pp. 391-4.

33. Cf. Ch. Larmore, **Patterns of Moral Complexity**, Cambridge, Cambridge University Press, 1987, pp. 36-39. For a similar critique, see also S. Benhabib, "Autonomy, Modernity and Community. An Exchange Between Communitarianism and Critical Social Theory," *op. cit.*, p. 8; D. Cornell, "Toward a Modern/Postmodern Reconstruction of Ethics," **University of Pennsylvania Law Review** 1985, 133:2, p. 323-4.

34. We must not aspire, argues MacIntyre, to produce a theory "necessarily to be assented to by any rational being, because invulnerable or almost invulnerable to objections," but rather to produce "the best theory to emerge so far in the history of this class of theories."

As regards the issue of validity, then, "we ought to aspire to provide the best theory so far as to what type of theory the best theory so far must be: no me, but no less." "The Relationship of Philosophy to History: Postscript to the Second Edition of **After Virtue**," K. Baynes, J. Bohman and T. McCarthy, eds., **After Philosophy**, Cambridge, MIT Press, 1987, pp. 418-419.

35. Cf. MacIntyre, **After Virtue**, *op. cit.*, p. 205.

36. On this point, see R. Bernstein, "Nietzsche or Aristotle? Reflections on Alasdair MacIntyre's **After Virtue**," **Soundings**, 1984, p. 6.

37. For a definition of practice, see MacIntyre, **After Virtue**, *op. cit.*, p. 175. On the difference between practices and techniques, cf. *ibid.*, pp. 180-1.

38. Cf. *ibid.*, p. 183.

39. Cf. *ibid.*, p. 181.

40. Cf. *ibid.*, p. 179.

41. *Ibid.*, p. 201.

42. *Ibid.*, p. 203.

43. *Ibid.*, p. 204.

44. *Ibid.*, p. 207.

45. *Ibid.*, p. 183.

46. *Ibid.*, p. 180.

47. Cf. MacIntyre, "The Relationship of Philosophy to History: Postscript to the Second Edition of **After Virtue**," *op. cit.*

48. Cf. MacIntyre, **Whose Justice? Which Rationality?**, *op. cit.*, p. 353.

49. *Ibid.*, pp. 361-362.

50. *Ibid.*, p. 362.

51. *Ibid.*, p. 363.

52. See **After Virtue**, *op. cit.*, p. 209.

53. MacIntyre comes closer to a reformulation of his standpoint in identity terms in his Lindley Lecture at the University of Kansas, "Is Patriotism a Virtue?" March 26, 1984, The University of Kansas.

54. Cf. M. Walzer, **Sphere of Justice**, *op. cit.*, p. 314.

gerald doppelt
beyond liberalism and communitarianism: towards a critical theory of social justice

Every universalistic theory of practical reason promises to provide a firmly grounded normative standpoint external to every particular society and tradition from which its way of life can be decisively understood and evaluated. Is there any really rational understanding and critique of society available from within the standpoint of its own historical forms of self-understanding? Does an understanding of the ethical life of a political community yield a possible framework for enlightenment and emancipation? Or, is this rather the highway of ideology, illusion, and resignation?

I will illuminate these questions indirectly through a reflection upon Sandel's "communitarian" critique of Rawlsian liberalism. My larger aim is to point the way towards the construction of an immanent critique of modern liberal-democratic society. To this end, I will argue that we require a conception of moral reasoning and political theory which goes well beyond the methodological resources of contemporary philosophical liberalism and communitarianism. But my immediate context of argument will focus upon Rawls's conception of (re)distributive economic justice (his argument for a welfare state) and Sandel's communitarian challenge to it. In this context, I will argue that Sandel's critique is effectively surmounted by a "communitarian" reading and defense of Rawlsian liberalism. But in turn, this attempt to ground Rawlsian social justice in the shared values underlying modern liberal political community opens the way onto gerald doppelt a yet more radical line of criticism. For Rawls's interpretation of modern liberal-democratic society misses its normative contradictions and thus fails to articulate or resolve its fundamental irrationalities and injustices. The illumination and critique of these irrationalities requires a broader and richer account of moral theory than what is available within philosophical liberalism or communitarianism. This summarizes the argument I will now present.

1. Rawlsian Economic Justice and the Communitarian Critique

Perhaps the closest thing to a litmus test for Rawls's theory of social justice is the capacity of his contractarian methodology to ground his principle of redistributive economic justice. Rawls's first principle of equal political and civil liberty is hardly controversial or at odds with the established structure of our political community. The second principle, however, requires the elimination of all inequalities of economic power, wealth, and income which do not demonstrably function, or are not made by the state to function, to raise the worst-off's standard of living above what it would otherwise be (i.e., in the absence of these inequalities).[1] This principle of justice is taken to justify a form of welfare-state and political redistribution of income which is quite contentious within our political life and otherwise violates many people's sense of justice and individual desert. Political theorists have attacked this conception from the left and from the right. More generally, Rawls's methodological critics have argued that his contractarian premises are too weak to ground anything like this principle of economic redistribution.

Sandel has developed the canonical communitarian version of this criticism.[2] It is especially interesting because Sandel indicates precisely what methodological conception Rawls's theory lacks but would have to have in order to ground and motivate an acceptance of Rawlsian economic redistribution. For Sandel, Rawls's argument requires a conception of personhood or moral identity essentially mediated by the concrete ends, bonds, common purpose, and joint projects of a historical community, whose attachments enter into a person's very sense of who he or she is and what his/her life is about. But Rawls's contractarian framework turns on a Kantian conception of personhood which detaches the moral identity of persons from all such particular ends, purposes, communities, common projects, shared values, and joint undertakings. Kantian personhood is essentially "unencumbered," mediated by nothing other than its bare capacity to choose what it will value, who it will become, and what sort of society it will sanction. Yet it is precisely this conception of personhood which, for Sandel, lies at the foundation of Rawls's construction of the "original position" (or contractarian situation), including his hypothetical deliberators, their overriding interest in abstract freedom, and the model of citizenship and society they are supposed ultimately to choose.

From Sandel's standpoint, the Kantian conception of "unencumbered" personhood is incoherent, impoverished and inadequate to the phenomenon of human identity. Beyond that, Kantian personhood cannot generate or sustain much in the way of allegiance or obligation to any given political order. It forecloses the possibility of raising the political order to everything it should and could mean to concrete people who, for Sandel, are always bound together by ties of community and tradition that are deeper and potentially more valuable than they normally understand. In this way, Sandel renews the critique of Kant made by Hegel, and the attack upon liberalism made by contemporary authors such as MacIntyre, Oakeshott, Bellah *et al.*, Walzer, and others.[3]

In the present context, I will focus upon Sandel's argument that Rawls's Kantian conception of personhood is simply too impoverished and empty to motivate or ground his conception of redistributive economic justice. For Sandel, the grounding and acceptance of such a conception requires precisely the kind of intersubjective identity, or "situated" conception of personhood, which Rawls's contractarianism excludes in principle. Rawls's second principle of justice—his "difference" principle—requires that a person think of his or her individual talents, abilities, character-traits, etc. not as grounds in themselves of personal merit and legitimate deserts, but rather as community assets (like natural resources in the public spheres) to be harnessed by the community on behalf of the common good. On this principle, only if everyone benefits from the division of labor and reward may individuals legitimately receive (unequal) rewards for their (scarce) individual talents and efforts. Sandel argues that the justification of Rawls's difference principle, with its welfare-state redistributions, effectively presupposes the very sort of attachment to the community, identification with the common good, intersubjective sense of oneself excluded by the Kantian conception. His argument proceeds as follows:

(1) Rawls's difference principle depends for its justification on treating individuals' talents, abilities, character traits, excellence, etc. as "common assets" which a just society should employ in order to benefit everyone.[4]

(2) This view of individual abilities and traits in turn depends on Rawls's blanket rejection of any meritocratic conception of individual difference in traits as proper bases for social inequalities of reward.[5]

41

(3) This anti-meritocratic conception effects a radical detachment of the moral identity of persons from their character or worth. On the resulting view, "...no one can properly be said to deserve anything because no one can properly be said to possess anything."[6]

(4) But if no one deserves anything, then on what basis can Rawls justify or motivate the benefits which every person is supposed to receive through the appropriation of individuals' talents as common assets at the disposal of a just society? This detachment of persons from their talents and character traits is but one more internal consequence of the Kantian conception of persons. Thus, the Kantian conception provides no basis for justifying the benefits and burdens allocated to individuals by the difference principle.[7]

(5) The only plausible basis for justifying an acceptance of the difference principle is an intersubjective conception of moral identity, on which my talents, abilities, and character traits belong to the community because it has already entered into my sense of who I am; its good and my good are essentially inter-related in my own self-understanding.[8]

(6) But this sort of intersubjective identity is excluded by Rawls's Kantian conception of persons. Therefore, the justification of the difference principle (the Rawlsian welfare-state, etc.) depends on a conception of persons excluded by Rawlsian liberalism.[9]

2. A Defense of Rawls's Conception of Economic Justice and its Kantian Foundation

On my reading of Rawls's system, the justification for his account of redistributive economic justice does not depend on a blanket rejection of any meritocratic conception of individual desert, though Rawls does in part reason in this way.[10] Rather, I will contend that, properly interpreted, the Kantian conception of personhood provides a firm foundation for a commitment to Rawlsian redistributive justice. From my standpoint, Sandel misunderstands the Kantian conception and denies it the affirmative normative content and mediated social meaning it increasingly assumes in Rawls's work. More generally, my argument is that the communitarian critique of liberalism in Sandel and other authors is blind to the fact that liberalism itself embodies an historical tradition, including an experience of political community and a concretely lived mode of common life. Freed from its universalistic self-misunderstanding, liberal philosophical conceptions, such as the Kantian ideal of personhood, can be grounded in a reading or interpretation of our political community and tradition. Indeed, it is so grounded in

Rawls's essays since **A Theory of Justice**.[11] But I am ahead of my argument. First, I will explain why Rawls's account of redistributive economic justice should not be read to depend on a blanket rejection of every meritocratic conception of what people deserve.

As Sandel emphasizes, Rawls regards individuals' acquired traits and characters as similar to their native endowments: both ultimately depend upon circumstances beyond a person's control and responsibility. Both are equally inappropriate bases of claims of individual merit or desert. Rawls treats this rejection of meritocratic notions of desert as opening the way onto the arguments for the difference principle. Rawls's blanket rejection of meritocratic notions is a weak and implausible link in his argument. As he recognizes, meritocratic assumptions are built into our ordinary moral discourse, judgments and practices— which, by Rawls's own method of "reflective equilibrium," a theory of justice is supposed to capture, not ignore or discount as irrational. Rawls is correct in his view that we do not praise, blame, reward, or penalize persons for traits which we regard as the outcome of circumstance, luck, the natural lottery, etc. On the other hand, our normative discourse rests on the assumption that people are responsible to some degree or another for what they make of their given endowments, circumstances, luck, etc.; to this extent their actions and character traits, acquired abilities and virtues are systematically regarded as proper bases for differential judgments of individual merit. Rawls's view that the efforts underlying the development of such individual traits are always and inevitably the result of circumstances beyond the control or responsibility of a person, is ungrounded and implausible.

Of course, our existing meritocratic conception may well misconceive where and how to draw the line between individual and social responsibility, culture and nature, personal merit and the mere play of social advantage, circumstance, or ideology. These conceptions undoubtedly misconstrue the proper rewards for individual merit and the line between universal rights and earned privileges. Our particular meritocratic assumptions may rest on an ideal of the person—e.g. possessive or competitive individualism—which should be rationally revised—given its tension with other ideals or norms built into our culture and tradition (e.g democratic equality, the Kantian ideal of human worth, etc.). Even so, such lines of criticism need not imply a blanket rejection of **any** notion of individual responsibility, merit, and desert; indeed, they typically assume some such notions— what persons **would** deserve if there were "genuine" equality of opportunity, respect for individual differences, democracy, community, virtue, etc. In sum, the general notion of individual merit and desert is so central to our practices and judgments that

43

a theory of justice cannot completely discount it without sacrificing its own plausibility.

In my view, the justification of the difference principle does not depend on a blanket repudiation of meritocratic notions. The Kantian conception, as I will read it, is both compatible with a limited role for meritocratic notions in the just society and rich enough to motivate the acceptance of the difference principle. This will be my two-pronged argument. The question upon which the acceptance of the difference principle turns is not, "Do persons ever deserve differential treatment or rewards of any sort based solely on differences of individual character, merit, or performance?" The question is rather, "Do persons deserve unequal income, wealth, economic authority, or power based solely on such individual differences?" In the standpoint of social justice, the question of whether the very notion of individual merit is defensible need not arise. The key problem concerns the proper basis for distributing or allocating "primary social goods": basic rights, liberties, opportunities, income, wealth, authority and power. Supposing that individuals do more or less inevitably differ in ability, character, merit, performance, etc. (even in a perfectly just society), are any of these differences appropriate grounds for an unequal distribution of basic political, civil or economic rights? What is and is not an appropriate reward or social form of recognition for individual merit, virtue, or achievement?

The justification and acceptance of the difference principle is fully compatible with the recognition of individual differences in merit, character, virtue, etc. Furthermore, it is fully compatible with informal practices which signify this recognition: the practice by individuals of communicating praise, blame, admiration, respect, disrespect, etc. to individuals on the basis of their contributions to Rawlsian justice, and the practice by groups of awarding various non-economic honors, accolades, or incentives to these same individuals. In Rawlsian society, no one enjoys any more civil or political freedom, income, authority or power **just** because he or she has more of those acquired talents, virtues, or broad human traits especially valuable within Rawls's just society. Nonetheless, it is rational to expect that such persons will and should continue to enjoy various sorts of unequal individual recognitions within the constraints of social justice. So, in Rawlsian society, persons **as individuals** may well earn unequal respect, recognition, praise, admiration, honor, status, etc.— just as long as it is compatible with broadly equal respect for their Kantian personhood (the equal worth of their rational capacities), and for the basic rights, liberties, mutual material benefits, etc. all deserve as Kantian persons. Rawls goes to the unnecessary and implausible extreme of voiding the whole notion of (unequal) individual merit because he is anxious to protect the more basic notion of that which all persons deserve simply because they are persons. He detaches the distribution of the primary social goods from the notion of individual merit and desert because these goods constitute the essential conditions of respect for all persons' rational capacities. Yet, Rawls's Kantian idea of what all persons deserve just because they are rational beings (capable of the just and the good) is compatible with various notions of what individuals deserve because they have developed particular traits or virtues which distinguish them from one another. In sum, Sandel is mistaken in contending that either the Kantian conception of personas or the difference principle requires a blanket rejection of all meritocratic conceptions. But what, then, is the Kantian argument for the difference principle?

3. Rawls's Kantian Ideal of Personhood

The Kantian argument for the difference principle—Rawls's conception of redistributive economic justice—depends upon a robust reading of the Kantian conception of personhood as a powerful normative ideal of human personality and society embedded in the public culture of modern liberal-democratic society. In **A Theory of Justice**, Rawls's Kantian conception of persons enjoyed an ambiguous and dubious status in the argument as a whole; the Kantian conception is introduced as one way of interpreting the picture of persons implicit in contractarianism.[12] However, in Rawls's subsequent essays, the Kantian conception assumes a far more central role in contractarianism which transforms the entire structure, content, and grounding of Rawls's theory of justice.[13] How? First, the Kantian conception becomes an ideal of human personality—a conception of the supreme good or value to be embodied in just institutions. Secondly, because this ideal is now incorporated into the "original position" as an assumed premise of its hypothetical deliberators, Rawls's theory of justice is no longer "value-neutral," no longer a strictly "deontological liberalism" which asserts the priority of the right over the good. Thirdly, this Kantian ideal is not a universal conception which is established by the hypothetical choice of purely rational deliberators under absolutely ideal circumstances. Rather, it is an historical ideal which is established by a reflection upon political tradition which does not occur within the original position. Rather, its results—the Kantian ideal of personhood—are built into the original position. This historicizes the whole contractarian situation, giving its deliberations and deliberators a specific and concrete moral identity which is validated through a non-contractarian mode of reflection. As a result, the burden of Rawls's theory shifts its weight from contractarianism to his normative, and indeed hermeneutical, reading of the ideals implicitly within modern

gerald doppelt

political culture and tradition. In effect, we have a kind of "communitarian liberalism" which seeks to ground its principles and conceptions in an understanding of national political communities with liberal-democratic traditions.

As I read it, the Kantian conception of personhood ties the moral identity of persons to the supreme value of their rational capacities for normative self-determination. This conception affirms that all normal persons have two central moral powers or capacities: (1) the capacity to determine, pursue, and revise their own conception of the good life, i.e., the kind of life most worth living; and (2) the capacity to acknowledge and respect this same capacity of self-determination on the part of other persons. The Kantian ideal further affirms that all persons have "two highest-order interests in realizing and exercising their moral powers."[14] Armed with this Kantian moral identity, Rawls's hypothetical deliberators desire or value, above all, being "a certain kind of person"—a person who is able to develop and exercise his or her "highest-order" powers of normative self-determination.[15] The desire to embody this ideal in social and political life motivates and justifies the choice of Rawls's two principles of justice in the original position.[16] This choice is based on the knowledge that the protection of Kantian self-determination for all persons depends on certain formal guarantees—the equal rights and liberties of democratic citizenship—plus guaranteed access to certain material resources—indeed, the highest possible standard of living which a modern welfare-state can deliver for all of its citizens. Thus Rawls's ideal of self-determination incorporates the understanding that the development and exercise of this capacity turns on the material circumstances of persons and not just their abstract or formal freedom and right to do or be this or that.

Suppose we move from Rawls's hypothetical deliberators to the citizens of his well-ordered just society. These citizens are not exclusively or primarily concerned with keeping out of one another's way, respecting one another's freedom of choice, as Sandel claims. They are motivated, instead, to participate in an economic and political system consciously aimed at providing everyone with the means to develop and exercise their capacities of self-determination, to pursue and realize a way of life which embodies their own normative judgment and will. Furthermore, this motivation is grounded in citizens' common attachment to the value of rational self-determination and to their society's shared work or project of bringing all persons within reach of realizing this value in their own ways of life. In Rawls's conception of a just society, its members are bound together by, and identify with, this common end and good. Thus, quite apart from its mode of justification, Rawlsian liberalism is "communitarian" in its social content and implications for political identity.

Sandel mistakenly identifies Rawls's standpoint with the classical liberalism of a Hobbes or Locke in which the ultimate motive of every individual for supporting the political order is the protection of one's own self-interest, freedom, or private property. Rawlsian liberalism is much closer to the spirit of T.H. Green, R.H. Tawney, and John Dewey. In these left-leaning understandings of liberalism, the moral development, self-determination, and rational capacity of each citizen is comprehended as a public good which animates the development of the whole society through the shared consciousness of its members. Needless to say, the question remains as to whether or not Rawls can succeed in justifying this full-blown Kantian ideal of persons and social justice. Similarly, the question remains as to whether or not Rawls's model of the just society (a reformed liberal-democratic, welfare-state capitalism) is stable and well-ordered, or rather works out to sustain many of the same privatistic, aggressive, divisive, and anti-liberal motivations which cut against the grain of his ideal of community in existing society. Yet in this context, my main purpose is to show that it is Sandel's reading of the Kantian conception of persons, not the Kantian conception itself, which is impoverished. For, if I am correct, in Rawls's Kantian conception, personhood is **not** detached from all normative commitments, shared ends, intersubjective identity, common projects and allegiances, etc., as Sandel claims. Rawls's Kantian conception is tantamount to an ideal of human personality which implies a shared, community-based sense of the good within the moral identity of persons. This shared sense of the good as normative self-determination provides the foundation for Rawlsian redistributive economic justice that is lacking in Sandel's reading.

Where and how has Sandel gone wrong? Sandel clearly sees what Kantian personhood is not, without attempting to see what concrete affirmative content it might yet have. He sees that Kantian persons do not identify with the particular values, ends, roles, or ways of life which they choose as distinct individuals. He finds this implausible and impoverishing because real person's essentially have such particular normative attachments, along with the ties of community they typically entail. Yet against Sandel, such particular normative attachments are an inappropriate basis for social justice. In modern liberal-democratic society, people have different normative attachments and legitimate disagreements concerning the best or right way to live. The pluralism and tolerance built into modern liberal-democratic consciousness and institutions are, for Rawls, essential and affirmative features of social justice. Thus the particular identities and attachments of particular persons and groups do not afford a basis for social justice.

Rather, social justice needs to be founded on some level of people's moral identity deeper and more universal than the particular values and attachments which differentiate them as individuals. The Kantian ideal meets this need, for it can plausibly be characterized as a shared value which commonly underlies the respect and protection we accord to particular ways of life and conceptions of the good which we reject for ourselves. This respect is based on the assumption that these particular ways of life embody the normative judgment and will of their agents and, as such, express their individuality, freedom, and moral powers or agency. In this way, the value of Kantian self-determination is a pre-condition of the value of many different particular ways of life and conceptions of the good, whose choice by individuals constitutes a concrete embodiment of their Kantian self-determination. As a result, Kantian moral identity only enters into the self-understanding of persons in the degree that they recognize, or identify with, the value of rational self-determination as the common unifying ground of the respect and value to be accorded to particular persons and ways of life.

Thus, while Sandel is correct in insisting that Kantian persons do not identify (exclusively or primarily) with the **particular** way of life or values they choose, he is incorrect to infer from this that they therefore have no concrete moral identity, value-commitments, or shared allegiances. Because he identifies Rawlsian personhood with the wholly abstract neutral "value" of bare personal choice in itself, he fails to consider what ideal of human powers, faculties, and self-objectification might be implicit in liberalism's affirmation of free choice, in particular free normatively grounded choice. For these reasons, he misses the positive normative content which informs Kantian moral identity.

Sandel's misreading of the Kantian conception of persons translates into a misunderstanding of Rawls's Kantian argument for the difference principle. He places too much emphasis on Rawls's rejection of meritocratic conceptions—which, I have argued, is inessential to the Kantian argument for the difference principle. He misreads this argument because he detaches the Kantian conception of persons from the theory of value and moral identity it presupposes. In his discussion of the difference principle, Sandel repeatedly asserts that on Rawls's Kantian conception, no one deserves anything.[17] A person has no intrinsic worth or value prior to institutional life. The "self" lacks any value or valued attribute which could serve as a moral basis for its claim to the material benefits or social use of individual assets dictated by the difference principle. Sandel holds that this inner poverty of the "self" of Rawlsian liberalism undercuts the justification of contemporary liberalism's favorite public programs and goods, e.g., affirmative action, welfare, economic redistribution, etc.

But this reading of Rawlsian liberalism badly distorts its normative impetus found in the work of Rawls and the democratic tradition he hopes to clarify. Ironically, Sandel paints himself into an extremist corner which is the exact opposite of the corner into which Rawls painted himself. In order to affirm the equal worth or universal desert of all persons (in the standpoint of social justice), Rawls is led to deny the very coherence of any notion of individual merit and desert. Conversely, in order to capture the detachment of Kantian moral identity from the notion of individual merit and desert, Sandel is led to deny or ignore liberalism's essential normative commitment to the moral worth of persons, the supreme value of their rational self-determination, and the notion of what a person deserves just because he or she possesses this capacity for self-determination. Yet, it is this normative commitment, under its Rawlsian interpretation and application to economic life, that explains what Sandel misses: the Kantian motivation for the difference principle, the liberal-democratic argument from human dignity to a Rawlsian-type welfare state.

4. Communitarian Liberalism?

In my defense of Rawls against Sandel, I have argued that Rawls's conception of social justice is rooted in a Kantian ideal of personhood which attaches individual moral identity to an essentially shared, intersubjective, and public conception of the highest good at stake in political life. Rawls's vision of a just society in which persons cooperate in order to sustain Kantian self-determination for all as a public good requires a fairly substantial sense of community among its members. In this sense, Rawls's framework can be understood as a "communitarian liberalism."

But there is a deeper and more fundamental sense in which his present argument points toward a "communitarian liberalism." Rawls grounds his argument in an interpretation of modern liberal-democratic society with its public culture and traditions of political discourse and judgment. Whereas many interpreters of modern society find only self-interest, power and manipulation, the dissolution of all tradition and community ties, the myth of the public good, false ideologies of legitimacy and social rationality, Rawls seeks to discover a shared rational basis for political community—indeed, an incipient if latent sense of community waiting to be brought to light, elaborated, and self-consciously strengthened through reflection.

gerald doppelt

Rawls's Kantian ideal captures a conception of persons that is "implicitly affirmed" in the public discourse of liberal-democratic society and is "congruent with our deeper understanding of ourselves and our aspirations...."[18] Through a critical reflection upon the liberal-democratic tradition of political judgment, we are supposed to discover that this very ideal of personhood has already entered into our moral identity, creating the ground of whatever unity and order is exhibited by our political community.[19] Indeed, Rawls thinks of his whole contractarian framework as providing a language for bringing to self-consciousness what is lived and enacted as the liberal-democratic tradition of discourse and judgment: "As a device of representation, the ideal of the original position serves as a means of public reflection and self-clarification."[20] Rawlsian liberalism is thus "communitarian" not only in the sense that his conception of a just society requires, in the ideal, strong ties of community based on common purpose and a shared intersubjective moral identity. It is also "communitarian" in the sense that he hopes to ground this philosophical conception upon a reading of the shared ideals and identity underlying the really existing modern political community.

Is Rawls's reading of modern liberal-democratic society reasonable and sound? Can it ground a theory of social justice for our time and place? In many ways, Rawls leaves his notion of a "public reflection and self-clarification" concerning tradition at an intuitive level. As I argue below, he does not confront the phenomenon of (1) disagreements over the nature of a tradition of discourse and practice, and (2) conflicts or tensions within it, and between it and other equally powerful discourses and practices in the same society. As a result, Rawls's conception of philosophical method and moral reasoning does not speak to the question of grounding one, as against other, rival interpretations of modern political discourse.

Nonetheless, Rawls's methodological notion of "reflective equilibrium" can be adapted to yield a way of grounding his Kantian reading of the liberal-democratic tradition. With this method, philosophical conceptions are grounded by the degree of "reflective equilibrium" which they can be made to exhibit with some ordinary, pre-philosophical class of judgments or body of discourse. "Equilibrium" exists when the philosophical theory yields results which more or less match the results of ordinary discourse. The equilibrium is moreover "reflective" when it results from our freedom and willingness to revise either the philosophical theory and/or our ordinary discourse, upon due reflection of the incongruities between them.

In this methodological context, Rawls's reading of the liberal-democratic tradition is an attempt to ground the Kantian ideal (as well as other features of the original position) by showing that as a philosophical conception, it can strike a reflective equilibrium with our most widely shared and characteristic judgments, or discourse, concerning political right and social justice. Put differently, the argument is that these judgments, as well as the tradition in which they are embodied, have a unity which is best interpreted as resting on the Kantian ideal. Interpreted in this way, our most common judgments concerning the civil and political rights of individuals, legitimate and illegitimate state action, the private and public sphere, the rule of law, what is and is not fair in political life, etc., all find their unity and grounding in the Kantian ideal—the underlying aim of preserving a person's freedom to determine his/her own way of life, and to a lesser extent, his/her freedom to participate as equals in the determination of public life as well (law, public policy, etc.).

To a point, Rawls's interpretation of modern liberal-democratic society is fruitful and sound. Its virtues emerge by way of a succinct contrast with Sandel's methodological framework. Sandel's communitarianism also posits some mode of critical reflection through which I (and others) might discover that certain ends or values are not just "mine" but "me" and that they are shared in an essential way by others.[21] Through such "enlightenment" concerning my authentic moral identity, the basis is laid for founding a larger conception of the good and firmer sense of community than what we started with. But, out of the totality of my social experiences, what in particular do I reflect on in order to uncover my true moral identity and an authentic prospect for heightened community? Sandel would have us reflect upon "our moral experience" within varying contexts of friendship, family, and the more and less inclusive communities in which we live.[22] But "moral experience" is too loose and abstract a notion to sustain any determinate epistemological conception of **critical** reflection. Supposing that we discover ourselves to have conflicting ends, common purposes, and moral identities in different spheres or contexts of life, how then do we determine which is most authentic or true? Why should the identity we discover to be implicit in one sphere or context of life have any relevance to the reconstruction of social life as a whole? How do we distinguish rational from voluntaristic or ideological forms of self-discovery or self-constitution? A genuinely **critical** reflection upon moral experience requires a more rigorous and determinate conception of both notions.

Rawls's framework is more fruitful in these respects. He argues not from an amorphous notion of our "moral experience," but from a shared democratic tradition which informs the moral experience of our entire society. Tradition—a more or less shared body of judgments and discourse governing a certain sphere of social

51

gerald doppelt life—provides a more objective, well-defined object of critical reflection through which we might discover a common moral identity or ideal of central relevance to political life. We critically reflect upon the claims, judgments, language arguments, symbolic acts, etc. which we make **from the standpoint of political justice, as citizens** to other members of the **political community,** in order to discover what we take to be fundamental to our sense of ourselves in **this global political context.** Furthermore, if a certain (e.g. Kantian) interpretation emerges form this reflection, it can be tested and revised in light of its ability to illuminate yet other aspects of our tradition-bound judgments of political right. Various rival interpretations can each seek to create their own optimal reflective equilibrium with the whole body of shared political judgments and discourse concerning justice characteristic of modern liberal-democratic society.

Furthermore, in my view, Rawls's Kantian ideal of persons succeeds in generating reflective equilibrium with much that is essential in our political tradition. Many of our shared judgments of political right do rest on the assumption that the value of a person's way of life, including his or her participation in public life, depends on its being, or becoming, a genuine embodiment of that person's powers of moral judgment and will; and not just an embodiment of blind luck, external circumstance, domination or coercion, bare impulse or appetite, ignorance, or irrational forces of personality or society. The protection and respect we extend to persons and ways of life different from our own rests on this assumption. It is this value of normative self-determination which is protected by the political rights, duties and liberties that are central to much of our political discourse and practice. Modern liberal-democratic laws, institutions, practices, and procedures are implicitly thought to protect the widespread aspiration of persons in our society to have a life of their own, to live, act, and think as free beings, to express their individuality and sense of worth in their ways of life and in the constitution of the public sphere. The Kantian ideal accounts well for many of the most basic claims of political right and justice made by the citizens and the polity in their various debates and relations to one another. To this extent, Rawls's "communitarian liberalism" succeeds in capturing and illuminating much of the ground of the unity and coherence exhibited by modern political discourse. Nonetheless, Rawlsian liberalism exhibits an inherently flawed understanding of modern social life, which I seek to expose in what follows.

5. Rawlsian Economic Redistribution and the Contradictions of Liberal-Democratic Society

Rawls's "communitarian liberalism" is unable to found an

adequate theory of justice for our time and place. His liberalism masks thoroughly fundamental conflicts within liberal-democratic society which are reflected in its tradition of discourse and its rival ideals of personhood. The Kantian reading of modern political life captures something basic within it, but is otherwise one-sided and in this sense "false." The Kantian ideal of "free and equal persons" is supposed to reveal the deepest and most fundamental idea within modern political life. Nonetheless, there are widespread attitudes, judgments, and practices concerning what is fair and unfair, right and wrong, legitimate and illegitimate in political and social life which embody **rival** ideals of (and aspirations for) full personhood which work against the Kantian ideal and need to be included within any adequate conception of the form(s) of moral identity underlying modern liberal-democratic society. Moreover neither Sandel's communitarianism nor Rawls's Kantian liberalism recognize that once we have discovered or recovered the moral ideal(s) or identity(ies) underlying our shared experience of social life, we might further discover that we have reasons for wanting to transform this underlying moral ideal or identity. For it might well embody incoherences and conflicts which work out in practice to sustain and legitimate a form of socio-political life with harsh and destructive scarcities in human goods and human worth. We require a paradigm of moral reason and political theory equal to the task of informing such an analysis of modernity. In this final section, I will argue that such a paradigm is necessary to overcome the impasse of Rawls's argument and take us well beyond the methodological resources open to communitarianism and Kantian liberalism.

Rawls's own method of reflective equilibrium can be employed to show that there are rival ideals of human personality presupposed by the modern political tradition. The most natural way to develop my point is to return to a consideration of Rawls's redistributive conception of economic justice, which I have defended against Sandel's critique. Rawls's conception clearly implies a degree of income-redistribution and political control over economic outcomes which sharply conflicts with rather widespread judgments in the modern polity and liberal-democratic tradition concerning what is fair and unfair, and what is legitimate for the state to do. Relative to these judgments, Rawls's difference principle drives a far too radical and arbitrary wedge in society between what individuals can earn or produce "on their own" in market relations and what they end up with, and can legitimately call "their own." Furthermore, relative to our political tradition of judgment, Rawls's principle gives the state a power to regulate and abolish inequalities of economic power and wealth that is "oppressive" and "unjust." Indeed, this is, or would be, the common response to the Rawlsian welfare-state among people and groups who otherwise disagree about the appropriate level, kind, and recipient of public welfare or welfare-rights in modern democratic society.

In sum, Rawls's conception of economic justice exhibits a profound disequilibrium with much established judgment, discourse, and practice—that part of the political tradition which fixes the role of the state in economic life and delineates the place of private property, market exchange, appropriation and accumulation, etc. within the public and private spheres of society. Rawls counts upon reflection to restore equilibrium. The reflective grounding of the Kantian ideal, and thus the principles of justice to which it leads, may convince persons to rethink those judgments which conflict with this ideal and the model of economic life it sustains. In effect, Rawls's "reflective equilibrium" strategy appeals to a reflection upon one part of the liberal-democratic tradition (one discourse or body of judgments within it) in order to provide the bases for rethinking and transforming another part of it. This philosophical strategy mirrors the contemporary left's strategy of grounding a socialist organization of production and economic life as an extension of established democratic values and principles into a sphere of life from which they have been irrationally (or unreflectively) excluded.

Form my standpoint, the fatal flaw in any such strategy is that it misunderstands the logic or rationality of that part of the modern political tradition of judgment which legitimates the broad contours of capitalist economic practice. This part of our tradition implicitly rests not on any Kantian conception of persons, but rather upon a rival bourgeois, or "competitive individualist" conception of persons. This conception or ideal of personhood is expressed in widely shared judgments, attitudes, discourses, and practices which justify the fairness of the social and economic inequalities in Western society: inequalities of property, wealth, income, professional privilege, economic power, training and skill, status, etc. Many persons take these inequalities to be more or less fair and legitimate, in principle if not always in practice, on the ground that they constitute the proper rewards for unequal individual achievement, talent, merit, character, rationality, effort, etc. Such judgments, and the practices which they sanction, are driven by a powerful bourgeois ideal of personhood which embraces the pursuit of allegedly scarce social status, professional standing, occupational achievement, economic security, material well-being, independent livelihood, economic power, and, underlying these, the scarce respect and recognition for one's person which are supposed to accrue to those who achieve these things. Rawls's Kantian reading of the modern liberal-democratic tradition misses the essential part of it, which undergirds the perceived legitimacy and justice of capitalist market relations and distributions, and rests on the implicit conviction that only through **these** relations are persons free to affirm their individuality and character. Within the standpoint of this bourgeois moral identity, competitive professional and economic performances of various kinds mark the measure of full personhood and human worth. Of course, I am not affirming the bourgeois ideal, which would be irrelevant in any case to my present argument. My point is rather that the bourgeois or "competitive individualist" conception of persons is in fact quite as powerful as the Kantian conception in the modern political tradition of judgment and sentiment.

A patriarchal ideal of persons also powerfully shapes the attitudes, judgments and practices of many persons concerning what is and is not just in socio-political life. This conception or ideal of persons posits an essential connection between full personhood and gender. It "idealizes" different roles and activities for men and women, and justifies laws, policies, institutions, decisions, etc. which "respect" these gender-based differences. The roles and activities of men require full rational and moral faculties assumed to be lacking or less present in women; these roles and activities and these alone betoken full personhood. Women are understood to possess other, lesser virtues which fit them for other, lesser roles and activities in society. This patriarchal conception of personhood informs widespread judgments concerning the fairness of inequalitieslin the rights, freedom, opportunities, offices, professions, income, salaries, powers, duties, and responsibilities of men and women in society. It also enters into the fact that whatever they do, men tend to gain more respect and recognition for what they do than is the case with women. This patriarchal conception of persons may be understood as a component of the liberal-democratic tradition, or as part of the wider cultural background of modern society. In either case, it is a powerful part of the shared moral identity of persons in modern liberal-democratic society, quite as influential in shaping the judgment, discourse, and practice of social justice as the Kantian and bourgeois ideals.

Thus, if we reflect upon the whole body of discourse and judgment concerning socio-political justice and injustice in modern liberal-democratic society, we do not recover simply one underlying Kantian ideal of persons as free and equal self-determining moral beings. We also recover rival bourgeois and patriarchal ideals which define full persons, in quite different and, indeed, more scarce terms. These ideals are rivals in several senses. First, they yield incompatible judgments concerning political justice in many contexts. A political redistribution of income, educational opportunity, health care, child care, or any other vital human resource which is arguably just and reasonable from the standpoint of the Kantian ideal, is unjust and contentious from the standpoint of the bourgeois or patriarchal ideal. Political measures which enhance all persons' ability to develop, exercise, or realize their powers of self-determination in personal or public life may well violate the morality of the market and drive a wedge between what individuals "get" and "what they earn"; or, may well violate the "morality" of patriarchy and drive a wedge between what individuals get and what is thought proper for their gender. Secondly, because these ideals are rivals in the first sene, they are rivals in the additional sense that they fuel many of the most basic political conflicts of liberal-democratic society at all levels of social and so-called "private" life. Thirdly, these ideals are rivals in the sense that they each are embodied in and sanction social practices whose effects tend to erode respect for the other ideals and persons' ability to realize them.

For example, the bourgeois ideal informs economic practices and interests which routinely reproduce harsh patterns of unemployment, poverty, mindless and self-stultifying forms of work, inequalities of educational and economic opportunity between classes, manipulative instrumental relations between persons in the labor process, etc. Such circumstances erode the opportunity and ability of many children and adults to develop, exercise, or preserve their moral powers of self-determination. The bourgeois conception of persons informs modes of economic life which reduce Kantian self-determination—the real freedom to embody one's normative judgment and will in one's life—to a hostage of scarce socio-economic circumstance and class position. It is equally clear that the Kantian ideal informs human interests and conditions of life (modern democratic citizenship, the state, rule of law, the public sector, etc.) which work to limit, and in some respects undercut, the role of market relations, private property and economic power, the competition for scarce goods, etc. in constituting social life.

Thus, on my analysis, the modern liberal-democratic tradition of judgment does not rest on the Kantian ideal of personhood alone. This Rawlsian position misunderstands the logic of modern liberal-democratic society and the tensions or incoherences embodied in it. Rather this tradition rests on rival ideals of personhood, each of which sanctions and inspires a way of life which in one degree or another undermines social, cultural, and psychological conditions hospitable to the satisfaction of the other ideal(s). Indeed, this same sort of conflict or inner tension obtains within the bourgeois conception of persons itself. This point requires clarification in order to appreciate the internal complexity of the bourgeois conception and the genuinely affirmative dimensions it has which Rawls neglects, to the detriment of his

conception of social justice.

One part of the bourgeois conception affirms the freedom of individuals to accumulate vast capitals and powers over the labor force, the structure of work, the location of investment and production, the goals or products of labor, etc. It idealizes the post or position of capital as the kind of individual achievement which signifies unusually scarce and valuable human powers, skills, abilities, character traits, etc. This ideal, along with the particular rights of private property which it entails, sanctions conditions of economic life in which many persons are unable to realize the more modest and minimal bourgeois ideals of individual achievement and human worth: the capacity to support oneself and one's family through gainful employment, the achievement of a decent or respectable standard of living by one's own labor, and the ability to do work requiring some respectable level of autonomy, responsibility, intelligence, rational judgment, skill and personal creativity. In this way, one part of the bourgeois ideal sanctions conditions of life in which the more modest aspirations engendered by other parts of the ideal are thwarted for many persons. As I read it, the bourgeois conception of persons entails a zero-sum struggle for scarce goods located within a hierarchy of value and human worth on which the more scarce the good, the higher it is. The social character of the goods idealized at the high end generates conditions in which many persons are unable to secure the more modest goods more modestly idealized at the lower end. This marks a conflict or tension within the bourgeois conception of persons which fuels many of the disagreements and struggles over economic life and public policy in modern liberal-democratic society. A more complete analysis of modern liberal-democratic society would also need to understand the place of a patriarchal conception of persons within its judgments and practices, and the conflictual relations between it and the other ideals.

The knowledge that there are conflicting ideals or moral identities implicit in our shared tradition of political judgment points to the necessity of going beyond Kantian liberalism, communitarianism, and communitarian liberalism. To be sure, Rawls's notions of reflection on tradition and "reflective equilibrium" can be employed (as I have in fact employed them) to uncover the conflicting ideals implicit in shared political judgments. Similarly, communitarians such as Sandel are able, at least in principle, to recover the shared identifications and normative attachments which give the people of this or that community a common moral experience, discourse, tradition, or practice. But if and when, in this way, reflection uncovers conflicting ideals and moral identities, neither Kantian liberalism nor communitarianism has the methodological resources for determining the full destructive impact of these conflicts upon the moral life of a society or the possibility of rethinking the political tradition in the interest of gaining a more coherent and less destructive conception of persons and society.

These tasks require that we go beyond a reflection upon a shared tradition, discourse, or body of judgment in order to comprehend the whole way of life embodied and sanctioned in tradition. For, it is only through a concrete sociological understanding of this way of life that we can determine if it entails destructive scarcities of human worth and value rooted in the conflicting ideals and moral identities built into the tradition itself. Does our established tradition or discourse of political judgment express and inform a way of life involving shared ideals and aspirations which are bound to be frustrated in large measure for many persons by the conditions of life which the tradition sanctions? Does the normative self-understanding underlying our tradition and discourse effectively sustain, or reflect, a way of life in which the good, and respect for the persons who are supposed to exhibit or achieve it, are **unnecessarily** and **avoidably** scarce? By the use of our moral and political imagination, can we re-invent the dominant political understanding of personhood, the good, and the right in light of the patterns of human frustration, deprivation, and suffering it entails?

We require a conception of moral theory and practical reasoning which embraces these questions. Such a conception might yield the knowledge that we have good reasons for transforming the (conflicting) moral identity and shared values which we have discovered ourselves to have. This way of understanding and transforming the social and human costs of the whole way of life informed by a political culture is not utilitarian. The costs are not assessed in utilitarian terms, relative to existing desires and their satisfaction. Rather, these costs ought to be understood and assessed as scarcities in the very kinds of good, personhood, human worth, and reciprocal recognition at the heart of our tradition of political judgment. Any conception of moral theory and practical reasoning equal to these tasks will sustain a much closer affinity to sociological inquiry and moral-political imagination than what is available within communitarianism or liberalism.

Contemporary liberalism has aspired to comprehend social justice and the modern polity without undertaking any critical evaluation of the conceptions of value exhibited in modern society. Liberal theorists have affirmed the adequacy of value-neutral foundations, or simple, uncontroversial value foundations, for modern social justice. The liberal tradition is thus founded upon the assumption that a theory of political right need not challenge the rationality of established desires, preferences, values, and interests. The "deontological liberalism" of Rawls's **A Theory of Justice** asserts the priority of the right over the good:

beyond liberalism and communitarianism

the right and just are characterized independently of any conception of the good life. Utilitarian liberalism grounds social justice upon the "self-evident" value of human happiness, the satisfaction of desire or preference in itself. Classical *laissez faire* liberalism bases its conception of political right and the "minimal" state upon the "incontestable" value of negative liberty, freedom from constraint, absolute "self-ownership." Rawls's recent "communitarian liberalism," as I have read it, seeks its grounding upon shared uncontroversial ideals such as the Kantian ideal of normative self-determination in the private and public spheres of modern society.

In this way, liberalism, in all of its variants, turns upon a conception of moral reasoning and theory detached from the task of rethinking the good and reconstructing established moral-political right and social justice for modern society. Such a theory must speak to conflicts over political right and justice which are rooted in latent conflicts between rival ideals of human worth and moral identity built into liberal-democratic tradition, discourse, and practice. Without an analysis, self-consciousness and rational mediation of these conflicting self-understandings, no possible conception of political right and social justice can be motivated or justified. Liberalism and communitarianism founder upon their inability to rethink and transform the moral identity they posit or uncover, in light of a more complex and less coherent normative reality then either is aware of.

The conception of moral theory advanced here seeks to comprehend and rethink modern liberal-democratic society from within the standpoint of its own historical forms of moral identity and framework of alternative normative and political possibilities. On my conception, both the object of critical reflection and its results are historically bounded in scope and validity; yet this non-universalistic understanding of moral theory may presuppose a method of reflection and critique with some universalistic presuppositions, application, and validity. Even so, such universalistic underpinnings by themselves would be too weak, abstract, procedural, and programmatic to produce any standpoint of real social understanding and well-motivated critique. The achievement of **this** standpoint hinges on the kinds of sociological and cultural specificity I have sought in this essay.

University of California, San Diego

ENDNOTES

1. John Rawls, **A Theory of Justice**, Cambridge, Harvard University Press, 1971, pp. 60-64, 195-284.

gerald doppelt

2. John Rawls, **Liberalism and the Limits of Justice**, Cambridge, Cambridge University Press, 1982.

3. Alasdair MacIntyre, **After Virtue**, Notre Dame and London, University of Notre Dame Press, 1981; Michael Oakeshott, **Rationalism in Politics**, London and New York, Methuen, 1982; Robert Bellah, *et al.*, **Habits of the Heart**, Berkeley and Los Angeles, University of California Press, 1985; Michael Walzer, **Spheres of Justice**, New York, Basic Books, 1983.

4. **Liberalism and the Limits of Justice**, *op. cit.*, pp. 69-71.

5. *Ibid.*, pp. 71-77.

6. *Ibid.*, pp. 85-86.

7. *Ibid.*, pp. 87-95.

8. *Ibid.*, p. 144.

9. *Ibid.*, pp. 177-179.

10. **A Theory of Justice**, *op. cit.*, pp. 101-106.

11. "Kantian Constructivism in Moral Theory: The Dewey Lectures 1980," **The Journal of Philosophy** 77, 1980, pp. 515-572; "The Basic Liberties and Their Priority," **The Tanner Lectures on Human Values**, Vol III, Salt Lake City, University of Utah Press, 1982; "Justice as Fairness: Political not Metaphysical," **Philosophy and Public Affairs**, 14, 1985, pp. 223-251.

12. **A Theory of Justice**, *op. cit.*, section 40, "The Kantian Interpretation of Justice as Fairness," pp. 251-258.

13. See note 11 above.

14. "Kantian Constructivism in Moral Theory: The Dewey Lectures 1980," p. 525.

15. *Ibid.*, pp. 533, 547-549.

16. *Ibid.*, pp. 524-527; "The Basic Liberties and Their Priority," *op. cit.*, pp. 18-20.

17. **Liberalism and the Limits of Justice**, *op. cit.*, pp. 85-87, 92-93.

18. "Kantian Constructivism in Moral Theory: The Dewey Lectures 1980," *op. cit.*, pp. 518-519.

19. "Justice as Fairness: Political not Metaphysical," *op. cit.*, pp. 4-5.

kenneth baynes
the liberal/communitarian controversy and communicative ethics

The recent exchange of views between liberals and their communitarian critics raises a number of issues important for the forms of democratic practice as well as for the kinds of justification appropriate to the political ideals embodied in democratic regimes.[1] It asks us to consider, for example, how a "politics of the common good" might differ from a "politics of rights," or what should be the proper role of judicial review in a constitutional democratic regime.[2] But it also asks us to reassess how claims about basic rights or distributive principles are best justified apart from, or prior to, their constitutional recognition. Do the political ideals and institutions we value require a general and coherent political morality for their defense (as Dworkin has argued), or is the interpretation and clarification of the shared meanings latent in our social practices via stories the most for which we can hope (as Walzer has recently claimed)?[3] The thesis developed in what follows is that so far the exchange between liberals and communitarians has revealed significant limitations and weaknesses on both sides: contemporary liberals have not sufficiently considered the social origin and justification of basic rights; whereas communitarians have not adequately addressed the nature and conditions of democratic citizenship. In both cases a broader framework of practical philosophical reflection is required for confronting these limitations. More specifically, in this essay I will consider three issues raised in the controversy:

kenneth baynes the liberal claim concerning the priority of the right over the good; the conception of the self or moral agency; and the justification of political ideals and institutions. I will then suggest how Habermas's communicative ethics, which takes as basic the idea that norms are justified only if they are ones which free and equal persons could agree to in a practical discourse, might provide a way of reformulating these issues within the framework of a proceduralist model of democratic justification.[4]

A central feature of contemporary liberalism is its assertion of the priority of the right over the good. One principal motivation behind this claim is the belief that questions of right or justice should outweigh or trump considerations of social utility or the common good, thereby securing for individuals a domain of thought and action free from intrusion by others. Individuals are guaranteed a right to develop freely their own identities and, in turn, to participate in the democratic process as autonomous citizens. Thus, many liberal rights—for example, most civil rights—impose limits or constraints on the pursuit of private and public interests, while other rights, including political and social (or welfare) rights, are intended to secure or render more effective the participation of individual citizens in shaping or defining the common good or democratic will.[5] In either case, however, the net effect of such rights is to remove certain items from the agenda of collective decision-making or majority rule.[6]

For many liberals, however, the assertion of the priority of the right over the good is also based on a second, deeper motivation. It suggests that the concept of right is to be defined prior to and independent of a conception of the good.[7] According to this view, individual conceptions of the good are invariably particular and diverse and thus cannot provide a suitable basis for justifying principles which define the basic terms of social cooperation. Rather, questions of justice are supposed to be neutral with respect to alternative conceptions of the good. For Kant, of course, rights were to be defined not with a view to the objects willed, but in connection with the universal features of practical reasoning (or moral agency). While contemporary liberals have resisted Kant's idealist metaphysics, they have generally followed him in defining the right independent of the objects individuals desire or ends they pursue. Rawls's model of "justice as fairness" defends the priority of the right through recourse to the idea of an "original position" in which hypothetical parties deprived of knowledge of their own conception of the good select principles for defining the terms of social cooperation between them. He nevertheless goes on to suggest that the original position "may be viewed as a procedural representation of Kant's conception of autonomy and the categorical imperative," appropriately stripped of its metaphysical baggage.[8] For Dworkin, alternatively, rights are introduced in connection with the egalitarian dimension of utilitarianism: they work to avoid a form of "double-counting" by insuring that, for the most part, personal rather than external preferences are counted in a process of collective decision-making where each person's vote counts as one.[9] Finally, according to Bruce Ackerman, basic rights are defined in a dialogue conceived as a *modus vivendi* whereby individuals agree to bracket their disagreements about the good for the sake of finding a common basis for resolving social conflicts: "When you and I learn that we disagree about one or another dimension of the moral truth, we should not search for some common value that will trump this disagreement; nor should we try to translate our moral disagreement into some putatively neutral framework; nor should we seek to transcend our disagreement by talking about how some hypothetical creature would resolve it. We should simply say **nothing at all** about this disagreement and try to solve our problem by invoking premises that we do agree upon."[10] Thus, despite other significant differences between them, each of these "deontological liberals" proposes a formula for determining the right independent of a particular conception of the good.

Communitarians have questioned the priority of the right over the good in both of these senses, e.g., as a moral trump and as an epistemological claim about the order of moral knowledge. Charles Taylor argues that, rather than reversing the relation between the right and the good in utilitarianism as Rawls suggests, liberalism merely advances its own alternative conception of the good life.[11] According to Taylor, we cannot resolve questions of right or justice by adopting a neutral stance toward the goods humans value; rather we must enter into the thicket of the "languages of qualitative contrasts" in order to make unavoidable, if difficult, choices from among the diversity of goods.[12] Similarly, in contrasting his own notion of "complex equality" to what he calls the "simple equality" of Rawls, Michael Walzer claims that arguments about rights and distributive principles must take into account the shared meanings of various social goods. Rights cannot be defined prior to the good since the nature and scope of distributive principles will vary with respect to different social goods.[13] Finally, Sandel and MacIntyre both argue that the liberal emphasis on rights rests on a social ontology which is morally bankrupt and which disregards the important role of tradition and community in defining rights and distributive principles.[14]

It would appear, then, that the disagreement between liberals and communitarians is clear. Liberals defend the priority of the right over the good on the assumption that there is no uncontroversial conception of the good that all citizens recognize as a common basis for defining the terms of social cooperation. Communitarians argue that the liberal attempt to define principles of justice without acknowledging the diversity of goods presupposed by different rights and distributive principles is to engage in an act of self-deception. However, a flair for the rhetorical on both sides allows the disagreement to appear sharper than it is. On the one hand, most liberals would concede that rights presuppose some notion of the good of citizenship (or at least the good of a system of fair social cooperation). Thus, in A **Theory of Justice** Rawls acknowledges that the definition of the right relies on a "thin theory" of the good which includes minimal assumptions about the nature of social cooperation. More significantly, in several recent essays, he claims that justice as fairness draws upon certain ideals widely shared in the public culture of democratic societies.[15] On the other hand, many communitarians (such as Taylor and Walzer) would surely place liberal rights high on any list of the diversity of goods valued in a democratic society. The important question is whether they can appeal to anything other than either social utility or prevailing beliefs and practices when those rights come into conflict with other ideals. It is unclear, for example, whether Sandel's "politics of the common good," which would allow a community to prevent a pornographic movie theater from opening, would also permit a neighborhood to enact zoning laws prohibiting a communal group from sharing the same household.[16] Priority is accorded to liberal rights not simply because they happen to be valued more than other goods or ideals—that is not necessarily true now and could certainly cease to be true in the future. Rather, certain rights have priority because of their fundamental role in securing equally the capacity of individuals to form and to pursue their own conception of the good and, thus, to shape their own identity within mutually defined and recognized constraints.[17] Thus, while it may be true that liberal rights are valued in part because they serve to promote a general conception of the good for democratic citizenship, one can argue equally well that certain forms of community are valued because they are ones that affirm the autonomy of individual citizens and permit them to pursue their own conceptions of the good within mutually defined and recognized constraints. Taylor's remarks are revealing in this regard. On the one hand, he states, "The citizen republic is to be valued not just as a guarantee of general utility, or as a bulwark of rights. It may even endanger these in certain circumstances." On the other hand, he immediately adds, "We value it also because we generally hold that the form of life in which men govern themselves, and decide their own fate through common deliberation, is higher than one in which they live as subjects of even an enlightened despotism."[18] Similarly, Walzer argues that the lines of demarcation that differentiate various social goods according to their own distributive principles should ultimately be ones that are democratically drawn: "Liberalism passes definitively into democratic socialism when the map of society is socially determined."[19] However, if liberal rights are to be defended in connection with a more general conception of democratic rule, then the priority of the right over the good may finally rest on a deep paradox: it rests on an argument for removing certain items from the agenda of collective decision-making in order that the decision-making process be made more fully democratic, that is, in order that the process exhibit equal regard for the autonomy of each member of the *demos*.[20] (I will discuss this paradox in more detail below.)

The critique of the priority of the right over the good is closely associated with a second issue in the dispute between liberals and communitarians—the conception of the self. In fact, the general strategy Sandel proposes for critically interpreting Rawls's theory of justice is to accept the two principles as stated and ask, "What then must be true of a subject for whom justice is the first virtue?"[21] His claim is that in the final analysis the self presupposed by the theory, which he describes as an "essentially unencumbered subject of possession," is both morally objectionable and internally incoherent. "Justice cannot be primary in the deontological sense because we cannot coherently regard ourselves as the kind of beings the deontological ethic— whether Kantian or Rawlsian—requires us to be."[22]

According to Sandel, what must be true of Rawls's conception of the self is that the self possess a unity and identity prior to its membership in any particular historical community and prior to its attachment to any specific ends. What is constitutive of the self is not any specific set of ends or attachments, but simply its **capacity** to choose. According to this "thin" view of the self, the self relates to its ends as a mere "system of desires." These desires can perhaps be rationally ordered according to their relative intensity, but they do not essentially determine the self's identity.[23] But, Sandel argues, such a distinction between the self and its ends ultimately undermines the very notion of moral agency itself. A self that exists prior to its ends must be a self "wholly without character, without moral depth," and thus "incapable of self-knowledge in any morally serious sense."[24] If all that justice protects is the capacity of an agent to make radically free—e.g., arbitrary—choices, it becomes unclear why it should even be valued as the first virtue of societies. Moreover, according to Sandel, the problem is not merely that the moral agent becomes a subject of radical choice deprived of any "qualitative distinctions of worth between different orders of desires," for "where the self is unencumbered and essentially dispossessed, no person is left for **self**-reflection to reflect upon."[25] In MacIntyre's apt phrase, moral agents have become ghosts—and, of course, ghosts don't exist![26]

In the alternative conception advocated by both Sandel and Taylor, human beings are conceived as "self-interpreting animals."[27] This suggests that our relation to our desires is not that of a "simple weigher" of preferences, but that the process of interpreting and evaluating those desires is **constitutive** of who we are. Moreover, our membership in specific historical communities also informs our attempts at self-understanding and shapes our self-identity. Thus, we are "thick" selves in the sense that we exist only **in** our individual and collective self-interpretations.[28]

However, it is debatable whether Sandel has provided the best reconstruction of the model of the self implicit in Rawls's theory.[29] While Rawls does describe his model-conception of the person as possessing two "highest-order moral powers," including the capacity to form, to revise and rationally to pursue a conception of the good, he does not deny the great extent to which our identity is socially constituted. In an earlier article, Rawls acknowledged that no degree of personal identity is "natural or fixed"; rather, he claimed, it depends upon the ideals and values fostered by a society and its institutions.[30] The real question at issue is whether it is possible, in the context of a plausible theory of moral psychology, to distinguish between certain capacities an agent has—such as the capacity to have and revise a conception of the good—and the exercise of those capacities in connection with varying content and within different situations. Sandel does not address this question of a moral psychology. Rather, by assuming that we can only have an intelligible model of moral agency if that model incorporates a notion of strong evaluations, that is, preferences that are constitutive of the self, he begs the question at hand. Furthermore, it is doubtful that Rawls must accept the description of his model of the self as "thin" and as a "simple weigher of preferences." A better characterization, I would like to suggest, is found in a model in which the agent possesses a hierarchy of motivations, or what Harry Frankfurt has called "first- and second-order" desires and valuations.[31] In this view moral autonomy is construed as the capacity to assess effective first-order desires in light of higher-order desires, as well as the capacity to integrate both levels of desires into a coherent sense of oneself in a reflective manner. My suggestion is that Rawls's description of the first highest-order moral power more or less parallels this description of a moral agent's second-order capacity to reflect critically upon and revise first-order preferences and desires. This model of moral agency could be developed further in connection with Kohlberg's description of a post-conventional level of moral reasoning characterized in terms of the agent's capacity for decentration, differentiation and reflexivity with respect to moral claims. Autonomous moral agency would then need to be understood not only as the capacity to formulate a coherent sense of oneself in a reflective manner, but also as the capacity to take sufficiently into account the viewpoint of others when assessing a norm or maxim of action.[32] If this reconstruction is at all plausible (as I believe it is), then the conception of the self that underlies Rawls's theory of justice would not be that of a "thin self," but that of an agent endowed with these general capacities for post-conventional moral reasoning.

Although Rawls might have replied to Sandel in something like the manner I have sketched, he chose instead to sidestep the deeper philosophical questions of a moral psychology and argue that "justice as fairness" need not rely on what he describes as a "general and comprehensive moral view" of the self.[33] His own response is to claim that his model-conception of the person with its two highest order moral powers is simply "a basic intuitive idea assumed to be implicit in the public culture of a democratic society."[34] According to Rawls, the further defense of a conception of moral agency as part of a comprehensive moral theory violates a "principle of tolerance" that must be observed in the attempt to justify principles of justice within a democratic society. While I agree that any acceptable principles of justice must be ones that could be publicly acknowledged by all members of a society, this sort of retreat from philosophical argument ultimately reflects an untenable division of labor between philosophy and the more mundane interpretation of everyday beliefs and practices.[35] To see why this is so, we must shift our attention from the conception of the self or moral agency to a third issue raised in the liberal/communitarian controversy—the nature of the justification of political ideals.

In "Justice as Fairness: Political Not Metaphysical" Rawls concedes that "it was an error in **Theory** (and a very misleading one) to describe a theory of justice as part of the theory of rational choice....There is no thought of trying to derive the content of justice within a framework that uses the idea of the rational as the sole normative idea. That thought is incompatible with any kind of Kantian view."[36] Thus the kind of justification that Rawls attempts is not "foundationalist" in the sense that it seeks to ground the principles of justice in a morally neutral conception of rational choice.[37] Conversely, Rawls also argues that the defenses of liberalism found in Kant and in Mill are inappropriate for a democratic order since they rely on "comprehensive moral views"—a notion of autonomy in the first case, utilitarianism in the second—which will inevitably be controversial in a society characterized by the "fact of pluralism."[38] Between the Scylla of foundationalism and the Charybdis of a comprehensive moral doctrine, Rawls would seem to have little room to navigate.

The strategy Rawls adopts for his constructivist approach is to argue from ideas that are assumed to be widely-shared in the public political culture of modern democracies. "Justification," he claims, "is addressed to others who disagree with us, and therefore it must always proceed from premises that we and others publicly recognize as true.... It goes without saying that this agreement must be informed and uncoerced, and reached by citizens in ways consistent with their being viewed as free and equal persons."[39] Thus, while there may not be a morally neutral ground, Rawls claims that there is nevertheless a common ground and one which does not entail controversial philosophical assumptions. However, at this point Rawls is confronted by what I shall refer to as the "paradox of democratic justification." In a democratic forum, claims about rights or principles of justice are legitimate only if they are ones that free and equal citizens would publicly accept; but if a meaningful distinction is to be maintained between *de facto* and *de jure* legitimacy, we need some criteria for determining whether an agreement reached is indeed between free and equal persons. In his earlier critique of Nozick, Rawls argued that in order to determine whether an agreement is voluntary, we need to know whether the background framework or "basic structure" of the society in which the agreement takes place is just.[40] This requirement now returns to haunt him: Since his theory of justice is designed to assess whether the basic structure of our society is just, Rawls cannot appeal **directly** to a common ground or an overlapping public consensus for the justification of his principles.

Rawls might reply that he does not make such a direct appeal to a public consensus and that to assume so underestimates the important role of reflective equilibrium in his constructivism.[41] Although the process of reflective equilibrium provisionally takes certain judgments and ideas as fixed, nothing is immune to criticism and revision. At an initial stage of "narrow reflective equilibrium," concrete moral judgments are dialectically confronted with moral principles of varying degrees of generality until a person arrives at a coherent set of moral beliefs. At the next stage, a condition of "wide reflective equilibrium" exists when an individual's coherent set of concrete moral judgments and moral principles is also corrected by, and brought into harmony with, a broader set of theories (theories of psychology, sociology, meaning, etc.) as well as various formal "conditions of rationality" (such as the conditions of generality, publicity and universality).[42] Thus, the principles of justice are not justified by a direct appeal to simply any set of widely-shared views, but by an appeal to views that have been refined and adjusted in a process of reflective deliberation.

This interpretation of Rawlsian constructivism also helps clarify the specific role performed by the original position in his argument. "As a device of representation the original position serves as a means of public reflection and self-clarification. We can use it to help us work out what we now think, once we are able to take a clear and uncluttered view of what justice requires when society is conceived as a scheme of cooperation between free and equal persons...."[43] The original position does not introduce any further moral assumptions than those already provided by the model-conceptions of the person and the well-ordered society; but neither does it shift the context of argument to a morally-neutral framework of rational choice. Rather, it is part of an exercise to help clarify ideas that you and I, who have been asked to find principles of justice, already recognize, or at least would recognize upon due reflection. It is an argumentative device that Rawls introduces in a public dialogue, quite literally, with us. It thus becomes less important (and is not surprising) that the parties in the original position unanimously chose the two principles—after all, they were constructed to select them. What matters is whether we, as free and equal citizens, (unanimously?) acknowledge the ideas employed in the construction of the original position as well as in its particular design. The reasoning that goes on inside the original position is part of a more general argument that we should accept the principles chosen there, and it is this more general argument that appeals to the presence of an overlapping consensus in our public culture.

While these qualifications suggest how Rawlsian constructivism differs from various forms of intuitionism and moral realism, they do not adequately deal with the paradox of democratic justification.[44] Why should we regard the principles as justified unless it is our beliefs that have been brought into a condition of reflective equilibrium as a result of a process in which we have participated? And, unless we have actually participated in the process, what reasons are there for preferring Rawls's characterization of impartiality in terms of the original position over other characterizations?[45] At this point, it is possible to push Rawlsian constructivism in either of two directions. Both have the advantage of seeing the justification of political ideals (or, more specifically, rights and distributive principles) within the context of a public dialogue. The first alternative, which is also found in the work of Bruce Ackerman and Charles Larmore, construes the public dialogue as a *modus vivendi*.[46] The second pushes Rawlsian constructivism in the direction of Habermas's communicative ethics. Although his recent writings suggest that

Rawls might be inclined more toward the first interpretation, I will offer some considerations in support of the second.

On the first interpretation of Rawlsian constructivism, the justification of principles for regulating the basic structure is the result of a public discussion, or as Rawls puts it, the use of "free public reason."[47] The principles must finally be ones that would be accepted by us or, at least, ones that it would be unreasonable for us to reject.[48] However, in this interpretation, not just any argument or consideration may appropriately be introduced into the public discussion. In view of what Rawls calls "the fact of pluralism," we cannot hope to reach an agreement about principles if appeal is made to what Rawls calls "general and comprehensive moral doctrines." Such a general and comprehensive doctrine, according to him, includes not only religious world-views and substantive moral theories (such as natural law, utilitarianism or Kantian autonomy), but also philosophical arguments and (non-common sense) theoretical assumptions from the social sciences.[49] His claim is that in a liberal democracy philosophical and social-scientific theories will also be controversial and thus cannot appropriately serve as a basis for agreement. Rather, the search for a consensus on the basis of which principles can be justified should only draw upon "fundamental intuitive ideas regarded as latent in the public political culture."[50] The search employs what Rawls elsewhere describes as a "method of avoidance" in which the guiding question becomes: "What is the least that must be asserted; and if it must be asserted, what is its least controversial form?"[51]

This interpretation is close to the model of "conversational constraint" proposed by Ackerman, and to the model of discursive legitimation offered by Larmore.[52] The idea is to remove from public discussion certain controversial claims, claims which finally come down to "a bare confrontation between incompatible personal points of view," so that a common basis for reaching agreement about principles can be established.[53] Rawls's particular strategy runs as follows: While it would be wrong to justify political principles by appeal to the notion that persons are free and equal moral beings on, say, Kantian or theological grounds, we are nevertheless entitled to appeal to this notion since it is widely shared in our public culture (even if, on a more personal level, this turns out to be so for a variety of reasons). If such a strategy is to be at all successful, Rawls must be able to draw a reasonably clear distinction between such comprehensive doctrines and the common sense or mundane beliefs latent in the public culture. Toward this end he suggests that there is "lots of slippage" between the beliefs that individuals hold and comprehensive doctrines so that it becomes possible to appeal to the former in a public debate without invoking the latter.[54] Among these intuitive beliefs, Rawls includes a "common sense political sociology" (which includes a belief in the fact of pluralism and its persistence in a democratic society) and a "reasonable moral psychology" (which presumably includes the model-conception of the person characterized by the two highest-order powers).[55]

However, it can certainly be argued that this strategy implies a moral epistemology of its own. It assumes, for example, that individuals have the capacity to distinguish between mundane beliefs and comprehensive doctrines, as well as between a public and non-public conception of their own self-identity. It also assumes that, for the purpose of justifying political principles, individuals are able and willing to set aside those comprehensive doctrines and personal points of view.[56] That is, it assumes that individuals can adopt a post-conventional form of moral reasoning characterized by the capacity for decentration, differentiation and reflexivity with regard to moral claims. Rawls's political conception of justice thus seems to imply a conception of the self or moral agency like the one indicated above.

Furthermore, Rawls must assume that the facts he cites are ones that would be acknowledged by all in a public discussion. Otherwise, they would not provide a suitable basis for establishing a broad overlapping consensus. Equally as important, "the guidelines of inquiry and publicly recognized rules of assessing evidence" used in identifying the facts must also be subject to public debate and discussion.[57] To be sure, such a debate could not consider such rules and guidelines all at once or in toto, but in principle the facts that help to define an overlapping consensus, as well as the standards of rationality for determining those facts, are also subject to public discursive justification. The public use of reason implies that present agreements are in principle always open to future discursive vindication.

These two considerations push Rawlsian constructivism in the direction of Habermas's communicative ethics. As with the first interpretation, the justification of principles regulating the basic structure is tied to the idea of a public discussion. But, on this interpretation, no prior constraints are imposed on the subject-matter that can be introduced into the discussion. Rather, each participant is free to introduce any argument or consideration she believes relevant. The interpretation of specific needs and preferences (or conceptions of the good, more generally) cannot be excluded in advance by fiat; rather, the question is whether there are good reasons—reasons that could not reasonably be rejected by any of the participants—for excluding some preferences or conceptions of the good from affecting the selection of principles of justice. Such an interpretation of the public justification of political principles reflects the basic idea of a communicative ethics, namely, that a norm is justified only if it could be agreed to by all concerned as participants in a practical discourse where no force but that of the better argument prevails.[58]

This characterization of a practical discourse is open to a serious objection: If there are no substantive constraints on what can be introduced into a practical discourse, what is to prevent the outcome from conflicting with some of our most deeply held moral convictions? What is to prevent the participants from agreeing to anything or, perhaps more plausibly, never reaching any general agreement at all?[59] A proper reply to this objection takes several steps, and will finally return us to the three issues we have already considered in the liberal/communitarian controversy.

The first step is to recall that on both interpretations, e.g., the *modus vivendi* and Habermas's ideal discourse, the characterization of the public discussion is itself supposed to specify an impartial standpoint for selecting principles of justice. Thus, it cannot be objected that the outcome of the public discussion might fail to be just since there is no independent standard of impartiality apart from the discursive process itself. Like Rawls's conception of justice as fairness generally, both interpretations present a case of pure procedural justice. The issue in dispute is which of the two interpretations of Rawlsian constructivism (or what further interpretation) better defines what it means to take an impartial standpoint, and I have already suggested why the first interpretation should yield to the second. The "method of avoidance" (Rawls) or "constrained conversation" (Ackerman) cannot *a priori* exclude considerations to which the participants would not agree. Any constraints that are imposed must be ones that could in principle be agreed to by the participants upon due reflection and deliberation.

However, to claim that any constraints imposed on discourse are subject to discursive vindication is not to assert that no constraints can be imposed. It is also important in this regard to distinguish between more and less fundamental constraints in terms of their constitutive role for a discourse.[60] Examples of a more fundamental constraint would be the stipulation that each participant have an equal opportunity to introduce arguments and considerations into the discussion or that each participant be provided equal access to information relevant to the issue under discussion. Habermas claims that constraints such as these can be derived from the general presuppositions of argumentation in a manner analogous to Grice's derivation of conversational maxims.[61] Nevertheless, even these constraints (as well as the success of their derivation) are in principle subject to discursive justification. To that extent, an element of the "paradox of democratic justification" persists even in the proceduralism of communicative ethics.

At a less fundamental level, many other constraints may well be imposed on discourses in view of the issues or tasks at hand. It is reasonable to assume, for example, that the basic rights and liberties specified in Rawls's first principle and contained in the U.S. Constitution would serve as constraints on most public debates, removing topics from the agenda because of their deeply personal nature or close connection with recognized spheres of privacy. However, discussion about the nature and scope of these rights is always something that can become the subject of public debate. As arguments about rights become more closely tied to specific interpretations of social goods, what counts as a good argument will no doubt depend more heavily on the shared meanings and practices that make up the everyday lifeworld. Thus there will be plenty of room for what Walzer (among others) refers to as "immanent critique." However, if there is a disagreement with the interpretation offered by "the (temporary) majority of sages" (Walzer), the grounds of that interpretation should themselves become the subject-matter of a practical discourse.

Similarly, it is important to distinguish between types of discourse according to the constraints required by the tasks at hand. Despite the complex interpenetration between the variety of more or less institutionalized discourses, the constraints on legal discourses will differ from the constraints on moral discourses, and both will differ again from the constraints imposed on political discourses.[62] While all discourses are implicitly oriented to the ideal of the uncoerced agreement of all, some will require further constraints on admissible forms of evidence and types of argument.

Thus, to return to the objection above, the model of communicative ethics neither assumes nor requires that most practical discourses will have a unanimous agreement as their outcome. A public debate about such political policies as welfare or affirmative action may well have little chance of ending in general agreement. But this is not necessary in a model of communicative ethics. What is required is that the compromises be considered fair in the sense that the rules regulating such discourses are themselves open to debate and in principle capable of general agreement at a deeper level of justification. At this deeper level, debates about basic constitutional rights or the preferred design of legal and political institutions are less suitably the subject-matter for a fair compromise or majority rule, since it is in the context of these rights and institutions that the other rules of decision-making are held to be fair.[63] For just this reason, the process for changing constitutional rights and the design of legal and political institutions is more complex and generally requires broader agreement. Finally, while a public moral-practical discourse about principles for regulating the basic structure is a discussion that requires unanimity, it is also a discussion that (for a variety of reasons) is unlikely to occur as such. Simulated discussions (such as Rawls's in **A Theory of Justice**) enter into the general public sphere, but they do not equally include us all and their claims so far have not received anything approaching a unanimous agreement. But it also does not seem likely that we can simply replace such hypothetical and invented dialogues by the mere telling of stories as Walzer suggests. Rather, what is also called for by a communicative ethics is a complementary theory of social institutions that reflects on the kinds of institutions necessary for expanding the possibility and variety of practical discourses within the public sphere at all of these different levels.[64]

The picture I have sketched is that of a network of various types of practical discourse ranging from the institutions for discussion and debate within the non-state public sphere—civil society in Hegel's sense—through the institutions of political, legal and constitutional debates, to the counterfactual ideal of an uncoerced moral-practical discourse as the final justification for these various forms of institutionalized debate. The constraints specified in the latter, while not in principle immune to debate, are derived from the general presuppositions of argumentation and from a model of post-conventional moral autonomy. However, this theory of communicative ethics also needs to be complemented by a critical social theory that reflects on the kinds of institutions required for that model of moral autonomy to flourish.

Let me conclude by briefly indicating how the three issues discussed above might be reformulated within the context of a communicative ethics. First, the priority of the right over the good is both preserved and transformed. It is preserved in the fundamental constraints imposed on a moral-practical discourse, e.g., the symmetry conditions and the right to equal participation. Further, as in the liberalism of Rawls and Dworkin, the general justification of basic rights is developed in terms of their role in securing the conditions for the autonomy of citizens by removing certain issues from the agenda of democratic decision-making. However, the grounds of this priority are altered since, in the final analysis, it is only within a practical discourse that the conditions required for individual autonomy, and thus the distinction between questions of justice and questions of the good life can be clarified and justified.

74

Second, the conception of the self that informs this defense of the priority of justice is not that of an "atomistic," "essentially unencumbered" or "emotivist" self, but that derived from a philosophical argument about the nature of post-conventional moral reasoning. A fuller defense would undoubtedly involve other philosophical and social-theoretic arguments about the normative core of modernity. Thus, in contrast to Rawls's recent arguments for a political conception of justice as fairness, I do not believe that the conception of the self that underlies his theory can be articulated without appealing to what he considers to be controversial philosophical and theoretical assumptions. However, I have also suggested that Rawls's belief that this appeal to such controversial assumptions must not be made, relies on an unduly restricted notion of the justification of political ideals.

Finally, the justification of rights and political ideals cannot proceed without reflecting upon "the conditions and presuppositions of the activity of justification itself."[65] I have argued that as a type of democratic justification, Rawlsian constructivism is better interpreted along the lines of Habermas's communicative ethics than Ackerman's model of "constrained conversation." But I have also suggested that it is unlikely (and undesirable) that counterfactual and hypothetical arguments introduced into a public debate might simply be **replaced** by a notion of storytelling (Walzer) or **dismissed** as the result of an unfortunate "urge to see social practices of justification as more than just such practices" (Rorty). Rather, such arguments reflect an element of unconditionality that "makes the validity (*Gültigkeit*) we claim for our views different from the mere *de facto* acceptance (**Geltung**) of social practices."[66] One aim of a critical social theory is to indicate how such arguments may become less counterfactual by becoming a more permanent and wide-spread feature of our public life and institutions.

State University of New York at Stony Brook

ENDNOTES

1. In this essay I will focus primarily on Michael Sandel's critique of John Rawls's theory of justice, but I also refer to Ronald Dworkin, Bruce Ackerman and Thomas Nagel as contemporary liberals, and Charles Taylor, Michael Walzer and Alasdair MacIntyre as their communitarian critics. For a good overview of this debate, see Amy Gutman, "Communitarian Critics of Liberalism," **Philosophy and Public Affairs** 14, 1985, 308-22; H.N. Hirsch, "The Threnody of Liberalism," **Political Theory** 14, 1986, pp. 423-449; and Robert Thigpen and Lyle Downing, "Liberalism and the Communitarian Critique," **American Journal of Political Science** 31, 1987, pp. 637-655.

kenneth baynes

2. For the contrast between "a politics of the common good" and "a politics of rights," see Michael Sandel, "Introduction" in **Liberalism and Its Critics** (New York University Press, 1984), p. 6; on the question of judicial review, compare Michael Walzer, "Philosophy and Democracy," **Political Theory** 9 (1981): 379-99 and Ronald Dworkin, "The Forum of Principle" in **A Matter of Principle** (Harvard University Press, 1985).

3. See Ronald Dworkin, "Liberalism" and his review of Walzer's **Spheres of Justice** ["What Justice is Not"] in **A Matter of Principle** and, most recently, Michael Walzer, **Interpretation and Social Criticism** (Cambridge: Harvard University Press, 1987), esp. pp. 65-6.

4. For Habermas's formulation of a communicative ethics, see "Diskursethik" in **Moralbewusstsein und kommunikatives Handeln** (Frankfurt: Suhrkamp, 1983); "Moralität und Sittlichkeit" **Merkur** 12 (1985); and "Gerechtigkeit und Solidarität" in **Zur Bestimmung der Moral**, ed. by W. Edelstein and G. Nunner-Winkler (Frankfurt: Suhrkamp, 1986); in this essay I treat Habermas's communicative ethics as a theory of political morality, comparable to Rawls's theory of justice, and thus leave aside the difficult question of whether it can also serve as a theory of personal morality as Habermas has claimed. A sharp critique of this latter claim is offered by A. Wellmer in **Ethik und Dialogue** (Frankfurt: Suhrkamp, 1985).

5. For an interpretation and defense of the expansion of rights along this line, see T.H. Marshall, **Citizenship and Social Class and Other Essays** (Cambridge University Press, 1950); see also Rawls, "The Basic Liberties and Their Priority" in **The Tanner Lectures on Human Values**, V. III, ed. by S. McMurrin (University of Utah Press, 1982): 3-87.

6. This way of viewing the function of rights is also mentioned by Rawls in "The Idea of an Overlapping Consensus," **The Oxford Journal of Legal Studies** 7 (1987), p. 14.

7. According to Sandel, this second motivation is distinctive of what he calls "deontological liberalism" (in contrast, for example, to the liberalism of Mill), **Liberalism and the Limits of Justice** (Cambridge University Press, 1982), p. 2.

8. **A Theory of Justice** (Cambridge: Harvard University Press, 1971), p. 256; I deal below with some of the recent developments in Rawls's argument; in short, he now attempts to base his "political conception" of justice more directly on a broad public consensus that avoids controversial theories and philosophical claims.

9. See especially the formulation in his reply to H.L.A. Hart in "Do We Have a Right to Pornography?" in **A Matter of Principle**, pp. 365ff.

10. Ackerman, "Why Dialogue?" **Journal of Philosophy** 86 (January 1989) p. 16.

11. "The Nature and Scope of Distributive Justice" in **Philosophical Papers**, V. II (Cambridge University Press, 1985), p. 291; see also his

"Justice After Virtue" in **Moralität und Sittlichkeit**, ed. by A. Honneth and W. Kuhlmann (Frankfurt: Suhrkamp, 1986).

12. See "The Diversity of Goods" in **Utilitarianism and Beyond**, ed. by A. Sen and B. Williams (Cambridge University Press, 1982), p. 132.

13. Walzer, **Spheres of Justice** (New York: Basic Books, 1983), p. 15.

14. See Sandel, **Liberalism and the Limits of Justice**, pp. 165f. and A. MacIntyre, **After Virtue** (University of Notre Dame Press, 1981), chap. 3.

15. **Theory of Justice**, chapter 7; for the more recent argument, see "The Idea of an Overlapping Consensus" and "The Priority of Right and Ideas of the Good" **Philosophy and Public Affairs** 17 (1988): 251-76 (which appeared after the present essay was written).

16. See Sandel, "Morality and the Liberal Ideal" **The New Republic** (May 7, 1984), p. 117 and the controversial Supreme Court decision in **Village of Belle Terre vs. Boraas** [discussed by Nancy Rosenblum in **Another Liberalism** (Harvard University Press, 1987), pp. 157-8].

17. See Rawls, "The Basic Liberties and Their Priority," esp. p. 50: "A liberty is more or less significant depending on whether it is more or less essentially involved in, or is a more or less necessary institutional means to protect, the full and informed and effective exercise of the moral powers in one (or both) of the two fundamental cases."

18. "The Nature and Scope of Distributive Justice," p. 245.

19. "Liberalism and the Art of Separation," **Political Theory** 12 (1984), p. 328.

20. See the similar suggestion offered by Norberto Bobbio in "The Future of Democracy": "Whatever may be the philosophical basis of these [basic] rights, they are the necessary precondition of the mainly procedural mechanisms, which characterize a democratic system, to work properly," **The Future of Democracy** (University of Minnesota Press, 1987), p. 25.

21. **Liberalism and the Limits of Justice**, p. 49.

22. *Ibid.*, p. 14; see also p. 180.

23. In this context Sandel refers to Taylor's distinction between the self as a "simple weigher" and "strong evaluator" of preferences; see Taylor, "What is Human Agency?" in **Philosophical Papers**, V. I, pp. 15-44.

24. *Ibid.*, p. 180.

25. *Ibid.*, pp. 167 and 180.

26. See MacIntyre, "How Moral Agents Have Become Ghosts,"

Synthese 53 (1982): 295-312; Sandel's description and critique of the "unencumbered self" is virtually the same as MacIntyre's critique of the emotivist self in **After Virtue**, chap. 3.

27. Sandel, **Liberalism and the Limits of Justice**, p. 179 and Taylor, "Self-Interpreting Animals" in **Philosophical Papers**, V. I, pp. 45-76. Although Taylor has developed his model of human agency in more detail than Sandel, I do not see any significant differences in their positions—see my introduction to Taylor, "Overcoming Epistemology" in **After Philosophy**, ed. by K. Baynes, J. Bohman and T. McCarthy (Cambridge: MIT, 1987), pp. 159-63.

28. Taylor, **Philosophical Papers**, V. I, p. 3.

29. See Rawls's own reservations about this in "Justice as Fairness: Political Not Metaphysical," **Philosophy and Public Affairs** 14 (1985), p. 239 n.21.

30. On the two moral powers, see "Kantian Constructivism in Moral Theory," **Journal of Philosophy** 77 (1980), p. 525 and **A Theory of Justice**, p. 505; the earlier essay, which included a response to a related criticism of his conception of the self by Derek Parfit, is "The Independence of Moral Theory" in **The Proceedings of the American Philosophical Association**, 1975, (quotation from p. 20); see also Norman Daniels, "Moral Theory and the Plasticity of Persons," **The Monist** 62 (1979): 265-87.

31. See the essays collected in his **The Importance of What We Care About** (Cambridge University Press, 1988); for an extremely helpful attempt to work out some of the problems raised by this hierarchical model, see Irving Thalberg, "Socialization and Autonomous Behavior," **Tulane Studies in Philosophy** 28 (1979): 21-39.

32. I develop such a model of moral agency in **From Contractarian Theories of Justice to Normative Social Criticism: Kant, Rawls and Habermas** (Albany: SUNY Press, forthcoming), chapter 4; see Rawls's own description of the stages of moral development in **A Theory of Justice**, pp. 462ff.; and J. Habermas, "Moralbewusstsein und kommunikatives Handeln" in **Moralbewusstsein und Kommunikatives Handeln** (Frankfurt: Suhrkamp, 1983), esp. pp. 130-143.

33. See "Justice as Fairness," pp. 225 and 239 n.21; see also "The Idea of an Overlapping Consensus," p. 3.

34. *Ibid.*, p. 234.

35. In this sense I think his later essays indicate a shift away from some of his remarks in **A Theory of Justice** on the nature of justification which allowed a greater role for theoretical arguments: "There is no reason to assume that our sense of justice can be adequately characterized by familiar common sense precepts, or derived from the more obvious learning principles. A correct account of moral capacities will certainly

involve principles and theoretical constructions which go much beyond the norms and standards cited in everyday life; it may eventually require fairly sophisticated mathematics as well" (p. 47); for a similar reading of Rawls's earlier view of reflective equilibrium, see Norman Daniels, "Reflective Equilibrium and Archimedean Points," **Canadian Journal of Philosophy** 10 (1980): 83-103.

36. P. 237 n.20; see the similar remark in "The Basic Liberties and Their Priority," p. 20 n.20.

37. For a discussion of some of the weaknesses in this sort of foundationalism, of which Hobbes is a classical example, see Arthur Ripstein, "Foundationalism in Political Theory," **Philosophy and Public Affairs** 16 (1987): 115-137.

38. *Ibid.*, pp. 246-7; and "The Idea of an Overlapping Consensus," p. 4.

39. *Ibid.*, pp. 229-30.

40. See "The Basic Structure as Subject" in **Values and Morals**, ed. by A. Goldman and J. Kim (Dordrecht: Reidel, 1978), p. 54.

41. See, for example, his remark in "The Idea of an Overlapping Consensus": "Here I assume that free and willing agreement is agreement endorsed by our considered convictions on due reflection, or in what I have elsewhere called 'reflective equilibrium' " (p. 5 n.8).

42. Rawls's distinction between narrow and wide reflective equilibrium is implicit in **A Theory of Justice**, p. 49 and explicitly stated in "The Independence of Moral Theory," p. 8: for a discussion see Norman Daniels, "Wide Reflective Equilibrium and Theory Acceptance in Ethics," **Journal of Philosophy** 76 (1979): 256-82.

43. "Justice as Fairness," p. 238.

44. These considerations also point to a weakness in David Brink's recent attempt to criticize Rawlsian constructivism from the perspective of moral realism, "Rawlsian Constructivism in Moral Theory," **Canadian Journal of Philosophy** 17 (1987): 71-90. Rawls's constructivism does not depend on an argument about the underdetermination of moral theory on the basis of appeals to ideals of the person, but on a specific conception of an acceptable public justification of political ideals and principles.

45. See, for example, Thomas Scanlon's alternative characterization of the impartial standpoint in "Contractualism and Utilitarianism" in **Utilitarianism and Beyond**, p. 121; Jürgen Habermas's discussion of impartiality in "Gerechtigkeit und Solidarität"; and Thomas Nagel's comments on the need for "a higher-order impartiality" to adjudicate between different orders of impartiality in "Moral Conflict and Political Legitimacy" **Philosophy and Public Affairs** 16 (1987), p. 216.

46. The notion of *modus vivendi* used here (and, I believe, by Larmore

kenneth baynes and Ackerman) differs from the interpretation offered by Rawls. Rawls describes a *modus vivendi* as a form of justification that appeals to a convergence of self- or group-interests apart from any common moral motivations and thus is closer to what I described earlier as foundationalism (see note #36) and what Nagel has called a "convergence theory" (p. 213). The sense of a *modus vivendi* employed here is closer to what Nagel has described as a "mixed theory," e.g., one that appeals to both moral conceptions **and** self- or group-interest as the situation may require (Nagel, p. 220). Thus, in **Patterns of Moral Complexity** (Cambridge University Press, 1986) Charles Larmore states that a framework for dialogue cannot be derived solely from a neutral model of rationality but must assume that the parties "wish to show everyone **equal respect**" (p. 61). Ackerman also rejects such an attempt to ground the framework for dialogue in a neutral model of rationality. What constitutes a *modus vivendi* for them is simply the fact that the grounds for dialogue are not found in a claim to moral truth or what Rawls calls a general and comprehensive moral doctrine. Thus, despite his own claim that a "political conception of justice" is not simply a **modus vivendi**, Rawls's "method of avoidance" seems congruous with that of Larmore and Ackerman (see Larmore's remarks on Rawls's approach, p. 125).

47. "The Idea of an Overlapping Consensus," p. 8.

48. See T. Scanlon, "Contractualism and Utilitarianism," p. 111 on the importance of this distinction.

49. "The Idea of an Overlapping Consensus," pp. 7-8.

50. *Ibid.*, p. 8.

51. *Ibid.*, p. 8; see also, "Justice as Fairness: Political Not Metaphysical," p. 231.

52. See Bruce Ackerman, **Social Justice in the Liberal State** (Yale, 1980), p. 9 and "What is Neutral About Neutrality" **Ethics** 93 (1983), p. 375; Larmore introduces a "a universal norm of rational dialogue": "When two people disagree about some specific point, but wish to continue talking about the more general problem they wish to solve, each should prescind from the beliefs that the other rejects, (1) in order to construct an argument on the basis of his/her other beliefs that will convince the other of the truth of the disputed belief, or (2) in order to shift to another aspect of the problem, where the possibilities of agreement seem greater," (p. 53).

53. Nagel, p. 232.

54. "The Idea of an Overlapping Consensus," p. 19.

55. *Ibid.*, p. 5, note #7 and p. 24.

56. "Justice as Fairness," p. 241.

57. "The Idea of an Overlapping Consensus," p. 8.

58. See Habermas, "Diskursethik" in **Moralbewusstsein und kummunikatives Handeln** (Frankfurt: Suhrkamp, 1983), p. 103; and "Moralität und Sittlichkeit: Hegels Kantkritik im Licht der Diskursethik," **Merkur** 12 (1985), p. 1041.

59. Walzer offers a similar criticism in **Interpretation and Social Criticism**, p. 11, note #9.

60. Again I have in mind something like Norberto Bobbio's notion of constitutional norms as preliminary rules which allow democratic debate to take place, see "The Future of Democracy," p. 25.

61. Unfortunately I cannot take up his argument here, see his "Diskursethik"; the first set of "Intermediate Reflections" in **The Theory of Communicative Action** (Boston: Beacon, 1984); and my discussion in **From Contractarian Theories of Justice to Normative Social Criticism**, chapter 3.

62. See Habermas, "Law and Morality," trans. by K. Baynes, in **The Tanner Lectures on Human Values**, V. VIII, (University of Utah Press, 1988), pp. 217-79, esp. p. 271ff.

63. See Claus Offe, "Legitimation Through Majority Rule?" in **Disorganized Capitalism** (Cambridge: MIT,1985), pp. 259-99 and Arthur Kuflik, "Majority-Rule Procedure" in **Due Process (Nomos V. XVIII)**, ed. by J.R. Pennock and J. Chapman (New York: NYU Press, 1977), pp. 296-32.

64. Such a complementary theory is argued for by Jean Cohen and Andrew Arato in "Civil Society and Social Theory" (unpublished manuscript).

65. Jeremy Waldron, "Introduction" to **Theories of Rights** (Oxford, 1984), p. 20 (though he may well have something else in mind than the interpretation I have given to his remark here).

66. Habermas, "Philosophy as Stand-In and Interpreter" in **After Philosophy**, ed. by K. Baynes, J. Bohman and T. McCarthy (Cambridge: MIT, 1987), p. 314.

jean cohen
discourse ethics and
civil society

We have before us two concepts: modern civil society and discourse ethics. The first is evocative of the themes of classical liberalism: the term "civil society" calls to mind rights to privacy, property, publicity, free speech, association, and equality before the law. The second, with its emphasis on the equal participation of all concerned in public discussions on contested norms, obviously refers to the principles of democracy. The current vogue in contemporary political theory is (once again) to view liberalism and democracy as antithetical. Defenders of the core tenets of classical political liberalism often see democracy, with its emphasis on majority rule and participation, as either illusory or, worse, dangerous to existing liberties unless suitably restricted.[1] Advocates of radical democracy, on the other hand, stigmatize the liberal tradition itself as the main impediment to achieving a participatory democratic society.[2] Nevertheless, I contend that the plausibility of each depends on its conceptual and normative relation to the other. Unlike the defenders of the status quo, i.e., of liberal democracy, however, I assume that the defense and expansion of acquired liberties depend on the **further** democratization of the institutions of modern society. I shall argue this thesis in three steps. First, by presenting the theory of Discourse Ethics as articulated in the works of Jürgen Habermas.[3] Next, by defending my interpretation of it as a theory of democratic legitimacy and basic rights. And, finally, by assessing the institutional implications of the theory by discussing its link to a coherent conception of a modern and potentially democratic civil society.

I. What is Discourse Ethics?

Discourse ethics is an attempt to articulate those rules and communicative presuppositions that make it possible for participants in a practical discourse to arrive at a valid, rational consensus on social norms. Habermas maintains that when the validity (normative rightness) of a social norm has been questioned, social actors have three alternatives: they can switch to strategic action; they can break off all discussion and go their separate ways; or they can continue to interact practically by entering into a critical discussion (practical discourse) about the validity of the norm in question. A practical discourse aims at a rationally motivated consensus on norms. Discourse ethics articulates the criteria which guide practical discourses and serve as the standard for distinguishing between legitimate and illegitimate norms.[4]

As such, it consists of two core tenets.[5] The first specifies the necessary conditions for coming to a legitimate rational agreement, the second articulates the possible contents (on a formal level) of such an agreement.[6] A norm of action is to be considered legitimate only if all those possibly affected would, as participants in a practical discourse, arrive at an agreement that such a norm should come into or remain in force.

What is to be considered as a rationally motivated agreement, however, has rather demanding preconditions. In order that all affected have an "effective equality of opportunity to assume dialogue roles," there must be a mutual and reciprocal recognition, without constraint, by all as autonomous rational subjects whose claims will be acknowledged if supported by valid arguments.[7] But in order that the dialogue be capable of producing valid results, it must be a fully public communicative process unconstrained by political or economic force. It must also be public in terms of access: anyone, capable of speech and action who potentially will be affected by the norms under dispute, must be able to participate in the discussion on equal terms. In addition to these procedural rules regulating the organization of interaction in the framework of a practical discourse, participants must also be able to alter the level of discourse and progressively radicalize the argument at all levels.[8] Nothing can be taboo in practical discourse: not the reserves of power, wealth, tradition, or authority. In short, the procedural principles underlying the possibility of arriving at a rational consensus on the validity of a norm involve **symmetry, reciprocity, and reflexivity**.[9]

Clearly, not all processes of coming to an agreement satisfy such conditions. Most actual processes of consensus formation are "merely empirical"—i.e. they have not been subject to the (reflexive) test of the criteria listed above. Nevertheless, and unlike most contract theorists, Habermas insists on an **actual** rather than a **virtual** dialogue because "only an actually carried out discourse allows the exchange of roles of each with every actor and hence a genuine universalization of perspective that excludes no one."[10] Only an actual practical discourse or real dialogue cooperatively engaged in by all potentially affected by the norm under question can lead to a rational consensus on its validity. For only under such conditions can we know that **we**, together (and not privately), are convinced of something. Accordingly, Habermas reformulates the Kantian categorical imperative along lines compatible with the procedural rules of argument. "Instead of prescribing to all others as valid the maxim which I will to be a general law, I have to offer my maxim to everyone with the aim of discursively testing its claim to universalizability. The emphasis has shifted from what each and every individual can will without contradiction to be a general law to what each and every one will recognize in consensus as a universal norm."[11]

The idea of rational consensus, however, involves more than the actual participation of every affected person in the relevant discussion. The *de facto* recognition of a norm by the community merely indicates that the norm could be valid. Its actual validity can be ascertained only if we make use of a bridge principle to establish the connection between processes of collective will formation and the criteria for judging a particular norm. This brings us to the second aspect of discourse ethics: the formal contents of agreements. Habermas maintains that norms of action upon which we agree must articulate generalizable interests. "Every valid norm must satisfy the condition that the consequences and side effects which result from their general observance could be accepted by all those concerned."[12] Of course, this principle requires, in turn, an actual dialogue in which the need interpretations and interests of everyone get a fair hearing and in which it becomes possible to discern whether there is indeed a common interest that can become the basis of a norm.

The question immediately arises as to how we can know that an empirical consensus is valid and whether a given norm really expresses general rather than particular interests. While I cannot go into these questions adequately here,[13] allow me simply to repeat the answer first proposed by A. Wellmer which is now embraced by Habermas: all consensus is only empirical. The idea of a rational consensus, if taken as set of meta-norms and not as a prefigured form of life, means simply that an empirical consensus has, as it were, been put to the test. To doubt the rationality of an empirical consensus means either to contest the justice of the particular procedure used, or to challenge the rationality of the participants. In either case, the doubt remains as an hypothesis that can be sustained only through proposing specific counter-arguments in the context of a new discussion. This means that any consensus on norms must be considered fallible and criticizable, i.e., open to new arguments.[14]

II. The Object Domain of Discourse Ethics

Thus far I have simply summarized Habermas's formulation of discourse ethics. As several critics have pointed out, however, it is unclear what, precisely, is the object domain of the theory. On the one hand, Habermas considers it a universalistic moral theory in the Kantian tradition. On the other, he also presents discourse ethics as the heart of a theory of democratic legitimacy that provides an alternative to traditional and neo-contractarian theories. To make matters even more complicated, Habermas has argued that, as a principle of legitimacy, discourse ethics can resolve the apparent rift between legality and morality by revealing the political ethic underlying law. The first question, then, is what exactly is the proper object domain of discourse ethics? Is it a theory of morality or a theory of political legitimacy? Can it be both?

It is my thesis that discourse ethics works best as a political ethic, i.e., as a theory of legitimacy and basic rights.[15] It provides, in short, the standard with which to test the legitimacy of socio-political norms. Indeed, terms such as "public dialogue," "general interests," "all those affected," "social norms," "valid consensus," and "practical discourse," evoke the categories of political philosophy.[16] The theory becomes unnecessarily overburdened when construed as more than this. I remain relativistic regarding which general theory works best with respect to the realm of **autonomous moral judgment**. It is possible, nonetheless, to defend discourse ethics as a political ethic without committing oneself to a specific moral philosophy.

Any differentiation between a general moral theory and a theory of political legitimacy, however, leaves a key question: how does one draw the boundary line between the two? The classical criteria of nineteenth century liberalism made famous by Bentham and J.S. Mill do not suffice. It is no longer convincing to maintain that the difference between the private (realm of autonomous morality) and the public (realm of legality) can be decided according to the criteria of what concerns only myself and what concerns others. Both morality and legality relate to societal norms. The private and intimate realms have always been constituted and regulated by law: even if what is constituted is the realm of autonomous morality that can enter into conflict with law.

Moreover, my interpretation of the discourse ethic along the lines of a principle of democratic legitimacy presupposes a sociological insight concerning the positivization of law and morality. Nevertheless, the theory rejects the total denormatization of politics and law and the depoliticization of morality as inevitable consequences of this process.[17] How can this apparent paradox be resolved?

To begin with, it is clearly Habermas's view (and my own) that the development of autonomous universalistic morality, as well as the emergence of a formal, differentiated system of positive law, must be seen as immense historical achievements. These developments, moreover, are linked to the emergence of a specifically modern conception of **democracy** and **rights**, representing the constitutive conditions of a modern version of civil society. There is, however, another side to this process. The uncoupling of positive legal norms from the body of privatized morality based on the principles (a process that accompanied the emergence of the constitutional states and capitalistic market economies) entails a potential conflict between the loyalty of the citizen to the abstract rules of the legal system (which are valid only for the area "pacified" by a particular state) and the "cosmopolitanism of the human being" whose personal morality makes general claims.[18] Even more important, since the decline of modern natural law theories and the rise of legal positivism, is the claim that laws have normative content beyond the correctness of the appropriate legislative and legal procedures; that they are binding independently of relevant sanctions, has been repeatedly disputed. The differentiation between legality and morality has involved the separation of politics from the everyday lives of the citizens and the denormalization of legality itself, at least according to much legal theory since the nineteenth century. Formal positive law, in one view, sets no concrete obligations as did traditional natural law—it does not command but only forbids. Thus, only those norms are allowed that delimit compatible scopes of action in which the individual can pursue his or her particular interests.

Moreover, when the law is understood as the will or command of the sovereign (Hobbes, Austin), and when constitutions and fundamental rights are declared to be only special instances of positive law, the results go beyond the separation of morality and law. In effect, legal positivism announces the denormatization of law, its transformation into a set of empirical facts. Obligation is turned into prudent behavior in the face of possible sanctions. It is thus difficult to see how such a conception of law can involve anything like a genuine political ethics grounding legal or political obligation. As a theory of democratic legitimacy, however, discourse ethics presupposes that there is a normative and rationally defensible component of legality and politics which accounts for the obligatory dimension of legal norms and the legitimacy of the socio-political system.

In his debate with Weber and Luhman concerning the foundation of legal-rational denomination, Habermas repeatedly pointed to the impossibility of deriving the legitimacy of the modern legal system, as a whole, solely from the formality and systematicity of legal procedures.[19] Law as legitimate authority rests on extra-legal sources of justification. References to constitutions as the ultimate source of authority, at least on the part of formally democratic states, implies that the legitimacy of law is ultimately parasitic on the principles of democracy—**popular sovereignty** and **basic rights**—embodied in constitutions and in the democratic process allegedly behind their development and maintenance. The principles of democratic procedural legitimacy underlie the authority of law. These principles, however, can no longer be defended as sacred "self-evident truths" as they were in theories of natural law and in republican theories of civic virtue. The purpose of discourse ethics, then, is to provide a contemporary equivalent of such theories while avoiding their dogmatic presuppositions.

I thus propose viewing legality in terms of the old reference of formal sanctions that potentially involve the legislative and juridical powers of the modern state on behalf of **valid** norms. Moral rules (unless they become legal rules as well) cannot call upon such enforcement. Accordingly, discourse ethics, as I see it, **would apply to the legal system as a whole, as well as to particular complexes of legal norms that depend not only on sanctions but also on the interpretation and compliance of those who are concerned**. In the first instance, I reinterpret **discourse ethics as a principle of democratic legitimacy**, in the second, as **a theory of basic rights**. Moreover, these two dimensions of discourse ethics imply a province of autonomous moral judgment beyond its reach which nonetheless is its own presupposition. Let me briefly address the later issue and then turn to the institutional implications of the theory.

I am assuming that discourse ethics pertains to the sphere of legality in two interdependent yet distinct dimensions: democratic legitimacy and basic rights.[20] Each of these touches on morality. However, even if we can say empirically where legality begins and morality ends by referring to formal sanctions, we have not yet addressed the **normative** question of where these boundaries ought to be. Of course, all modern societies draw a boundary between legality and morality, but they draw these boundaries at different places. In the case of disputes, the issue inevitably arises whether the **boundaries** should be drawn from the point of view of legality or of morality, public discourse or private moral reflection. In such cases, at least in the first, discourse ethics must be considered superior to any monologically attained moral standpoint. This is so because only with an actual discussion among everyone potentially affected by a norm can **we** find out what, if anything, is common to us all—what should be the domain of legal regulation, what forms of political decision-making are legitimate, what could be left to the moral individual's personal judgment, and upon what we must compromise.

Discourse ethics thus has a **double** status: its specific object domain comprises institutional social relations, the legal and political system as a whole, and particular laws and rights. It also provides a way to decide the boundary question between morality and political justice. This by no means entails the collapse of the boundary between the two. On the contrary, a realm of autonomous judgment for the moral individual is thereby preserved. At the same time, positive law is protected from the potentially incapacitating interference of totalizing moral judgments without thereby being delivered into the hands of legal positivists. Indeed, once we restrict the relevance of discourse ethics to questions of **democratic** legitimacy and rights, **it leaves room for a variety of moral principles in the private sphere. Without judging the internal adequacy of any of these**, the discourse ethic adjudicates between them only in cases of conflict over general societal norms. Thus, the autonomy of conscience is respected by the principle of democratic legitimacy even though the latter brings principles to bear on the domains of law and politics. Although in this case, too, processes of discursive will formation decide the boundary between private and public, they cannot entirely abolish the private. Indeed, the meta-norms of discourse themselves provide for the autonomy of the individual moral conscience. If all those affected must have an effective chance to assume dialogue roles, if the dialogue must be free and unconstrained, and if each individual can shift the level of the discourse, then practical discourse presupposes autonomous individuals with the capacity to challenge any given consensus from a **principled** standpoint. The very rules which underlie argument and the cooperative search for consensus predicate the distinction between morality and legality. By articulating the meta-norms of the principle of democratic legitimacy and rights, the discourse ethic provides the justification for the autonomy of morality, grounding, as it were, its own self-limitation.

89 It is, moreover, the very *raison d'être* of discourse ethics to

provide a formal principle of legitimacy for societies which are pluralistic and composed of individuals with distinct and differing conceptions of the good life.[21] Even in a situation closely approximating the requirements of symmetrical reciprocity, there is no basis for assuming either the absence of difference or the absence of change. No consensus, no matter how unanimous or long lasting, can know itself to be permanent. Every consensus is, after all, only empirical and thereby open to challenge and revision. Thus, moral consciousness, differing ways of life, and experiments with new ways must all be granted autonomy from the current consensus on what is just.

One might object, nonetheless, from the point of view of a moral consciousness, that a separate theory of ethics for the realms of law and politics is unnecessary. As a moral subject, I obey the law because it is right and, in the case when it is morally wrong to do so, I would disobey the law, whatever the consequences to myself. Morality is certainly wider than legality—from both an objective and subjective point of view. Formal law cannot regulate every domain of action; whereas, from the subjective point of view, morality ought to. The moral consciousness could grant the necessity of law and sanctions because we are not gods, not always moral, and are, thus, in need of external constraint in certain cases. But if the moral component of the law is equivalent to what a moral actor could monologically arrive at (Rawls), then there is no need for a separate ethical theory. Why develop a discourse ethics at all?

There are, in the modern context, two reasons why we cannot move directly from morality to legality or re-synthesize them, as it were. First, as is well known, we moderns live in a plural moral universe—the multiplicity of value systems, modes of life, and identities would be violated if laws or political decisions were made from the point of view of any one of them. Every good liberal thus can argue against the totalization of any single moral standpoint to the whole of society. To do so would lead either to the subjugation of individual dignity and rights to the concerns of general welfare, or to the violation of the integrity of those who do not share the particular concept of the good life that has come to prevail. Not all action, not even all moral action, can (or ought to) be institutionally regulated.

The second and more compelling reason why we cannot equate the obligatory dimension of social/political norms with what motivates even the post-conventional moral actor, is that the genesis of legality, unlike morality, **must be discursive in principle**. Habermas himself conflates morality and legality because he rightly sees that moral testing involves an inner virtual dialogue to which the rules of argument apply. It would thus seem possible, if one followed these rules and considered the need-interpretations and potential side-effects of a maxim on all others, that one could arrive at the same judgment that an actual discourse would yield. The core difference between virtual and actual dialogue would, nonetheless, remain—only an actual dialogue in which all concerned could participate on equal terms of mutual recognition would yield or reaffirm a **we**, an emergent or already existing solitary collectivity, with a collective identity and, therefore, the capacity of articulating a general or common interest. As Hannah Arendt pointed out long ago, **only in a public space can a public opinion emerge.** Even imagining an ideal moral subject who is able to consider all the possible arguments of everyone involved, the monologically attained judgment would not converge with the political judgment of a duly constituted public because the relevant emergent collective identity would be missing. At best, an idealized, self-reflective moral judgment could imply tolerance of others and of different arguments,[22] but it could not yield the solidarity of a collectivity or an understanding of what our collective identity is and our general interests might be; this, however, is the object domain of institutionalized norms. Indeed, it is quite possible that a judgment could be moral and yet not be just. According to our interpretation, discourse ethics implies that the justice of justice, that the obligatory normative force of law, derives from democratic will formation and the articulation of a general interest in the norm. From the point of view of morality, a law imposed, e.g. by an **enlightened despot**, might well be moral, and it might even articulate a general interest (the common good); yet even so, it would not be just. For even if it happened by chance that what the enlightened despot decided is the common interest were to coincide with what the community would have agreed upon, given the chance, justice would still be violated because it requires that those potentially affected by a norm determine it for themselves, in a process of collective will formation. Only in this way does the norm obtain obligatory force. Moreover, only in this way is the autonomy of those affected preserved intact. Indeed, autonomy takes on a special significance in the framework of the discourse ethic conceived politically. In addition to the now standard understanding of autonomy as the capacity to choose one's own ends (for Rawls, one's "plan of life"), and to subject conventionally held or traditionally prescribed norms to the "test of reason," autonomy, for Habermas, involves the capacity to distance oneself from one's social roles and their content (attaining reflexive role distance), and to take into account the standpoint of others involved in a controversy. This does not require that individuals define themselves independent of their ends; rather, it is a necessary precondition for developing a "rational" collective identity and assessing what general interests may be ascertained with regard to its maintenance.

91

III. Institutional Implications

It should be clear from the above discussion that discourse ethics does not prescribe a particular form of life. The interpretation of discourse ethics as a theory of political justice would, nevertheless, imply that without determining entire forms of life, the conception leads to a specific organizational model of political practice.[23] Nevertheless, I will insist that no single model of democratic institutions flows from the theory. Moreover, none should be derived from it, if democratic theory is to avoid an authoritarian turn *vis à vis* existing (even if deficient) patterns of democracy. In spite of this, discourse ethics should and does have a link to an institutional level of analysis. Moreover, the principles of democratic legitimacy, and the basic rights which they ground, imply an open-ended plurality of democratic forms and hence projects of democratization that presuppose both modern civil societies and a critical relation to them.

While institutional or organizational questions should not be confused with the issue of legitimacy,[24] it would nevertheless be misleading to conceive of democratic legitimacy without democratic institutions. To do so would imply that democratic organization is merely one form of domination among others, and democratic legitimacy simply an ingenious way of justifying domination. Democratic theory must be able to indicate at least the **minimum conditions**, on the level of organization, for democratic institutions. In short, democratic legitimacy minimally requires the establishment of actual discourses in the level of organization.

The most obvious example of the institutionalization of discourse in the political realm is the creation of the parliamentary public sphere, along with its "societal presuppositions"—public spaces, guaranteed by rights, for discussion, association, and cultural exchange on the terrain of civil society. Habermas argues that the claim of "bourgeois" democracy from the beginning was to link all politically consequential decision-making to legally guaranteed discursive will formation of the public.[25] Accordingly, the structure of domination itself, the state, was to be penetrated with the principle of accountability to a valid consensus formed in the political public sphere. But, as many have pointed out, including Habermas, the claims of bourgeois democracy have hardly been adequately realized. While the principles of formal democracy (universal suffrage, majority rule, protection of minorities, representation, alternation, freedom of the press, assembly and opinion) are "freedom-guaranteeing," the organization or institutionalization of these rights has been selective at best and is, today, increasingly bureaucratic.[26] The possibility of participating in public opinion formation and genuine political discourse and, hence, of influencing political decision making, is considerably restricted through the segmentation of the voter's role, competition of elites, vertical opinion formation in party apparatuses, manipulative techniques of the mass media, culture industry, etc. Thus, locating the necessary minimum for democratic legitimacy in contemporary political institutions seems quixotic. Rather than appear as instances of actual discourse, these institutions apparently reinforce the purely counter-factual character of the principle of democratic legitimacy. The standards of discourse ethics seem to lift the democratic veil off the political practices of mass democracies rather than find institutional supports for them.

Nonetheless, it is not impossible to avoid the thesis of institutional decline and the corresponding temptation to diagnose all existing political institutions in mass democracies as one-dimensional and undemocratic. The unattractive choice plaguing democratic theory since Rousseau, between rather undemocratic yet "realistic" elite theories of democracy and excessively utopian normative/participatory theories, can be avoided. If one proceeds from the standpoint of civil society rather than the political system, a way opens up beyond the antinomy between the positive normative developments in modernity and institutional decline. Let me explain.

A. Civil Society and Rights

By "civil society" I have in mind a social realm differentiated from the state and from the market economy.[27] A modern civil society includes **plurality**: institution or culture, communication, assembly; **privacy**: a domain of autonomous individual moral choice; and **legality**: the structure of general laws and basic rights that protect and demarcate plurality, publicity and privacy from the state and, in principle if rarely in practice, the market mechanism. With respect to the rights, I stress their operation on two levels. First, as Hegel already insisted, the institutionalization of rights in a legal system belongs to institutions of civil society. Second, on a deeper level, rights implying the limitation of the modern state reconstitutive of civil society as a **modern** i.e., differentiated, society. I thus conceive of civil society as involving a classically liberal stabilization of societal institutions on the basis of rights. However, I also conceive of it as a framework that has the **immanent possibility** of becoming more democratic and whose norms call for democratization. The first aspect can be explored on the level of a theory of rights, the second as a theory of democracy.

93

I claimed earlier, without explanation, that both the principle of democratic legitimacy and the liberal principle of rights are justified by the same set of meta-norms that discourse ethics articulates. It is my thesis, indeed, that basic rights, as legal institutions, require discursive validation and opportunities for participation in public discourses. Discursive validation plays a role on the level of the constitutional origin of rights, but also on the level of the renewed participation necessary for their sustenance and expansion. This second dimension depends on the processes of cultural transformation which in turn depend on the chances to assemble, associate, and articulate positions publicly on the terrain of civil society. Why?

At issue is the relationship between the assertion of rights and the legalization of rights. It is undoubtedly the case both that rights in the modern sense presuppose the positivization of law and that they cannot be simply reduced to positive law. The rights that we have can become effective and stable only when embodied in constitutions and legal codes. But such rights are paradoxical: formally they represent a voluntary self-limitation of state power that could be annulled by a legislative act—e.g., in England, 51% of Parliament could abolish any right. But rights do not simply emerge, nor are they sustained or expanded as mere acts of positive legislation. What the state could take back on the legal-constitutional level, it cannot take back, in fact, if certain social-historical conditions are fulfilled, and it ought not take back from a normative point of view. Discourse ethics points to the conditions of the **cannot** on the sociological side and the ought on the philosophical side.

First, the survival and expansion of basic rights depend very much on vital political cultures that allow and even promote the mobilization of concerned constituencies on behalf of rights. The claims of individuals to protection by basic rights would be hollow indeed if these could not be backed up by public discussion, assembly, or even civil disobedience, and social movements. The principle of rights thus requires the possibility of participation in societal public spaces.[28] Discourse ethics has obvious relevance here, for it requires precisely that institutionalization of discourse in civil society that is so crucial for the positing and defense of rights.

Second, discourse ethics points not only to the sociological process of creating and expanding rights, but provides the basis for a theory of rights which not only argues for fundamental rights, but also helps us isolate the central clusters of rights from among them. Accordingly, the two sets of rights most fundamental to the institutional existence of a fully developed civil society are those that secure the integrity and autonomy of the person (privacy rights) and those having to do with free communication (assembly, association, expression). However, all rights, including those securing moral autonomy, require discursive validation. From this point of view, it might appear that the rights of communication are the most fundamental since they are constitutive of discourse itself and, hence, the key institution of modern civil society: the public sphere. The appearance is due in part to the already discussed sociological primacy of rights to communication.

In point of fact, however, discourse ethics logically presupposes **both** classes of rights. By basing rights not on an individualistic ontology, as classical liberals have done, but on the theory of communicative interaction, we have strong reason to emphasize the cluster of rights of communication. It would certainly be arguable that other clusters of rights, e.g., privacy, suffrage, are required to maintain this key complex. The rights of privacy would be affirmed because of the need to reproduce autonomous personalities without which rational discourse would be impossible. Such would be the result of a purely Habermasian deduction of rights from discourse ethics understood as the sum total of practical philosophy. In my argument, however, legality and morality, justice and autonomy, **discourse ethics** and **moral self-reflection** represent **two pillars of ethical life irreducible to each other**. From one we can reason to rights of communication, from the other, to the rights of autonomous personality. Both are preconditions of actual discourse seeking to be rational; thus, both are required as preconditions of democratic legitimacy. From this point of view, the rights of communication point us to the legitimate domain for formulating and defending rights. The rights of the personality identify the subjects who have the right to have rights.

Even if it were shown that such rights are only selectively institutionalized in contemporary capitalist mass democracies, **they are nonetheless institutionalized**. Moreover, the right to have rights has come to be recognized as a core component of democratic politics.[29] The significance of the institutionalization of rights is thus the open possibility of fighting for their fuller realization and expansion. This conception of civil society accordingly points to a key set of existing social institutions as the **minimum framework** for the institutionalization of democratic legitimacy. By implication, contemporary forms of democratic institutions, at least those secured within civil society and those that secure them (laws, rights, parliaments), are two-sided. They internalize, as it were, an antinomy between democratic norms and insufficient institutionalization as a set of dual possibilities of development. On this basis, one can move either towards a more democratic civil society and polity, or towards one increasingly bureaucratized and functionalized by the requirements of administration or the capitalist economy.

B. The Organization of Democracy

In denying the legitimacy of deducing one organizational form from discourse ethics, I imply that different models of democracy are compatible with the principle of democratic legitimacy. The affinity of discourse ethics with a plurality of forms of democracy links us to civil society in two ways. **First, the existing forms of formal and representative democracy and civil society, political and juridical, presuppose one another. Second, only on the ground of civil society can an institutionalized plurality of democracies be conceived.** Let us examine these two claims in turn. (1) To begin with, formal representative democracy and modern civil society share one key institution that "mediates" between them, the institution of the political sphere. The frameworks of politically relevant public discussion (the media, political clubs and associations, party caucuses, etc.) and parliamentary discussion and debate are continuous. As even Marx noted, it is, to say the least, inconsistent (even if temporarily possible) for a parliament, formally a body of discussion and debate, to eliminate or even to severely limit political discussion in society.[30] But equally important is that existing forms of politically relevant publics in society, through their built-in logic, imply the eventual establishment of such a public sphere within the institutional framework of the state itself. Furthermore, a plural, dynamic civil society finds in a parliamentary (among others) structure of compromise the most plausible general framework in which the conflicts of member groups and individuals can be politically mediated, conflicting and rival interests aggregated, **and** the possibility of reaching a consensus, explored. Parliamentary structures of interest aggregation and conflict mediation, on the other hand, work well only if there is a more or less open articulation of these on the social level.

(2) It is our contention that while modern civil society logically presupposes and (historically) facilitates the emergence of representative democracy, it is equally important that it also makes historically possible the **democratization** of representative democracy. This is precisely in line with the implication of discourse ethics to defend existing formal democracy and, simultaneously, to demand further democratization. Both the complexity of and the diversity within contemporary civil societies call for the posing of the issue of democratization in terms of a variety of differentiated processes, forms, and *loci* depending on the axis of division considered. Indeed, there is an elective affinity between the discourse ethic and modern civil society as the terrain on which an institutionalized plurality of democracies can emerge. Two sets of distinctions are relevant in this regard. The first and more general

has to do with the institutional differentiation between the state, civil society, and the economy. The second concerns differentiation or pluralization within each sphere.

Marx made the point long ago that if democracy is restricted to one sphere (the state) while despotic forms of rule prevail in the economy or in civil associations, then the democratic forms of the first become undermined. On the other side, all of historical experience after Marx indicates that differentiation poses limits to democratization. The requirements of the state's and the economy's steering mechanisms must be respected in order for them to function efficiently. This, as is well known, militates against total democratization of either along the lines of direct participatory models. Yet it would be fallacious to conclude that no democratization is possible in these domains. On the contrary, once one takes into account the different logics of the coordinating mechanisms of each sphere, it becomes evident that there are forms of democracy adequate to each, even if these vary according to the relevant structural conditions.

As we have already indicated, formal representative democracy, on the level of the state, articulates the minimum degree of democratic participation required by modern interpretations of the citizenship principle. Needless to say, this requires both the rule of law and formal equality in the sense that every adult, regardless of function, social affiliation, or ascribed characteristics must be admitted as a citizen. On the other side, the limits posed to direct participation by virtue of the very existence of a state whose functions are coordinated through power relations, and which is defined by the monopoly of the legitimate use of force, are obvious. The separation of powers, the rule of law, and requirements of efficient bureaucratic functioning guided by the principles of due process, all preclude the direct participation of everyone in policy making on the state levels. At most, participants here work indirectly through parliamentary supervision, control, and publication. Further democratization of a formally democratic polity must respect these limits.

At the same time, in almost all representative democracies, national structures can be complemented by local and regional ones that, in principle, allow for more direct participation than is usually the case today. Moreover, in some countries, structures of functional representation, albeit in rather undemocratic, corporatist forms, complement territorially based representative structures. These are, in principle at least, open to more democracy and participation, the old dream of Durkheim and the philosophical pluralists.[31] What seems to be missing everywhere is the institutionalization of total social input by **local** and **functional** bodies in global open, public procedures that share legitimacy with already established representative bodies. Hence, there is the eventual weakening of many bodies of more direct participation. The ever renewed call for a second parliamentary chamber of the guild socialists, Austro-Marxists, and other democratic socialists, all the way down to some contemporary social movements, point in this direction. Of course, the exact device for democratization in this area cannot be at issue on a prior, pre-abstract context.

The notion of functional representation already touches on questions of economic democracy. It is clear, however, that insofar as the economy is concerned, the requirements of efficiency and market rationality, implied by the systematic role of money as a coordinating mechanism, can be disregarded in the name of democracy only at the cost of both. Here the levels of representation and participation must be reconciled with the social needs of production and consumption. Forms of economic democracy need not be as universalistic (i.e., inclusive) as those of the polity; yet as the institutionalization of mechanisms of collective bargaining, co-determination, and representative workers' councils that elect managers show, democratization is not *per se* incompatible with efficient functioning.

The plurality of democratic forms that are possible **and** desirable with respect to the economy would include, among others, consumer and producer cooperatives, employer and union representation within corporate bodies, workers' councils which elect managers, grievance committees, etc. Each of these could in principle be made compatible with efficiency requirements and with one another (or at least the loss of efficiency implied by them could be within acceptable limits). The further democratization of the economy would involve the institutionalization of these various forms of participation without thereby differentiating the economy, society, and the state.

It is our central thesis that democracy, on the societal level itself, can go much further than on the level of the state or the economy because the primary coordinating mechanism is communicative interaction itself. Leaving aside the systematic aspects of this claim,[32] it is inductively certain that the functioning of societal associations, public communication, cultural institutions and families allows for potentially high thresholds of toleration for direct participatory forms and collegial decision-making. Of course, the possibility for open, unlimited experimentation with the exact level of various forms of participation is provided only where there is already an articulation of pluralities in the forms of associations, publics, and informal groups guaranteed by rights. Only where these exist is there a possibility for small scale participation to become, as de Tocqueville insisted, the real substance of democratic local government and the heart of a process of self-education that leads to a democratic political structure. In modern civil societies which are often linked to what are, in effect (if not in form), quasi-oligarchical political practices, the foundations for independent pluralities from voluntary associations to universities and even churches are well established. While they are not always democratic and rarely involve genuine participation **in the context of democratic norms**, these structures are ever present targets for democratization. We see relevant conflicts over this issue in many contemporary associations almost continually—the latest focus being, e.g., the Catholic Church, male clubs, unions, and universities, which repeatedly have their day.

In his **Strukturwandel der Offentlichkeit**, Habermas argued for the democratization and politicization of existing corporate entities as one of the possible solutions to the decline of the public sphere.[33] It is clear that the principle of democratic legitimacy, when linked to the theory of civil society, leads to a revitalization and extension of this kind of alternative for three reasons. First, participation in modern societies is ultimately only virtual if there is no small scale participation in addition to representative parliaments. Second, discourse ethics in this context cannot validate the suppression of existing pluralities in the name of one all-inclusive discursive process. Third, the democratization of existing pluralities is more compatible with the preservation of modern structures than their "totalization" by some kind of council model. The latter imply the re-embedding of steering mechanisms (administration, market) in direct social relations and thus conflict with the presupposition of a modern civil society, namely differentiation. Nevertheless, the limits to democratization on the level of steering mechanisms would be in part compensated for by the democratization of societal associations that may indirectly influence the state and economy as well.

The norms of the public sphere in civil society, even if distorted, represent a constant demand for overseeing, control, and democratization of existing forms of association. Originally a form of society-generated discursive control over state-bureaucratic power, the **liberal** public sphere has declined precisely to the extent to which private associations became transformed into large-scale organizations that attained a quasi-political character and took on tasks of economic and political steering. The normative demands of publicity in the new situations thus inherently imply the public exposure and the democratization of these private associations. Historically, just such developments, along with the renewal of alternative publics outside formal organization, have complemented processes that defend the liberal public sphere. The renewal of political public life is an ever present potentiality on this side of the overall process.

Beyond the norms of publicity itself, two components of discourse ethics militate for the plurality of democracies: the **critique of the exclusion of anyone at all concerned** and the stress on **actual** participation. In fact, all existing forms of democracy have built in processes of exclusion. Liberal representative democracy in the nineteenth century model excluded passive citizens. Modern representative democracy *de facto* diminishes the relevance of (if not formally excludes) those who are not members of strong voluntary associations or party organizations. Direct democracy excludes those who do not seek public happiness first and foremost, i.e., the politically inactive. Territorial democracy discriminates against producers, industrial democracy against consumers. Federalism reduces the importance of weak members of the federation and of dissenting individuals and groups within each member unit, and centralizing democracy provides no incentive for potentially important self-governing units. While no combination of these principles precludes exclusion altogether, a plurality of forms of democracy contains the promise of more meaningful participation on several levels which are otherwise reduced in importance.

To summarize: democratic legitimacy and basic rights interpreted in the sense of discourse ethics strongly imply a plurality of democracies for which modern civil society represents the institutional terrain of potentiality in two ways: (1) the differentiation of state, society, and economy as institutional spheres allows democracy and democratization to be defined according to the different logics of these spheres, and (2) the structures of plurality—actual and potential—in civil society itself allow the possibility of the democratization of the all-important social sphere in terms of **participation** and **publicity**, for this sphere is the locus of the principle of democratic legitimacy.

Thus, while discourse ethics does not call for a specific form of political life, and while a plurality of democratic forms, rights, and even non-democratically structured institutions are compatible with it (provided the latter are democratically agreed upon as necessary), it **does** exclude certain forms of life. Discourse ethics is incompatible with forms of life based on domination, violence and systematic inequality. It thus militates for the further "modernization" of those institutions of civil society that are based on such relations.

Today, the question of democracy has migrated back to the sphere in which it first emerged—that of civil society. The further democratization of formal democratic policies must be posed with

discourse ethics and civil society

reference to society and not simply to the state or the economy. Discourse ethics, as we have interpreted it, together with a revised theory of civil society, not only allows for such an approach, but as an ethics of democratization, demands it as well. If the principle of rights based on discourse ethics implies the protection of modern civil society, the principle of democratic legitimacy implies its democratization beyond the liberal-democratic model.

Columbia University

ENDNOTES

1. For the best defense of rights-oriented liberalism, see Ronald Dworkin, **Taking Rights Seriously** (Cambridge: Harvard University Press), 1978. The best recent discussion of the liberal ideal of neutrality is in Charles Larmore, **Patterns of Moral Complexity**, (Cambridge, England: Cambridge University Press), 1987.

2. See Carole Pateman, **Participation and Democratic Theory**, (Cambridge, England: Cambridge University Press), 1970; and **The Problem of Political Obligation: A Critical Analysis of Liberal Theory** (New York: Wiley), 1979. See also, C.B. Macpherson, **The Life and Times of Liberal Democracy** (Oxford, England: Oxford University Press), 1977; and **Democratic Theory** (Clarendon Press), 1973. See, finally, Benjamin Barber, **Strong Democracy** (Berkeley: University of California Press), 1984.

3. Habermas, Jürgen, "Diskursethik: Notizen zu einem Begrundungsprogram," in **Moralbewusstsein und kommunikatives Handeln** (Frankfurt: Suhrkamp Verlag), 1983, pp. 67-86. This is Habermas's definitive statement of his version of the theory of discourse ethics. For earlier versions, see also: **Legitimation Crisis** (Boston: Beacon Press), 1975, Chapter 3, pp. 95-117; "Wahrheitstheorien," **Wirklichkeit und Reflexion: Festschrift für Walter Schulz** (Pfullingen), 1973; and "Reply to My Critics," **Habermas: Critical Debates**, eds., John B. Thompson and David Held (Great Britain: MacMillan), 1982, pp. 254 ff.

4. For a good summary, yet one which precedes the publication of "Diskursethik" *(op. cit.)* see Thomas McCarthy, **The Critical Theory of Jürgen Habermas** (Cambridge, Mass.: M.I.T. Press), 1978, pp. 272-357.

5. What follows is a restatement of the core assumptions of discourse ethics that are shared, despite different formulations, by the two main proponents of the theory, Jürgen Habermas and Karl-Otto Apel. We rely for the most part on Habermas's version. Whether discourse ethics can be given a transcendental (Apel), universal-pragmatic (Habermas) or only historical (Castoriadis) foundation, and whether rational argument

jean cohen

(Habermas) or decision (Heller) is to have ultimate priority in relation to our "choice" for such an ethic, remain open questions. An impressive debate between Cornelius Castoriadis and Habermas in Dubrovnik in 1982 convinces us that equally good arguments can be given for historicity and universality. It also becomes clear from this debate that the common element in the two positions is the duality of levels of analysis: stronger types of argumentation for the meta-level (the procedural level of institutionalization) are necessary than for the historical level (that which is already instituted). For the works of Apel upon which we rely, see **Towards the Transformation of Philosophy** (London: Routledge and Kegan Paul), 1980, Ch. 7, pp. 225-285; and "Normative Ethics and Strategic Rationality: The Philosophical Problem of a Political Ethic," **The Graduate Philosophy Journal**, Vol. 9 No. 1, Winter 1982, pp. 81-109.

6.   The two dimensions are separable, with the first having priority, a point not entirely clear in McCarthy but having now been explicitly stated by Habermas in his reply to Lukács in Thompson and Held, **Habermas: Critical Debates**, p. 254. See also Apel, "Normative Ethics," pp. 100-101.

7.   See McCarthy, p. 325; Albrecht Wellmer, **Praktische Philosophie und Theorie der Gesellschaft** (Konstanz: Universität Konstanz Universitätsverlag Konstanz GMBH), pp. 10-11, and Apel, **Transformation**, pp. 258-259, 227.

8.   See Habermas, "Wahrheitstheorien," pp. 251-252, quoted in McCarthy, pp. 99ff for the most recent formulation of the rules of argumentation.

9.   For a succinct formulation in English, see Seyla Benhabib, **Critique, Norm and Utopia** (New York: Columbia University Press), 1986, pp. 284-285.

10.   Habermas, "Reply," p. 257. See also Wellmer, **Pracktische Philosophie**, pp. 33-34.

11.   Habermas, "Diskursethik," pp. 77.

12.   *Ibid.*, pp. 75-76 (my translation).

13.   For a full discussion, see Andrew Arato and Jean L. Cohen, **Civil Society and Social Theory** (Cambridge, Mass: M.I.T. Press) (forthcoming), Chapter __. "In this chapter, we take up the debate around Habermas's reliance on the concept of general interest in his moral theory. We argue, in brief, that Habermas insists that discourse ethics brings need interpretations into discussions on norms, and that only if norms express general interests in addition to being the product of a general agreement, are they legitimate and the consensus 'rational.' But since the binding character of an agreement derives from the meta-norms of discourse, what is the role of the concept of general interest— what does it add? Indeed, if 'general interest' refers to raw need interpretations, Habermas would be open to Hume's objection that a

discussion on needs and interests must remain inconclusive. If, on the other hand, 'general interest' refers to the objective interest of a group, this cannot be used as the criterion for the rightness of a norm without authoritarian implications. For it opens the door to the Jacobin/Leninist claim to the possession of objective truth on the part of self appointed elites, collapsing thereby the categories of truth and rightness so carefully distinguished by Habermas. Nevertheless, the concept of general interest is crucial to a political ethic, for interests are in part the stuff or content of discussions in the political domain. Our solution is that 'general interest' as a category must cede priority to the concept of 'common identity.' In a pluralistic society, discourse provides the way to discover who 'we' are, what we have in common apart from our differences, what our collective identity is, and what aspects of it are worth preserving. The norms securing our common identity become part of the content of legitimate norms and the foundation of social solidarity. A collective identity that has as its core component the principles of democratic legitimacy and rights, presupposes a post-traditional, post-conventional orientation to our traditions—such that we can question and discuss those aspects of our common identity that become problematic. Thus it is possible to have a democratic political culture which applies the principles of critical self-reflection to itself, thereby avoiding the charge of authoritarianism. Once such a 'rational' collective identity is established, that is, once the relevant political culture is able to act in a post-traditional way towards itself, and once its basic principles and norms are agreed upon (again, always open to revision), then it becomes possible to establish the general interest of the political community. This would comprise those institutional arrangements necessary for the 'material' reproduction of the relevant collective identity. Here there is room for the observers or social-scientific, 'objective' point of view to enter in. In short, we can be told that in order to preserve our collective identity, our political culture, our principles, such-and-such an institutional arrangement is necessary. This can then be debated and argued; but the normative component must be established independent of and prior to such claims. This is, as far as we can see, the only way in which the category of "general interest" can enter into the theory of discourse ethics without authoritarian implications."

14. Albrecht Wellmer, "Praktische Philosophie," pp. 46-47. For a more recent and far more critical analysis of discourse ethics see Wellmer, "Zur Kritik der Diskursethik," **Ethik und Dialog** (Frankfurt: Suhrkamp verlag), 1986, *passim*.

15. Here I am in agreement with Agnes Heller, "The Discourse Ethic of Jürgen Habermas," **Thesis 11**, No. 10/11, 1985, pp. 5-17; and A. Wellmer, "Zur Kritik," pp. 51-55.

16. See the various formulations in Habermas, "Diskursethik," *passim*.

17. E.g., the position of legal positivists and sociological system theorists such as Niklas Luhmann, **The Sociological Theory of Law** (Routledge), 1972.

18. Habermas, **Legitimation Crisis**, pp. 87-89.

jean cohen

19. Habermas, **Legitimation Crisis**, pp. 95-117. See also, **The Theory of Communicative Action**, Vol. I (Boston: Beacon Press), pp. 254-270.

20. This is not, of course, Habermas's position. He sees discourse ethics as a general moral theory and as a political ethic.

21. This is, of course, the goal of John Rawls in **A Theory of Justice** (Cambridge, Mass.: Harvard University Press), 1971. However, Habermas, unlike Rawls, provides a principle of **democratic** legitimacy and not simply or even primarily a theory of political obligation. Rawls's theory works well to legitimate basic liberties and even state redistributive policies. But it does not provide a theory or principle of democratic legitimacy since no actual dialogue, no actual participation in collectively (discursively) testing political/legal norms is required by Rawls. Instead, he settles for monological testing along Kantian lines—a process appropriate to moral questions but not to political questions of legitimacy.

22. This is the Rawlsian model. John Rawls, **A Theory of Justice**, *passim*.

23. Axel Honneth. The opposite charge, namely, that the discourse ethic is so formalistic that it has no institutional consequences, has two variants: one that accepts the project of a discursive ethics but searches for institutional mediation, and one that contests the project as a whole. For the first, see Jean L. Cohen, "Why More Political Theory?," **Telos** 49, Summer 1979, pp. 70-94; Jack Mendelson, "The Habermas-Gadamer Debate," **New German Critique** 18, 1979, pp. 44-73. For the second, see Seyla Benhabib, "Modernity and the Aprorias of Critical Theory," **Telos**, No. 49, Fall 1981, pp. 39-59; Steven Lukes, "Of Gods and Demons: Habermas and Practical Reason," in Held and Thompson, **Habermas: Critical Debates**, pp. 134-148.

24. Habermas, **Communication and the Evolution of Society** (Boston: Beacon Press), 1979, pp. 183, 186-187.

25. Jürgen Habermas, "Die Utopia des guten Herrschers," **Kultur und Kritik**, p. 383.

26. Habermas, **Theory of Communicative Action**, Vol. II (Boston: Beacon Press), pp. 343-373.

27. For a fuller discussion, see Andrew Arato and Jean L. Cohen, **Civil Society and Social Theory**, *op. cit.*, forthcoming.

28. See John Rawls, **A Theory of Justice**, pp. 382-391 for a discussion of civil disobedience as justified in a democratic polity. See also, Ronald Dworkin, **Taking Rights Seriously**, pp. 206-222 and **A Matter of Principle** (Cambridge, Mass.: Harvard University Press), 1985, pp. 104-116; and Habermas, "Ziviler Ungehorsam-Erstfall für den demokratischen Reichtsstaat," **Die Neue Unübersichtlichkeit** (Frankfurt: Suhrkamp), pp. 79-99.

29. Claude Lefort, "Politics and Human Rights," **The Political Forms of Modern Society** (Cambridge, Mass.: M.I.T. Press).

30. Ksrl Marx, **The Eighteenth Brumaire of Louis Bonaparte,** (New York: International Pub.) 1963, pp. 66-67, 106.

31. G.D.H. Cole, **Guild Socialism Restated** (New Brunswick: Transaction Books), 1980; Harold Laski, **Studies in the Problem of Sovereignty** (New Haven: Yale University Press), 1919; Harold Laski, **The Foundations of Sovereignty and Other Essays** (New York: Harcourt Brace and Co.), 1921.

32. See Arato and Cohen, **Civil Society and Social Theory,** op. cit.

33. Jürgen Habermas, **Strukturwandel der Offentlichkeit** (Berlin: Luchterhand), 1962, pp. 263-277.

II.
ethics in historical
perspective

rolf zimmermann
equality, political order and ethics: hobbes and the systematics of democratic rationality

All the great philosophical texts challenge us persistently to reinterpret and reexamine their arguments, their ways of looking at a problem, and their proposals for solving such problems. In this, a hermeneutic endeavor may lay claim to systematic relevance to the extent that it not only uncovers difficulties which are immanent in the text, but also encounters problems which suggest permanently interesting questions. Hobbes leads us to such a question when we consider the stringency of his thought in **Leviathan** and comparable texts.

The question here concerns the tension between a general concept of human equality and the political order which, as its rational complement, awaits further definition. With Hobbes, this question becomes a central theme of modern ethical-political theory and, at the same time, Hobbes's answer provokes the suggestion that rational political rule is only possible under conditions of democracy. I will show that, for reasons immanent in Hobbes's text, there is a problem regarding the democratic mediation of power which cannot be dealt with within the framework of his theory. This leads to the question of the appropriate relationship between the equality of men,* their participation in democratic processes, and the claims of rationality; the latter being connected with both the introduction of a fundamental principle of equality and with the discursivity of

rolf
zimmermann

democratic participation. From a systematic point of view, I make a plea for a historico-hermeneutic conception of modern democratic rationality, within the framework of a coherence theory of practical truth. In this way, the "linguistic fallacy" of the so-called formal-pragmatic ethics will be avoided.

I. Natural Equality and Voluntative Equality

If we stick to the main text in Hobbesian theory, **Leviathan**, we must refer, in particular, to Chapter 13: "Of the natural condition of Mankind, as concerning their Felicity and Misery," to find the important points of departure for his argument. Hobbes begins by making an observation in favor of the natural equality of men. He connects this with the idea of self-preservation, a consequence of which is that, in the case of conflict about goods of one kind or another, men are driven by the natural interest in self-preservation to settle these conflicts. As a result, this basic situation leads to the war of all against all. Therefore, in order to avoid this war of all against all, a power is required which will establish an equilibrium between men. The installation of such a power in the shape of the sovereign state is made possible by, on the one hand, what we might call the peaceable passion of fear of death and, on the other, reason, which is able to suggest principles of peace in the form of laws of nature.

As soon as one pursues the details of this sketch, the following question, in particular, is of interest: what function does the equality of men claimed by Hobbes in fact assume? My thesis is that Hobbes's theory has to be supplied with a completely different concept of equality than the concept of natural equality if we are to regard it as even internally consistent.

Let us begin by looking more closely at Hobbes's arguments in favor of natural equality. These gain their strength from Hobbes's acknowledgement that men have different physical and mental capacities (cf. **Leviathan**, Chs. 8, 11), but, at the same time, denies that it is possible to infer from this some kind of inequality in principle. He skillfully distributes the burden of proof by presenting a possible counter-thesis, with points of view that cast doubt on the idea of inequality in principle. With regard to physical abilities, it can be argued that someone who is physically stronger—in whatever way—can be killed by the guile of a weaker person. Something similar holds true with regard to mental abilities. It should be noted that Hobbes differentiates between the scientific knowledge which is acquired through intellectual training and the prudence which is gained through experience, where only the latter is of interest to begin with. And, indeed, while acknowledging all the empirical differences, why should it be disputed that knowledge which is acquired through experience can, in dealing with the appropriate objects, lead to approximately similar results?

In this way, Hobbes attempts to safeguard his thesis concerning the natural equality of men. The thesis claims, then, that there are no natural relations of subordination or domination which might distribute men's entitlements and positions differently from the very beginning. Every imaginable social relationship between men must therefore be conceived in terms of their natural equality. Nonetheless, in sharply contrasting this position with Aristotle's, Hobbes also reveals to us more about a different concept of equality:

*I know that Aristotle in the first book of his **Politics**, for a foundation of his doctrine, maketh men by nature, some more worthy to command, meaning the wiser sort, such as he thought himself to be for his philosophy; others to serve, meaning those that had strong bodies, but were not philosophers as he; as if master and servant were not introduced by consent of men, but by difference of wit: which is not only against reason; but also against experience. For there are very few so foolish, that had not rather govern themselves, than be governed by others: nor when the wise in their own conceit, contend by force, with them who distrust their own wisdom, do they always, or often, or almost at any time, get the victory. If nature therefore have made men equal, that equality is to be acknowledged: or if nature have made men unequal; yet because men that think themselves equal, will not enter into conditions of peace, but upon equal terms, such equality must be admitted. And therefore for the ninth law of nature, I put this, **that every man acknowledge another for his equal by nature**. The breach of this precept is **pride**.*

Ch. 15, pp. 100f.[1]

Whereas the first part of the passage underlines the difference between the ancient and modern epochs, a textual difficulty for Hobbes's own system arises from the second part. We are forced to recognize, to our surprise, that, for Hobbes, men's attitudes to each other, in the sense of seeing-each-other-as-equals, are evidently much more important than a possible objective proof of their natural equality. In spite of his own reflections, devoted to the natural equality of men, Hobbes formulates a different idea. He now tells us that even if men were unequal by nature, it would secure peace to assume that they are equal. Since both the thesis of natural equality and the possible counter-thesis of natural inequality are compatible with this kind of demand for equality, a different concept of equality is evident. We might speak of voluntative equality as opposed to natural equality (equality "by will" as opposed to equality "by nature"). This voluntative equality either can be assumed as an empirically existing attitude, or it can be made a normative requirement at a theoretical level.

As soon as one takes note of the difference between natural and voluntative equality, one finds illuminating support for voluntative equality in Hobbes's reflections on the state of nature. Once we assume voluntative equality in principle, and if we allow that conflicts can arise between men by virtue of their initial equal opportunities and equal entitlements, Hobbes, with the intensification of the *"bellum omnium contra omnes,"* can be seen to merely describe the extreme situation of permanent conflict. This extreme situation can, nonetheless, be read as a *reductio ad absurdum* of the supposition of voluntative equality; faced with the prospect of a situation of uncontrollable conflict, it is far more advisable to work in advance as hard as possible towards inequality. Other people's claims to equality must be impeded before one comes under risk oneself and before the necessity of fighting arises, as Hobbes says at another point.[2] Seen in this way, the state of nature demonstrates the impossibility of holding onto voluntative equality. Since it would make no sense to view the state of nature as a *reductio ad absurdum* of natural equality, the difference between the two concepts of equality is underscored. Furthermore, this view emphasizes the central function which falls to the supposition of voluntative equality with regard to men's willingness to enter into the state of peace on equal terms. This state of affairs further prompts the question of how we are supposed to assess the conceptual means which Hobbes has at his disposal to ground his principle of equality.

If we look back to Chapter 13 with this in mind, the difference between natural and voluntative equality, which has clearly emerged from our discussion of Chapter 15, can be elucidated as follows. The decisive sentence here is: "From this equality of ability, ariseth equality of hope in the attaining of our ends" (Ch. 13, p. 81). The "equality of ability," according to Hobbes, refers to the way in which men are equipped by nature. Thus, with regard to their **objective possibilities**, we might say all men are equal. It does not follow from this, however, that this objective possibility must direct men's consciousness in acting. This would only follow if men were to incorporate, as part of their **subjective perspective in acting**, the objective possibilities of their "equality of ability." The "equality of hope in the attaining of our ends" represents, for Hobbes, this subjective perspective. The phrase "**our** ends," in particular, gives expression to the change of perspective. The factual "ariseth" shows the ambivalence of the transition from objective possibility to subjective perspective. Strictly speaking, therefore, Hobbes could, at most, say the following: (1) if men are equal in respect to their objective possibilities in acting, and (2) if they become aware that they are equal in this way, and (3) if they use awareness of objectively equal opportunities in acting as a basic orientation in pursuing their ends (in acting); then it follows that (4) every man regards every other man as someone who pursues his ends with the awareness that the chances of his actually realizing these ends are equal to everyone else's.

We thus do not find a deduction of the subjective-voluntative attitude towards equality from objective possibilities, but rather a mere combination of natural and voluntative equality or, we might now say, a combination of objective equality according to possibility, and subjective equality according to reality. Subjective equality according to orientation in acting, however, is compatible with objective inequality according to abilities and possibilities in acting. For one might say, in spite of objective inequality according to possibility, that we wish to mutually attribute to one another, as humans, equal opportunities in acting, at least in principle.

This shows that the decisive premise which Hobbes requires for the further progression of his thought must in fact be understood in the sense of voluntative equality. Putting this differently, one might say that the argument initially brought to bear by Hobbes, which shows that, by and large, there is no inequality between men by virtue of different mental or physical abilities, is too weak to allow us positively to infer a concept of equality in principle. Such a conclusion cannot simply be drawn from facts of nature, but rather requires an act of mutual interpretation by people who conceive of each other as equal. The concept of voluntative equality formulates a **principle of social relationship** which, by its very meaning, admits no exception.[3] We can also say that voluntative equality points people to a self-understanding according to which they confront each other as social beings. The intention here is not to distinguish humans as primarily social beings. Even if we assume that every person begins by pursuing his or her own interests, this does not prevent us from viewing the social relationship to others as guided by the principle of equality.[4] This is in keeping with the fact that, when the concept of equality emerges most tangibly in Hobbes, i.e., in Chapter 15 (cf. above), the dominant theme is a concern to formulate "laws of nature" which will enable men to co-exist peacefully. However, "laws of nature" are, on Hobbes's conception, rules of reason which, in the form of principles of peace, can be acquired through reflection. However much this underscores the status of voluntative equality as a principle of social relationship, it also brings to light the difficulties which arise for Hobbes's theory as soon as we regard the putative derivation of this principle from the idea of natural equality as unviable.

2. Voluntative Equality, Democracy, Rationality

To begin, it is obvious that an appeal to voluntative equality, on the grounds that only with it could people be persuaded to enter the state of peace on equal terms, is circular. For, of course, it presupposes the idea that we must conceive the move to the state of peace as the closing of a contract among equals. Reason's principle of peace presupposes itself, as it were. A further possibility would be an explicitly normative justification of the principle of equality now under debate. We can, however, expect nothing from Hobbes's theory in this respect. This is due to the thesis of ethical subjectivism which Hobbes puts forward: all our moral predicates and judgments are colored subjectively by our passions and, to this extent, there is no possibility of achieving objective foundations in this sphere. The sentence, *"bonum ergo relative dicitur ad personam"* (**De Homine**, Ch. 11) expresses this succinctly.

Even this brief outline is sufficient to make it clear why Hobbes, for reasons immanent in his theory, cannot provide a normative foundation for voluntative equality. What is left, then, since the idea of natural equality is also no longer at our disposal? Well, Hobbes might presuppose voluntative equality as a principle of social relationship in such a way that he claims it as a fact, i.e., a fact in the sense that it would have to be assumed that voluntative equality had already become dominant *qua* self-understanding of mankind. An anchoring of a principle of this sort in the dimension of human passion or inclination might then always be already present. The supposition here is that men share a mutual interpretation of their selves as equal in principle—whereby we can leave aside for the moment the question of why they do so.[5] This way of looking at things also does justice to Hobbes's emphatic claim to have grounded ethical-political theory as a science, since for this he requires voluntative equality as a fact of human self-understanding. To see this clearly we have to pursue the question of how Hobbes's moral subjectivism, as already outlined, might possibly be made compatible with the idea that something like objective knowledge in the dimension of morality and politics is admissible. The answer to this takes, as its starting point, the distinction which Hobbes introduces between two kinds of knowledge:

There are of KNOWLEDGE two kinds: whereof one is **knowledge of fact**: *the other* **knowledge of the consequence of one affirmation to another.** *The former is nothing else but sense and memory, and is* **absolute knowledge**; *as when we see a fact doing, or remember it done: and this is the knowledge required in a witness. The latter is called* **science**; *and is* **conditional**; *as when we know, that,* **if the figure shown be a** *circle, then any straight line through the centre shall divide it into two equal parts.* And this is the knowledge required in a philosopher; that is to say, of him that pretends to reasoning.

Leviathan, Ch. 9, p. 53

The fact that Hobbes here relates knowledge of fact to sense and memory, as though it were self-evident, directs us back to his remark at the beginning of **Leviathan**. Sense is, for Hobbes, the origin of all our ideas and concepts, and memory always refers back to sense. We need only take note of this as the background of the discussion since it is not decisive for the actual distinction which Hobbes makes here. Rather, what is important is his description of factual knowledge as absolute, in contrast to the merely conditional knowledge which is characteristic of science. By "absolute" Hobbes clearly does not mean something mysterious; but rather factual knowledge's non-conditional, unrestricted sense of validity which we always already have in the case of simple empirical statements, e.g., there is a chair here, Hans is bald, Fritz caused a car accident, etc. Empirical statements which we make in this way are true without reservation and are, in this sense, absolute. This is why it makes sense, for example, to swear as a witness to facts which are completely certain. The witness swears without any "ifs and buts" that something specific is or was the case. It is obvious, in contrast, that it would make no sense if someone were to swear that every circle, through the center of which there is a straight line, is divided into two equal parts. Here we are dealing with truth from concepts, an analytic truth, the validity of which depends exclusively on the meaning of the terms used. Now, these truths of thought have the peculiarity that they are always, according to their logical form, hypothetical-conditional. This also naturally holds true even if we don't think primarily of geometrical examples; we might take another example from Hobbes (Ch. 4, p. 21): a man is a living creature (if he be a man, he is a living creature). It seems, therefore, easy to understand why Hobbes emphasizes the conditional character of scientific knowledge; this is the knowledge which we have before us in analytic sentences and sequences of sentences, in conditional-knowledge sentences. In contrast to this is factual knowledge in the form of empirical-synthetic sentences which, unlike scientific knowledge, has an absolute court of validation, namely, reality. Hobbes's favorite science, geometry, is thereby brought into a more general perspective, one which permits an adequate evaluation of his general idea of science. Pursuing ethical-political philosophy as a science thus simply means to conduct an examination which takes its orientation from the guiding idea of analytic truth. Thus, Hobbes's battle-cry is not "more geometrico," but rather "more analytico."[6] For this reason, it is also easy to

rolf
zimmermann

understand why Hobbes defines the discipline of ethics as that science which demonstrates consequences from the passions of men. This corresponds to the conditional character of analytic knowledge, as does his explicit definition of political science as dealing with "consequences from the institution of commonwealths" (cf. **Leviathan**, Ch. 9). Bearing these clarifications in mind, it is possible to understand how, on the one hand, a moral subjectivism is put forward (cf. above), while, on the other, there is a striving towards an objective science of ethics and politics. The solution to the puzzle is that this science must be conceived from the point of view of conditional-analytical knowledge.

This means that the problem of finding sufficiently general premises from which relevant consequences may be drawn becomes all the more obvious. Speaking theoretically, the only chance of advancing lies in the attempted working out of the conditions under which men already evaluate and act in a subjectively moral manner in such a way that we would be able to interpret the, as it were, subjective position which each individual holds as one which is subject to general conditions of human nature. No one can evade these general conditions and, to this extent, they must be recognized by everyone, even if individual convictions and actions admit no common denominator. These general conditions of human nature could provide a non-controversial point of departure for drawing analytic consequences which might count on general recognition.

For this reason, Hobbes's endeavor to introduce a general principle of equality *qua* natural equality fits in with the internal logic of his conception just as much as does the interest in the principle of self-preservation—which is to be understood in a no less general way. This shows just as convincingly, however, that my critique of the guiding idea of natural equality leaves us with absolutely no other choice than to make use of the concept of voluntative equality in its stead, the latter concept being understood in the sense of a normative fact which has been proven to hold true generally.[7] What happens, however, if we insert the concept of voluntative equality into the structure of Hobbes's theory in this way?

To begin with, the result is a **historical** relativization of the premise, for we cannot assume voluntative equality to be a trans-historically valid principle of social relationships. Conversely, such an assumption is general enough to do service as a premise in the way desired—having the sense of an epochal fact.[8] To the extent, therefore, that Hobbes believes his laws of nature, the articles of reason, to be "immutable and eternall" (**De Cive**, Ch. III, Sec. XXIX) he is subject to misapprehension. If anything at all is

116

"immutable and eternall" then, at most, it is the structure of analytic knowledge, in the sense of the conditional use of reason. The principle of voluntative equality, of course, is not analytic but synthetic, as is Hobbes's presupposition of fear of death which, *qua* peaceable passion, provides the point of departure for peace contract settlements. Seen in this way, voluntative equality does not follow from a generic principle of reason, but, rather, reason, *qua* conditional reason, on the presupposition of voluntative equality and fear of death, gets a chance to formulate rules of equality more precisely. Correspondingly, the directive to seek peace which Hobbes understands as his first law of reason, if it were to be made more explicit, would have to run as follows: if you are guided by the passion of fear of death, and if you wish to live securely and commodiously, and if you accept voluntative equality as a principle, then, if it is possible at all, endeavor to achieve peace on equal terms. Hobbes then gives these terms a more precise formulation as the terms of a contract. Thus, only if voluntative equality is always presupposed, does reason have a chance of orienting the move to peace towards a contract constructed in an egalitarian way.[9]

If we hold onto this as a provisional result then, to be sure, a further difficulty for Hobbes's theory results from the central position of the premise on voluntative equality; moreover, it is one which calls this theory systematically into question. This difficulty concerns the equality of men in their relationship to the sovereign power. Having seen that Hobbes, for reasons of internal consistency, lays claim to voluntative equality as a historical fact, we need only express this fact somewhat differently in order to become aware of the critical point.

This historic fact simply means that we take account of the actually existing individual wills of people, in the sense of a social self-understanding of voluntative equality. The assumption must be made, at least for the sake of argument, that people would agree with such a self-understanding. However, if the very premise of the institution of the political commonwealth by contract is forced to refer to the empirically existing wills of people, then the question of how these wills are to be taken account of once the contract has been closed is unavoidable. It then makes no sense to understand the fact of voluntative equality retrospectively in a weaker way than before. If one has to presume that men's wills demand that, from the perspective of each individual, there is equal social respect, then this must be understood as the articulation of a historical fact which must be taken account of systematically. Rational recognition of the sovereign power in terms of the construction of the contract requires, at one and the same time, the rational mediation of the individual wills of the political commonwealth. Such a rational mediation may then, however, only be conceived in the form of the democratic participation of the individuals, leaving aside for the moment the institutional details of such a participation.

With this result we can formalize Hobbes's concept of sovereignty to a considerable extent. Sovereign power is nothing more than a decision procedure for political conflict resolution. This conflict resolution loses its authoritarian features to the degree that democratic mediation can make a rational contribution to conflict resolution. **Equality, Political Order, and Democracy thereby form a systematic unit.** With this result we also gain a conceptual basis for investigations which go beyond Hobbes's theory.

I will turn to these after I have demonstrated the contradiction which now becomes apparent between Hobbes's ethical subjectivism and the systematic connection between voluntative equality and democracy as just shown. Democratic participation would make little sense if the chances of rational social mediation and conflict resolution were hopeless, or reducible to a minimum, from the very beginning. Nonetheless, this is what we would have to accept if Hobbes's ethical subjectivism holds good. I have already called attention to this subjectivism and the way in which it makes the possibility of rational ethical argument seem slight. Strictly speaking, for Hobbes it makes absolutely no sense to ask about the truth or falsity of those judgments which refer to the concepts of good and evil. Why? It makes no sense for Hobbes because he founds the subjectivity of the ethical dimension on a sensualistic materialism. Every person is exposed in different ways to the causal influences of the external world and to the influences of other people; these act as stimulants on his sensory organs and, depending on the situation and on the physical constitution of the person in question, release certain effects. Since the causal situation of every person is different in the way just described, the conversion of causal influences into judgments is also different in each instance, and even varies in the case of each individual (cf. **Leviathan**, Ch. 4). In this way, Hobbes denies, from the very beginning, the possibility of a cognitive moment of moral judgment.

In taking note of this foundation of ethical subjectivism we must simultaneously reject it. An ethical subjectivism which dispenses with a phenomenology of value judgments, and possible intersubjective foundations for these, fails to be effective. As soon as we distribute the burden of proof here in an appropriate way, we cannot avoid taking a cognitive moment into consideration, in the case of judgments concerning questions of good and evil; for the unprejudiced eye, this cognitive moment emerges on the basis of examples from our normative language. It means, for example, distinguishing the fundamental difference between value judgments and mere expressions of feeling. If I say, "I find the death penalty repulsive," I say something other than, "The death penalty is unjust." In the second case, I commit myself, in a certain way, to the attempt to provide a justification in response to the question, "Why?" In the first case, in contrast, there is no expectation that a justification necessarily follows. An explication on the cognitive level, with regard to a relevant group of judgments concerning questions of good and evil, points to a social dimension of intersubjective discursive rationality. However, if the possibility of cognitive mediation can be demonstrated in this way, then there is an important additional result from the argument so far. Previously, it became clear that the move to democratic participation follows from voluntative equality; now it becomes clear that the move to cognitive-intersubjective mediation follows from democratic participation; therefore, cognitive mediation follows from voluntative equality. The contradiction between Hobbes's ethical subjectivism and the presupposition of voluntative equality can be brought to this abstract conclusion. It is also evident that Hobbes's authoritarianism now becomes redundant, given that it merely represents the janus-face of ethical subjectivism; where there are more subjective moral judgments, the political decision-making is more authoritarian.

3. Voluntative Equality, Justification, History: From Hobbes to Dworkin

This critique of Hobbes provides us with a systematic framework for a more extensive treatment of the question of the guiding concept of voluntative equality. I will now illustrate this framework briefly with reference to Locke, Rousseau and Kant. In doing so, I hope, with the help of clarifications found in R. Dworkin, to find a solution to the problem of grounding which is linked with the concept of voluntative equality.

In Locke's writings, voluntative equality *qua* principle of social relationship is not grounded by way of natural equality, but rather is conceived, on the basis of the law of nature/reason, as a principle which is just as fundamental as the latter. The question of the character of this law remains unclarified, even if Locke rightly takes the unavoidable premise of voluntative equality as his point of departure. He assigns this premise--more clearly than does Hobbes--the status of an explicit societal presupposition.[10]

The premise of voluntative equality is articulated most decisively in Rousseau; it simply has a different name - *volonté générale* (the *general will*). To be more precise: the concept of voluntative equality, as a principle of social relationship which is in turn a principle of equal respect, may be understood as an explication of the rational kernel of the *volonté générale*. The *volonté générale* is in fact a *volonté égalitaire*--a desire for equality that expresses the condition under which the political community may be constituted. This is, of course, not the whole story with regard to Rousseau; nonetheless, use of the formulation *volonté égalitaire* throws light on a number of problems; for example, both the recognition of voluntative equality as the highest principle of social regulation, and the necessity for unanimous recognition of this principle--which may then, analogously, be noted in Rousseau--become comprehensible, as does the remark, "the *volonté générale [égalitaire]* always aims for what is right." Understood as a principle of social relationship, it undoubtedly does this.[11] The problems which must be dealt with in Rousseau become clearer if we understand the "general will" as a principle of voluntative equality, and distinguish this from the subordinate, though also important, questions of democratic participation and rational societal mediation which remain unresolved in Rousseau.

The move from Rousseau to Kant bears out this train of thought to the extent that we find in Kant a clear concept of volition guided by principles, and an explicit reservation with regard to the idea that rigorous principles of will can be derived from characteristics of human nature.[12] In addition to this, Kant's terminology can help us to grasp the status of the concept of voluntative equality, in the sense of a principle of social relationship as we encountered it in the foregoing. What we are dealing with here may be described as a maxim, although we must, for the moment, leave open the question of whether it satisfies the law of practical reason in the Kantian sense. To be sure, it is a very interesting maxim, since the principle of voluntative equality, *qua* presupposition of politico-social intersubjectivity, would be a **universally shared** subjective principle of volition. In the context of my critique of Hobbes, the reference to a normative fact which is to be presupposed historically, corresponds to this. In this way, the problem of grounding with which we are now concerned becomes clear. This problem leads, I believe, to the following alternatives. Either we accept here an idea of grounding which is conceived—in whatever way—according to the Kantian model, that is, based on a structural concept of reason, **or** we conceive the principle of voluntative equality as a historically situated, and, as it were, unavoidable, principle of human self-understanding—a principle which allows no rational **historical alternatives.** I will argue for this second possibility.

An important step in understanding the concept of voluntative equality consists in seeing this principle as the recognition of a basic right to equality which represents, if you like, a politico-social **self-definition of men and women.** By means of the concept of a basic right to equality that must be attributed to every member of any politico-social community conceivable *for us*, the guiding idea of voluntative equality is, from the point of view of every individual, given a kind of permanence by definition, in that *every* member is provided with an established right, an entitlement in principle. At the same time, the universalistic sense of such a process comes to fruition. As R. Dworkin shows, in particular, what we are dealing with here is a very abstract right to equal treatment which is held by men and women *qua* human beings:

...a natural right of all men and women to equality of concern and respect, a right they possess not by virtue of birth or character or merit or excellence but simply as human beings with the capacity to make plans and give justice.[13]

Dworkin's formulation also provides evidence for his thesis that this kind of conception of a basic right to equality is rooted so deeply that it cannot be contested by any more radical concept of equality, because it is unclear what the latter would look like (cf. *ibid.*). In working out a concept of equality of this kind, Dworkin can not only point to the general presupposition on which Rawls's "original position" rests; he can also, over and above this, argue convincingly for the thesis that the clearest concept of equality is one which understands equality as a matter of an individual right that is mutually acknowledged:

...equality defines a relation among citizens that is individualized for each, and therefore can be seen to set entitlements as much from the point of view of each person as that of anyone else in the community.[14]

With this clarification, we receive a kind of definition of voluntative equality which, though abstraction, provides the tradition of natural right, since Hobbes, with its own emancipation. The appeal to nature is now merely metaphorical; it is replaced by a self-definition of people, the achievement of which consists in the fact that it takes as its basis the most abstract principle possible under which they can confront each other as moral beings. Seen in this way, Kant's concept of moral autonomy is also taken into account, although in such a way that we understand voluntative equality as a self-imposed moral principle which, while permitting us (with Kant) to conceive of people as beings capable of duty, does not claim to derive voluntative equality from a fundamental structure of reason. Rather, it is a matter of understanding that reason's achievement in establishing a principle of voluntative equality is historically mediated.

This, however, must also lead to a revision of traditional strategies for grounding moral principles of a fundamental nature. If we grasp concepts such as voluntative equality or that of a basic right to equality, in both their historicity and rationality, then the mode of justification of such principles can itself be only a historical one. It now makes no sense to look beyond the basic right to equality for even more fundamental grounds on which we might appeal; rather, our concern now must be the unfolding of the moral potential of a basic right to equality by means of an interpretation of the connection between morality, law and politics, in the context of the relevant traditions. A principle such as voluntative equality, or that of a basic right to equality, can be justified hermeneutically by way of the potential for action and reaching agreement which they make available for appropriate spheres of *praxis*. It is a matter of justification through coherence. As I understand them, Ronald Dworkin's writings provide solid support for this thesis, not least due to their conscious orientation towards the anglo-saxon tradition of moral right and politics.[15]

To be sure, strong fundamentalist or objectivistic claims to provide foundations, such as those currently raised by Habermas or Apel, will not be satisfied by this. However, the claims raised by "German fundamentalism" can themselves be understood only in the context of the moral distress provoked by recent German history. I will therefore conclude by describing a curve from Hobbes to Habermas which will make this clear and, at the same time, provide support for my systematic thesis.

4. Democratic Ethics, Decision, Consensus: Between Hobbes and Habermas

Habermas's political theory can be introduced from the start as the ideal-typical antithesis to Hobbes:

The "power" of the public sphere is, according to its own idea, an order in which power itself dissolves: **veritas non auctoritas facit legem**....*Pouvoir as such is, by means of a public sphere that functions politically, made the subject of debate. This is supposed to transform* **voluntas** *into a ratio which,* **qua** *consensus concerning that which, in the general interest, is of practical necessity, produces itself in the competition between private arguments in the public sphere.*[16]

This position not only provides us with the ideal-typical alternative to Hobbes; it also contains *in nuce* the systematic program which Habermas, with his consensus theory of theoretical and practical truth and with his so-called formal-pragmatic theory of language, has been trying to carry out to the present day. Corresponding to this is Habermas's occasional reference to the "darkness of pure decision" or "decisionism gone blind," dangers to which we fall prey when we fail to take account of the rational potential of discursive processes of reaching agreement in an adequate way.[17]

With this, Habermas also provides a terminological qualification of Hobbes's doctrine which has become influential since Carl Schmitt. Schmitt characterizes Hobbes as the "classical representative" of the "decisionistic type"[18] and appeals to the formula just cited *("auctoritas, not veritas...")* in support of this. Over and above this, we find in Schmitt repeated attempts to demonstrate an analogy between his own systematic reflections, which might be described as a kind of "existential decisionism," and Hobbes's theory. Schmitt's notorious definition of the political sphere, using the friend/foe antithesis, is behind his reference to Hobbes. To the extent that one understands this antithesis in an abstract way as the expression of the idea of conflict, the two theorists do indeed show points of contact here; yet, Schmitt's theory goes far beyond this common ground.[19]

Thus, if Habermas frequently argues energetically and polemically against decisionism, it is because he has Carl Schmitt's theory, in particular, before his eyes; the fact that Schmitt's theory is, in addition, associated with the Nationalist-Socialist ideology lends support to the accusation that all decisionistic theories are irrational. Even while completely rejecting Carl Schmitt's theory, however, we must make a supplementary differentiation here. What is so unattractive about Schmitt is, in particular, his rigorous denigration of the possibility of democratic-discursive potentials for resolving social and political conflicts, such as those recognized by the liberal tradition. His critique of parliamentary democracy is of particular relevance here--a critique which has grim political consequences.[20]

Once one refuses to follow Schmitt along this mistaken path, the problem of decisionism takes on a different slant, one which is in tune with the democratic reading of Hobbes's theory which I have just proposed. The question of how we are to conceive the democratic-discursive rationality of social and political problem-resolution (supposing this is assumed) must be answered in view of the claim that *"veritas"* may be achieved. The willingness to engage in discursive processes of understanding and the institutionalization of discursive-participatory procedures by no means automatically guarantees theoretical or practical truth—at least, not if one allows the concept of truth to retain its selectivity *vis à vis* the concepts of thinking, considering-to-be-true, and believing. To put this somewhat differently: the principle of discussion-free-from-domination introduced by Habermas, which is supposed to provide a consensual truth-criterion in some form or other (for instance, the "ideal speech situation"), cannot do this. What it does achieve is a convincing formulation of a radical democratic principle in the liberal traditions, one which fastens on to the guiding ideas of equality and freedom. What we gain by this is primarily an ethics of democratic-discursive participation. However, the acknowledgement of social and political decisions is compatible with such an ethics. Seen in this way, a discursively mediated decisionism would not be a sign of irrationality but, rather, the expression of pragmatic reason and tolerance.

Naturally, consensus is desirable and, within the framework of a democratic ethics, to be regarded as a higher good. This is, however, something quite different from consensus in the sense of a criterion of practical truth that must be accepted for structural-systematic reasons. As is well known, Habermas tries to introduce such reasons by way of a linguistic-theoretical attempt to provide a foundation for his discourse-ethics and for his theory of rationality.[21] If this ambitious program were to succeed, then one could indeed show that even the orientation towards voluntative equality, or towards the basic right to equality, is itself founded in yet more fundamental dimensions of reason that provide the historical processes in which moral convictions are formed with an objective foundation. Over and above this, one could show that the norms and decisions selected within the framework of discursive processes are ultimately bound by the telos of an objective consensus.

No matter how fascinating such a program may appear at first glance, the theses which support it remain unproven. It is simply not clear how one might obtain basic moral principles through an appeal to so-called fundamental norms of possible speech. It is certainly true that our language contains a potential for reaching agreement discursively, one which is expressed formally in practical and ethical sentences and which represents the dimension in which moral convictions develop for us. But from the fact that men and women are linguistic creatures to whom a potential of this kind is available, it does not follow that they, *qua* linguistic creatures, must share specific material convictions-- even if these are of a very general nature. Whether or not I am willing to adopt an attitude of intersubjective equality is a question not of my linguistic competence but rather of my psychic and moral disposition-- even if this is mediated through language. One has to be careful here if one is to avoid introducing the paradigm of a "linguistic fallacy." Voluntative equality follows just as little from linguistic competence and linguistic equality as it does from a putative natural equality. And no consensus theory of practical truth follows from a fair, reciprocal, democratic supposition, no matter how much this is mediated discursively.[22]

hobbes and democratic rationality

This is **not** contradicted by the fact that we have to conceive of the principle of voluntative equality, as it emerged from the discussion of Hobbes's theory, as well as the idea of a basic right to equality as introduced by Dworkin, in the sense of a consensual fact. Rather, this merely means that such indispensable basic concepts of ethical orientation attain dominance by way of a complicated process of discursive-cognitive and historico-motivational mediation, thereby gaining the right to claim a voluntative consensus, on the basis of which politico-social self-conceptions of people are defined. Thus, here too, we must make a distinction between a voluntative consensus and a veritative consensus.

This demonstrates the dilemma of the idea of a "formal-pragmatics" or "universal-pragmatics." The failure of this idea is a result of mixing two conceptually distinct aspects; the structure of language, on the one hand, and social context, ethical attitudes and historical development, on the other. For this reason, Habermas cannot confer on his concept of a discourse ethics, or on his very special concept of communicative action, the dignity of a language-theoretical deduction in any substantial sense.[23] Language is a necessary but not a sufficient condition for a discourse-ethics and for communicative action.[24] With regard to these latter notions, all that is required on the part of language is the presupposition that it itself is powerful enough to enable us to communicate in the interest of providing reasons, arguments and justifications, whenever this is necessary to satisfy the demands of social rationality. And, evidently, language is powerful enough to open up this dimension of rationality. It seems to me, therefore, that Habermas's concern with the theory of language is an unrequited love. Just as nature is not the interpreter of our human condition, language as such is not the enchanted princess of emancipation.

University of Konstanz

Translated by Maeve Cooke

ENDNOTES

*When referring specifically to Hobbes's views, the author and editor have retained Hobbes's use of "man," rather than modify for gender neutral language, in order to avoid historically inaccurate modification.

1. Quotations from the M. Oakeshott, Oxford, Basil Blackwell, 1960 edition of **Leviathan.**

2. Cf. Hobbes, **The Elements of Law, Natural and Politic,** ed. F. Tönnies, 2nd edition, London, Cass, 1969, part 1, Ch. 14, sect. 13.

rolf
zimmermann

3. The equipment of men with "rights" in principle which, even in the state of nature, makes possible both the transference of rights and obligation, is to be understood in exactly the same way. Cf. B. Barry, **Warrender and His Critics**, in M. Cranston/R.S. Peters, eds., **Hobbes and Rousseau**, New York, Anchor Books, 1972.

4. This fact is underlined in a way appropriate to the present context by the contrast with Aristotle to which Hobbes attaches so much importance (Cf. **De Cive**, ch. 1). For Aristotle, the "natural definition" of man as a community animal (*zoon politikon*) in no way excludes the possibility that men confront one another as social creatures which conceive themselves as unequal (citizens-slaves).

5. Cf. also G.S. Kavka, **Hobbesian Moral and Political Theory** Princeton, Princeton University Press, 1980, ch. 7, who makes some similar points.

6. Cf. Th. Hobbes, **Thomas White's De Mundo Examined** (Latin translated by H.W. Jones, London, Bradford University Press, 1976), p. 26: "Now philosophy, i.e. every science, must be treated in such a way that we shall know from necessary deductions that the conclusions we draw are true. Philosophy should therefore be treated logically, for the aim of its students is not to impress [others], but to know with certainty."

7. As a point of interest, stronger and weaker attempts to argue for the concept of natural equality can be found in Hobbes. The argument in **De Cive** is weak: "...they are equalls who can doe equall things one against the other; but they who can do the greatest things, (namely kill) can do equall things. All men therefore among themselves are by nature equall..." **The Philosophical Works**, Vol III, ed. H. Warrender, Oxford, Clarendon Press, 1983, Ch. 1, sect. III, p. 45. In this way one would also be able to show that tigers, lions, etc. and men are equal by nature.

8. In the present context it is a question of working out the systematic status of the premise of voluntative equality. The question of how such a premise was historically constituted in the context of the 17th century is, of course, in need of further examination. Consideration of this question means, above all, that we see Hobbes as a child of his time and show connections with his mode of thinking which allow us to understand such an extensive concept as that of voluntative equality as the articulation of a new view of man. To this extent, the required historical interpretation would have to be both more differentiated and more comprehensive than that provided by C.B. Macpherson, **The Political Theory of Possessive Individualism**, Oxford, Oxford University Press, 1962. Cf. also for further material, P. Zagorin, **A History of Political Thought in the English Revolution**, London, Routledge & Kegan Paul, 1954; Ch. Hill, **Puritanism and Revolution**, London, Panther Edition, 1969; Q. Skinner, "History and Ideology in the English Revolution," **The Historical Journal**, Vol. VIII, 1965; Q. Skinner, "The Ideological Context of Hobbes's Political Thought, **The Historical Journal**, Vol. IX, 1966.

9. The hypothetico-conditional form which, e.g., J.W.N. Watkins (**Hobbes's System of Ideas**, London, Hutchinson, 1965) emphasizes,

is thus preserved, even if voluntative equality is introduced as a normative premise.

10. Cf. J. Locke, **Two Treatises of Government,** ed. P. Laslett, Cambridge, Cambridge University Press, 1966, 2nd Treatise, ch. II, sect. 14ff., ch. VI, sect. 54.

11. Cf. J.J. Rousseau, **Contrat Social,** Livre I, ch.6, Livre II, chs. 1,4,6, Paris, Gallimard, 1966.

12. Cf. I. Kant, **Grundlegung zur Metaphysik der Sitten,** Akademieausgabe, Bd. IV, S. 411f, 425. Very illuminating also is P. Riley, **Will and Political Legitimacy,** Cambridge, MA, Harvard University Press, 1982, ch. 5.

13. R. Dworkin, **Taking Rights Seriously,** New Impression, London, Duckworth, 1981, p. 182. Cf., chs. 1, 12 and pp. 356f., "...the idea of equality is meant to suggest content for the ideas of respect and autonomy."

14. R. Dworkin, "What is Equality?" Part 2, "Equality of Resources," **Philosophy and Public Affairs,** Vol. 10, no. 4, 1981, pp. 340f. Cf. Dworkin's comments on the differences between his conception and Rawls's, *ibid.,* pp. 338ff. Cf J. Rawls, "A Kantian Conception of Equality" in J. Raijchman/West, eds., **Post-Analytic Philosophy,** New York, Columbia University Press, 1985, for a contrasting point of view.

15. Cf. R. Dworkin, **A Matter of Principle,** Cambridge, MA, Harvard University Press, 1985. R. Dworkin, **Law's Empire,** Cambridge, MA, Harvard University Press, 1986. In contradistinction to Rorty, I believe that it is by all means possible to "historicize" even Dworkin, Cf. R. Rorty, "The Priority of Democracy to Philosophy," in M.D. Peterson/R.C. Vaughan, eds., **The Virginia Statute of Religious Freedom,** Cambridge, MA, Cambridge University Press, 1987.

16. Cf. J. Habermas, **Strukturwandel der Oeffentlichkeit,** Neuwied 1964, p.95.

17. Cf. J. Habermas, **Towards a Rational Society,** Boston, Beacon Press, 1970.

18. Cf. C. Schmitt, **Politische Theologie,** Berlin/W.: Duncker & Humblot, p. 44.

19. Cf. C. Schmitt, **Der Begriff des Politischen,** Berlin/W.: Duncker & Humblot, 1979/1932), pp. 26f, 64f.

20. Cf. C. Schmitt, **Die geistesgeschichtliche Lage des heutigen Parlamentarismus,** Berlin/W.: Duncker & Humblot, 1975.

21. Cf. J. Habermas, "Diskursethik—Notizen zu einem Begründungsprogramm" in **Moralbewusstsein und Kommunikatives Handeln,** Suhrkamp, Frankfurt, 1983; also, J. Habermas, **Theory of Communicative Action,** Beacon Press, Boston, 1984.

rolf
zimmermann

22. Cf. E. Tugendhat, "Langage et éthique", **Critique**, Oct., 1981, pp. 1067ff.

23. Cf. E. Tugendhat, "Habermas on Communicative Action" in G. Seebas/R. Tuomela, eds., **Social Action**, Dordrecht, Reidel Publishing Company, 1985, pp. 179-186.

24. For more on this, cf. R. Zimmermann, **Utopie—Rationalität— Politik. Zu Kritik, Rekonstruktion und Systematik einer emanzipatorischen Gesellschaftstheorie bei Marx und Habermas,** Freiburg/München, Alber, 1985, part II; also, R. Zimmermann, "Emancipation and Rationality. Foundational Problems in the Theories of Marx and Habermas," **Ratio**, Vol. 26:2, 1984.

axel honneth
atomism and ethical life: on hegel's critique of the french revolution

Ever since Lukács, or at least since Joachim Ritter's famous treatise on the subject, we have known beyond all doubt that Hegel's political philosophy is inextricably bound up with the French Revolution. However, it is still a matter of controversy how and in what manner Hegel incorporated the course and the achievements of revolutionary action into his thinking on political theory and made them the point of reference for his own philosophy. Joachim Ritter believes Hegel was convinced that the French Revolution signified the historical breakthrough of that principle of the formal right of freedom by virtue of which subjects are free, via their division from one another, to realize their being-as-self.[1] Jürgen Habermas has supplemented this somewhat affirmative interpretation by putting forward the critical thesis that Hegel was so quick to raise the revolutionary process of the assertion of abstract law to the heights of an objective process of world history because he wished to avoid creating a hazardous relation between his own philosophy and revolutionary *praxis*.[2] And finally, Andreas Wildt has countered both interpretations with the provocative thesis that, in his lifelong tussle with the French Revolution, Hegel was actually not concerned with the realization of an abstract right of freedom, but with the historical conditions that made possible the assertion of such relations of solidarity as could not be precisely laid down in a legal code.[3]

This brief summary of three pertinent interpretative approaches shows how varied the answers hitherto have been to the question axel honneth   of Hegel's use of the French Revolution as the central principle of his political philosophy. Yet, in the course of discussions over the last thirty years researchers have more or less come to agree that the center of Hegel's exposition of revolutionary activity was occupied by precisely that politico-philosophical problem about which Ritter speaks only briefly in the conclusion to his study: namely that of how the social mediation of legal subjects—who are free and equal, formally speaking—occurs within the overarching context of a moral community.[4] With a view to this central problem, I propose an interpretation that initially seeks to distance itself from the discussion just sketched by determining Hegel's relation to the French Revolution not substantively, but with respect to the history of how it developed. In the course of his philosophical development, Hegel had to switch from an internal to an external critique of the Revolution, because he had forfeited not only his original idea of communicative ethical life but also the concept with which he had been able to encapsulate the full breadth of revolutionary aims and then refer them back internally, as it were, to practical political occurrences. While still in Jena, Hegel was able only to explain the political difficulties of revolutionary upheavals intrinsically: as the problems involved in achieving an institutional balance between freedom, equality and fraternity—and then only for such a time as he endeavored to interpret the inclusion of formally equal legal subjects within the overarching whole of universal ethical life with respect to the referential model of a higher-stage intersubjectivity. For it was only the conception of an intersubjectively structured ethical life which permitted him to understand the revolutionary demand for "fraternity" in terms of creating contexts of solidarity in which formally free and equal subjects could, in turn, be related to one another communicatively. However, as soon as Hegel clandestinely attempted to substitute that substantialist conceptual model for the model of ethical life based on a theory of intersubjectivity, he had to renounce the immanent reference to revolutionary goals and could only refer to political occurrences "externally," from the vantage point of a substantive state. The notion of an agency of state bereft of intersubjectivity takes the place of the idea of fraternity, an agency against which the revolution, not reduced to the twin demands for freedom and equality, can be measured. In order to provide at least a rough outline of the groundwork for the many implications of this suggestion, I shall first sketch Hegel's Jena interpretation of revolutionary occurrences and then, in a second step, contrast this with his substantialist interpretation of ethical life.

I.

130   As a young man, Hegel had, if we take up Franz Rosenzweig's description,[5] perceived the revolutionary occurrences in France

initially from the philosophical horizon of a deeply Romantic ideal of community. With his slant toward the moral potential for integration afforded by the Early Christian communities, and his enthusiasm for the Greek *polis*, it must at first have been the reports of a new, highly expressive form of political public sphere that enabled him to be caught up in the sway of the Revolution. According to Rosenzweig, it was not long, however, before that other, normative side to revolutionary upheaval became uppermost in Hegel's thought, a side he had elucidated via an intensified consideration of Kant's moral philosophy. He had learned even before this time, namely in Frankfurt, to conceive of the Revolution as the legal anchoring of universal principles of freedom in the stage of world history.[6] Finally, when moving from Frankfurt to Jena, and this is also to be gleaned from Rosenzweig's description, Hegel took his third, and this time decisive, step in the politico-philosophical understanding of the French Revolution. At the same time, with his insight into those economic conditions which made possible the new legal universalism, an entity he is later to term as a whole "civil society," he slowly became convinced of the dissociating force exerted by a form of societalization which was grounded solely in the freedom that was formally secured from the arbitrariness of isolated subjects.[7]

It was by combining these three theoretical steps that Hegel finally developed a philosophical-historical referential system in the framework of which he determined, systematically, the difficulties facing the political realization of the revolution, and concomitantly assigned its place in the context of world history. This construction orients itself toward the idea, outlined in his essay on natural law, of a history of human ethical life in which progress in the given relations of this life is to be accomplished by gradually overcoming those still extant instances of one-sidedness and particularization.[8] In Hegel's eyes, the French Revolution was initially allocated a double-edged role in the scheme of this developmental process, in that it brought about the individual's emancipation to formal freedom only at the price of institutionalizing an intrinsically disintegrative, and therefore negative, sphere. For, on the one hand, revolutionary *praxis* had aided those abstract rights of freedom by functionally dove-tailing with the expanding market system, which consequently gained institutional validity and thus opened up a legal space in which individuals could realize their respective interests; yet, on the other hand, precisely this process of legal emancipation created a social zone for persons objectively severed from one another, and this, the central problem which arose from the revolutionary upheaval, brought about the trend toward a decay of ethical unity in the first place. For Hegel, then, the real challenge posed by the age must have been the question generated by the Revolution, namely, how that sphere of abstract freedom which had been won through political struggle could itself be embedded in an overarching context so that it would not unleash its atomizing capacity *ad infinitum*, but rather become a positive formative element in an ethical community. In essence, Hegel started looking for an answer to this question the moment he clearly conceptualized the atomistic premises of modern natural law.[9] The politico-philosophical treatises which he wrote in his first years in Jena stand out because they, in principle, expect the Revolution itself to engender those social forces which are necessary to solve the problem.

Hegel made this surprising turn as a result of the historico-philosophical concretization of the overall framework of a conflict-laden Becoming of ethical life which he undertook in Jena. The notion of love—indebted to Hölderlin[10]—as the reconciliatory power which could always lead one beyond the stages of a severed ethical life had, meanwhile, under the influence of Fichte, become transformed into a theory of the relations of human recognition, a theory which was not intended to explain the further development of the ethical conditions of life.[11] According to this theory, it is the intersubjective claim of individuals to reciprocal recognition which, in the course of human history, gradually leads via struggle to an augmentation in individual autonomy and social solidarity. Hegel discerned in the demand for "fraternity" precisely that notion of a goal that—at the stage of disintegration called forth by the progress of abstract law reached thus far—marks the form of reciprocal recognition by means of which, at a higher level, it would be possible to generate an ethical totality. Admittedly, if the Revolution is to unleash such forces of communicative reconciliation after the event, then its false, limited understanding of itself must first be corrected. The agents of the Revolution must, to a certain extent, learn first that an overarching form of reciprocal recognition is necessary so as to recreate ethical cohesion following the individual's emancipation to formal freedom, and that this recognition cannot be introduced by anchoring it in law.[12] Hegel's early Jena writings, especially the **System of Ethical Life** and the first drafts on "Real philosophy" can be understood as the attempt to bring about the self-enlightenment of the revolution with respect to its tasks. A rudimentarily sketched theory of stages of social recognition constitutes the philosophical core of these works; this theory is the only approach to an internal critique of the French Revolution to be found in Hegel's *oeuvre*.

In the **System of Ethical Life**, Hegel, for the first time, outlined three stages of reciprocal recognition—even if this is still in the guise of a schematic form of representation borrowed from Schelling. The pattern by which these stages evolve shows clearly that they refer back to the structural problems of the Revolution. The process which establishes the beginnings of social relations is initially described as the subject's gradual extrication from his/her determination by nature. According to Hegel, this "gradual growth" of individuality ensues via two stages of reciprocal recognition, the differences being assessable in terms of those dimensions of the respective subject which find practical affirmation in them. In the relationship of "parents and children," in other words in the family, individuals recognize each other reciprocally as loving beings in need of emotional sustenance.[13] The sublation of this "unification of feeling," as Hegel puts it, is followed by a second stage of recognition, that of contractually-regulated exchange relations between property owners, which is still, however, dealt with under the heading of "natural ethical life."[14] The path intended to lead to this new state of social relations is depicted as being a process of legal universalization. The practical links between subjects and the world, which were pertinent at the first stage, are now stripped of the merely particularist conditions for their validity and are transformed into universal, contractually guaranteed legal claims. The subjects now recognize each other as the bearers of legitimate property claims and are thereby first constituted as owners of property; in the act of exchange they refer to one another as "persons" to whom the formal right to freedom in realizing their interests is accorded. The reasons with which Hegel implicitly justified continuing to allocate this stage of formal legal relations to the state of "natural ethical life," characterized by the "principle of singleness," clearly reveal those arguments which had already prompted him to denote the sphere of abstract law as a zone of negativity. If society is organized such that it is informed solely by legal forms of recognition, then the subjects are also included in it solely in terms of negative freedom and are thus without any overarching mutuality.[15]

Hegel contrasted the two initial forms of recognition in quite different forms of struggle, and it is this distinction which is of direct significance for the reference back to the French Revolution. In their capacity as different shapes taken by crime, these acts of destruction, which are described in a chapter devoted to them,[16] relate back to the previous stage of ethical life because they comprise forms of the negative expression of that formal freedom which subjects had been accorded by the implementation of legal relations. Hegel did not, however, proceed only to elucidate how already established relations of recognition are respectively violated or challenged by such acts in which individual freedom is exercised negatively; rather, he demonstrated, in the course of his description, that a form of awareness of the reciprocal dependency of subjects arises from the struggles resulting from the criminal's challenge. The given legal relation of recognition is no longer suitable with respect to such dependency: individuals now finally confront each other having taken the challenge posed by different crimes upon themselves—no longer as self-referential actors, but as self-confident "members of a whole."[17] If the chapter on "Crime" is interpreted against the background of these findings, then it would seem logical to view it as Hegel's depiction of the formative process which leads from the stage of a legal relation of recognition to a new stage of ethical unification. The criminal, by violating the formal rights of other persons, makes it an object of common knowledge that the identity of each single person is dependent on the community of all others. To this extent, the same social conflicts that challenge the legal relations of natural ethical life first prompt individual subjects to recognize themselves reciprocally as dependent on one another and yet as completely individuated persons.

However, in the course of his remarks, Hegel went on to address a third stage of recognition leading to relations of solidarity among members of a society; yet he addressed this only in the form of an implied presupposition. In his presentation of "absolute ethical life," which follows the chapter on crime, he asserted that a specific relation between subjects, which he termed the concept of "reciprocal perception," forms the intersubjective basis for a future commonality.[18] The argument he followed suggests in many places a differentiation between three forms of recognition which must be distinguished from one another in terms of both "why" and "how" practical confirmation of recognition occurs. In the emotional relation of recognition to the family, the human subject is recognized as a concrete being which exhibits needs; in the cognitive-formal relation of law, it is recognized as an abstract legal entity; and, finally, in the emotionally enlightened relation to the state, it is recognized as the concrete universal, namely as a unique subject. If one differentiates more carefully between the institution and the mode of respective relation of recognition, then the theory of stages Hegel has in mind can be reproduced in the following chart:

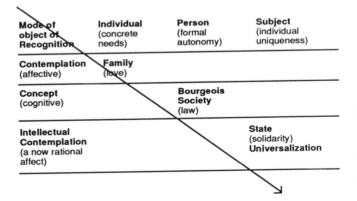

Mode of object of Recognition	Individual (concrete needs)	Person (formal autonomy)	Subject (individual uniqueness)
Contemplation (affective)	Family (love)		
Concept (cognitive)		Bourgeois Society (law)	
Intellectual Contemplation (a now rational affect)			State (solidarity) Universalization

If this concept does in fact designate a form of reciprocal relation between subjects that goes beyond mere recognition—and this is suggested by the label "perception," borrowed from Schelling—then the presentation of the **System of Ethical Life** quite obviously evidences a double reference back to the occurrences of the Revolution. On the one hand, Hegel attempted, in the description, to locate a positive meaning in the terrorist outgrowths of the Revolution after the event, viewing them as a formative process by virtue of which the participating subjects have to become aware of the fundamental relations of solidarity that obtain and which could provide the basis for the integration of abstract rights of freedom within the overarching context of an ethically integrated commonality. On the other hand, with his scheme of the stages of recognition, Hegel demonstrated indirectly that the revolutionary goal of "fraternity" cannot precisely be achieved along the formal route of an institutionalization of rights taken by the extreme Jacobin factions [19] Hegel wished, if these pointed remarks are true, to initiate a learning process by describing an ethical process of learning. The **System of Ethical Life** is intended to instruct the revolution as to the political path to be taken if the process of social atomization, already factually commenced, is to be transformed into a formative moment in a new form of ethical unity.

II.

Hegel admittedly, as can be seen from the above, was only able to formulate such an intrinsic critique of the French Revolution for such a time as he regarded its potential for political ideas to be an appropriate expression of the goals harbored in the forms of therapy he proposed. The theoretical presupposition for the immanent correction to the self-understanding of the revolution, which he undertook in the **System of Ethical Life**, is to be found in the significant fact that, at the beginning of the new century, he rediscovered the slogan of "fraternity" as a label for the program which he himself hoped would be the solution to the socio-political problems of the day. In Jena, Hegel conceived of the mediation of particular and universal and, thus, of the reconciliation of a divided society in terms of communicative ethical life. Here, the universality of solidarity that has occurred by free will—and in which free and equal subjects recognize each other reciprocally as partners in mutual life who are dependent on and yet independent of each other--is held to comprise the ethical unity of the functional matrix of society. It was this conceptual model alone which allowed Hegel the fleeting chance to refer immanently to the historical process of the French Revolution. The slogan of "fraternity" enabled him to recognize the programmatic expression of the goals he himself set: to preserve politically the emancipatory results of the revolutionary implementation of formal rights of freedom by encouraging public consciousness of an overarching context of solidarity that absorbs its atomizing after-effects.

Yet, this intersubjectivist model of ethical life, which Hegel constructed by means of his theory of the stages of social recognition, was from the outset tainted by the ambiguity of his fluctuation between the Classical *polis* and the post-traditional concept of community. These are adjacent to each other in Hegel's early Jena writings: the idea of a pre-reflexive, community generated by links to a tradition and not subjected to examination; **and** the idea of a reflexive form of solidarity resulting from the formation of a moral consciousness among all individuals.[20] Even at this time, Hegel did not attempt to transpose the higher stage of intersubjectivity contained in his model of ethical life onto the mechanism of political will formation itself. Rather, while in Jena, he still was able to conceive only of the institutional structuring of the ethically integrated society, the social foundations of which he believed to be a life shared in solidarity, in the form of a monarchy along corporate lines. These differentiations, which were internal to the theory, become redundant, however, once Hegel, while still in Jena, started substituting the theoretical construct of a self-referential Spirit of a philosophy of consciousness for the model of the intersubjective formation of consciousness contained in the doctrine of recognition. With the restructuring of the underlying concepts that this entailed—as a result of which the history of ethical life is no longer explained in terms of the structures of a struggle for recognition, but, rather, as a stage in the self-movement of Absolute Spirit—a transformation of the model of ethical life occurred in Hegel's thought which has important consequences. If the Absolute is now conceived of in line with the model of a self-understanding essence, then the mediation of particular and universal within absolute ethical life can no longer be regarded as the outcome of an intersubjective relation, but must, rather, be viewed as a relation of that essence to its members, thought of as accidental attributes.[21] From now on Hegel must, therefore, ineluctably think of ethical reconciliation of the divided society solely in the form of a subordination of individual will to the essential authority of the state.

In this substantialist model of ethical life, which is the theoretical successor in Hegel's thought to the conception based on a theory of intersubjectivity, processes of reciprocal recognition between subjects have lost any constitutive function they once had. Hegel has so very consistently switched the "relation of essence to these persons"[22] that he can now conceive of the state as a space free of intersubjectivity. This has significant consequences with respect to his relation to the French Revolution: he could no longer view the slogan of "fraternity" as the political expression of a reconciling force that he had originally assumed could potentially effect the ethical reconciliation of society. The moment he took up a substantialist concept of ethical life, Hegel embarked on an external critique of the French Revolution. He criticized the terrorist outgrowths of the Revolution by measuring them against a yardstick foreign to them, namely substantive agency of state. He was, admittedly, thenceforth never to contest its world-historical ability to implement abstract law in practice, but he was also never to expect it to have the capacity to solve, politically, the divisions it had brought about. Finally, with masterful insight, Hegel reduced the effects of the Revolution solely to the emancipation of the individual to formal freedom. And he was able to incorporate this revolution all the more smoothly as a positive component of world history because the problems it had left unsolved made the state appear, all the more clearly, to be the guarantor of ethical reconciliation.

Johann Wolfgang Goethe Universität, Frankfurt

Translated by Jeremy Gaines

ENDNOTES

1.   Joachim Ritter, "Hegel and the French Revolution," **Hegel and the French Revolution. Essays on 'The Philosophy of Right'**, tr. R.D. Winfield, Cambridge, MA, MIT Press, 1982.

2.   Jürgen Habermas, "Hegels Kritik der französischen Revolution," **Theorie und Praxis**, Frankfurt, Suhrkamp, 1971, p. 128ff.

3.   Alexander Wildt, "Hegels kritik des Jakobinismus," **Aktualität unf Folgen der Philosophie Hegels**, ed. Oskar Negt, Frankfurt, 1970, p. 265ff.

4.   Above all, recent English debates have shown that this politico-philosophical problem lay at the core of Hegel's critical engagement with the French Revolution. Cf., for example, Charles Taylor, **Hegel**, Cambridge, Cambridge University Press, 1975, Part Four, Chapters XIV and XV; Steven B. Smith, **Hegel's Critique of Liberalism. Rights in Context**, Chicago, University of Chicago Press, 1989, Chapter 3.

5.   Franz Rosenzweig, **Hegel und der Staat**, Aalen, 1982, reprint of the Munich and Berlin edition of 1920, Part Three: Tübingen.

6.   *Ibid.,* Part Four: Berne.

7.   *Ibid.,* Part Seven: Jena, in particular p. 158ff; cf. also Rolf Peter Horstmann, "Über die Rolle der bürgerlichen Gesellschaft in Hegals politischer Philosophie," **Materialien zu Hegels Rechtsphilosophie**, ed. Manfred Riedel, vol. 2, Frankfurt, Suhrkamp, 1975, p. 276ff.

axel honneth

8. Georg Wilhelm Friedrich Hegel, "Über die wissenschaftlichen Behandlungsarten des Naturrechts," **WW, Theorie-Werkausgabe**, vol. 2, Frankfurt, Suhrkamp, 1970, p. 434ff, above all Chapters III and IV.

9. Cf. above all *Ibid.*, Chapters I and II.

10. Cf. on this point Dieter Henrich, "Hegel und Hölderlin," **Hegel im Kontext**, Frankfurt, 1971, p. 9ff.

11. Cf. on this the more recent, pioneering work by Ludwig Siep (**Anerkennung als Prinzip der praktischen Philosophie, Untersuchungen zu Hegels Jenaer Philosophie des Geistes,** Frieburg and Munich, 1979) and Andreas Wildt (**Autonomie und anerkennung. Hegels Moralitätskritik im Lichte seiner Fichte-Rezeption,** Stuttgart, 1982). These two studies were preceded by Manfred Riedel's major essay, "Hegels Kritik des Naturrechts," **Studien zu Hegels Rechtsphilosophie,** Frankfurt, 1969, p. 42ff. On the complex as a whole, see the first, preliminary interpretation I put forward in **Zwischenbetrachtungen. Im Prozeß der Aufklärung** eds. Axel Honneth, Thomas McCarthy, Claus Offe, Albrecht Wellmer, Frankfurt, Suhrkamp, 1989.

12. This is the central and to my mind accurate argument which Andreas Wildt develops in his presentation of the Hegel's relation to the French Revolution. Cf. Andreas Wildt, "Hegels Kritik des Jakobinismus."

13. Georg Wilhelm Friedrich Hegel, **System der Sittlichkeit**, Hamburg, 1967, p. 17ff.

14. *Ibid.,* p. 26ff.

15. *Ibid.,* p. 33.

16. *Ibid.,* p. 38ff. ("On the Negative or Freedom or Crime").

17. *Ibid.,* p. 50.

18. *Ibid.,* p. 54.

19. This is what I understand Andreas Wildt's suggestion to be in his "Hegels Kritik der Jakobinismus."

20. On this internal tension within Hegel's concept of ethical life cf. the incisive deliberations by Vittorio Hösle, **Hegels System**, vol. 2, **Philosophhie der Natur und des Geistes**, Hamburg, 1987, p. 471ff.

21. Cf. Michael Theunissen, "Die verdrängte Intersubjektivität in Hegel's **Philosophie des Rechts**" in **Hegels Philosophie des Rechts** ed. Dieter Henrich and Rolf Peter Horstmann, Stuttgart, 1982, p. 317ff., in particular Chapter 2 (p. 322ff.).

22. *Ibid.,* p. 328.

michael kelly
the gadamer/habermas
debate revisited:
the question of ethics

The debate between Hans-Georg Gadamer and Jürgen Habermas had a rather ironic feature in that its path and conclusion seemed to contradict their notions of philosophical discourse.[1] The path did not conform to Habermas's notion of communicative action oriented to understanding, because Habermas's interest in the dialogue was admittedly to establish his differences with Gadamer and, as a result, his action in the debate was more instrumental than communicative; and the conclusion did not conform to Gadamer's notion of a dialogue that culminates in a fusion of horizons, for the two participants were farther apart at the end of the dialogue than they had been at the start. It is perhaps because of this irony that some commentators on the debate have recommended a mediation between Gadamer's and Habermas's viewpoints. Such recommendations are themselves Gadamerian in spirit, although most have been proposed from the perspective of Habermas's recent theory of communicative action.

One issue that was not a part of the original debate between Gadamer and Habermas was the status of philosophical **ethical** theory. This is both surprising, because many of the terms of the debate would clearly apply to ethics as well as to social theory, and not surprising, because neither Gadamer nor Habermas focused on ethics before or during the debate. Since the debate

michael kelly

has subsided, however, both philosophers, though particularly Habermas, have become more involved in ethics.[2] For this reason, but especially because of its obvious relevance to ethics, I shall investigate the implications of the Gadamer/Habermas debate for philosophical ethics by asking: How is critical ethical reflection possible? I shall discuss the differences between a conception of ethical reflection partially derived from Gadamer's philosophical hermeneutics and partly from Habermas's recent "discourse ethics" based on the theory of communicative action. In the final section, I shall explore the possibility of a mediation of these two conceptions of philosophical ethics.

I.

The basic principles common to Gadamer and Habermas are, according to Thomas McCarthy,

recognition of communication as a "universal medium" of social life, awareness of the historicity of human existence, and the ideal of dialogic resolution of practical questions.[3]

The common ground in ethics is that language—more specifically, dialogue (Gadamer) or discourse (Habermas)—is the medium of ethical life. This means that ethical norms can be understood, justified, and criticized dialogically or discursively, and that ethical conflicts can be resolved in the same manner. The dialogue or discourse that serves as a medium for ethical life is both an actual practice of reflection in which we are always already engaged and an ideal to which the actual practice is always oriented.

The basic philosophical problem that arises in relation to their shared dialogic conception of ethics is the same one discussed in the general debate - the philosophical basis of critique. Habermas insists on the need for a procedural theory that can provide criteria to justify ethical norms, distinguish moral-rational resolutions of moral conflicts from merely prudent-instrumental compromises, and make distinctions between the ethical and non-ethical constituents of a particular tradition. A hermeneutic ethical theory, by contrast, denies the possibility of such a procedural theory and must, without it, explain how norms can be justified, conflicts resolved, and traditions defended. The ultimate issue in this debate, therefore, concerns the possibility of critical ethical reflection based on dialogue/discourse.

Although Gadamer never explicitly developed an ethical theory, and despite the fact that, at times, he seems to deny that a theory is either possible or necessary, some of his basic hermeneutic concepts—solidarity, *die Sache*, and experience, are readily applicable to ethics. Of these, the main ethical concept is "solidarity," because, according to Gadamer, this concept is constitutive of the concept of ethical action: for all ethical actions, whether individual or collective, are based on norms, and all valid norms are social in the sense that they must be recognized as valid by other individuals. Solidarity is constituted by the set of ethical norms which individuals recognize as valid, which they have in common already. Insofar as ethical actions are based on social norms that take the concrete, if general, form of solidarity, then solidarity is a presupposition of these actions.[4] It is also a goal of these same actions in the sense that it is always only partially realized and always fragile because of the many conflicts and disagreements between people about ethical norms. For example, people may disagree about which norm applies to which action, about how to interpret the norm they agree does apply, or about whether a once valid norm should still be considered valid. Solidarity is thus a goal of ethical actions because it must be constantly reaffirmed and redefined. This constant reaffirmation and redefinition of solidarity is, as we shall see below, the task of critical ethical reflection.

The concept of solidarity can be further clarified in terms of Gadamer's concept of *die Sache*,[5] which he introduces in his account of the structure of a dialogue. He argues that the goal of a dialogue between two or more participants is not to establish one participant's viewpoint as the only true one, but to come to some understanding between them concerning the *Sache*, subject matter, topic, or object, of the dialogue. It is this *Sache*, not the participants or their viewpoints, which determines the structure and goal of the dialogue. It also determines the truth of the dialogue, for the "truth" is a result of a "fusion of horizons" of the participants' viewpoints about the *Sache* in question. The similarity between *die Sache* and "solidarity" is as follows: each ethical action has a common *Sache* by which it is constituted—a norm or, in general, solidarity. Individual agents do not determine the moral rightness and orientation of action, for both are determined by the norms of the action in which they are engaged. Solidarity, thus, is to ethical action what *die Sache* is to dialogue.

Solidarity has a similar role in relation to ethical reflection, because ethical reflection, like ethical action,

*presupposes that we are already shaped by the normative images or ideas [**Vorstellungen**] in the light of which we have been brought up and that lie at the basis of the order of our entire social life.*[6]

141 Ethical reflection presupposes concrete, substantive norms which are currently held to be valid in particular ethical actions,

practices, and societies, and which shape whatever solidarity exists within and between them; it is one of the practices of ethical life. In addition, it presupposes the norms (e.g., concerning rationality and justification) that govern its structure and task as well as the norms on which it reflects. Thus, ethical reflection not only presupposes solidarity, it is also constituted by it.

But ethical reflection cannot be merely descriptive, nor can it uncritically legitimate the validity either of the norms it presupposes or those which constitute it:

...[the presupposition of norms] does not at all suggest that these normative perspectives remain fixed immutably and would be beyond criticism. Social life consists of a constant process of transformation of what has been previously held valid.[7]

Ethical reflection is the practice of criticizing currently valid ethical norms and solidarity. Such critique begins when several existing norms come into conflict with one another or new norms emerge as possible replacements for old ones, forcing reflection on the various possibilities and a choice of norms by which agents of a particular action or participants in a specific practice or society will henceforth abide. When this happens, the problem that arises is not one of the universal foundation of the ethical norms in question, but of doubt and choice concerning which norms the agents and participants will now accept as binding. The stimulation of reflection by doubt is the "process of transformation of what has been previously held valid." Because this process is part of the life of ethical tradition, the practice of ethical reflection and critique is also part of this tradition. Moreover, since solidarity is what constitutes this tradition in general, it is necessary for ethical reflection and critique.

The hermeneutic notion of experience helps to explain how it is possible for ethical critique to develop as part of ethical tradition.[8] According to Gadamer, a genuine experience is not one which confirms what we already know about the world, but one which challenges and even negates what we know. All genuine experience is thus negative in this sense. Applied to ethics, this means that a genuine ethical experience is one which arouses doubt in us about an ethical norm that we hold to be valid. The negativity of ethical experience is thus what accounts for the moments of doubt which arise in ethical actions and practices and which stimulate reflection on the norms in question. Another feature of experience related to its negativity is its openness. Since we can expect our experiences to be negated, experience remains open to other experiences which negate it and which may open it up to a broader solidarity. This openness is what prevents ethical solidarity from becoming static and dogmatic, that is, immune to criticism; for no concrete solidarity can exclude the possibility of future refutation or emendation. It is thus the moments of negativity and openness constitutive of ethical experience which make it possible for ethical critique to develop within a general ethical tradition.[9]

The purpose of ethical critique is to illuminate and resolve ethical agents' experiences of doubt. In doing so, it assumes the standpoint of ethical experience rather than usurps it in the name of a neutral theoretical standpoint. This means that critical reflection does not need a procedural theory that is neutral with respect to any particular ethical tradition in order to criticize that tradition; if ethical reflection is already a part of ethical tradition, all it needs to begin and to continue to operate is the process of ethical experience itself. The norms that govern this process—solidarity—become the material for critical reflection whenever conflict and doubt emerge concerning them. Moreover, not only does ethical reflection not need such a procedural theory, it cannot have one; as a part of ethical tradition, ethical reflection is historically conditioned. This means that the norms constitutive of ethical reflection are themselves historical. For example, the concept of rationality at the heart of Habermas's theory of communicative action, which will be discussed below, is historically specific: it is a modern, Enlightenment conception of rationality. The philosophical consequence of the historical conditionedness of ethical reflection is that it is impossible for the critical task of such reflection to be based on a strictly procedural theory. Ethical reflection is immanent to ethical life and thus cannot be founded on, or appeal to, a procedural theory that claims to be neutral with respect to the historical solidarity that constitutes this ethical life.

But the question still remains: How can ethical reflection be **critical** if it presupposes the valid norms of the ethical practices on which it reflects, and if the norms that determine ethical reflection are also historically conditioned? It would seem that, as Habermas will argue below, this presupposition of conditionedness precludes the possibility of critical ethical reflection. To show that it does not, however, I shall discuss an ethical theory about which similar claims can be made, albeit not in exactly the same or such explicit terms.

Kant's ethical theory is an excellent, if unexpected, example to illustrate the hermeneutic claims about ethical reflection, because, to begin with, he must presuppose the maxims that are to be tested by the categorical imperative.[10] By definition, maxims do not start out as valid universal laws; but they are valid as maxims. The problem with these maxims, for Kant, is that their validity is subjective and thus restricted. To overcome this restriction, the maxims must be examined using the categorical imperative to test whether they are, at the same time, universal. But, since a maxim remains a maxim even when it passes the test and becomes at the same time a universal law, the introduction of the categorical imperative does not affect the presupposition of the validity of the maxims; it only universalizes this validity. What we have here, rather than a contrast between invalidity and validity, are two different types of validity, distinguished by their subjective or universal scopes, which also have different grounds: the subjective validity of the maxims emerges from the ethical practices in which the maxims first arise, whereas their universal validity is established by ethical reflection. In the latter case, ethical reflection does not create the maxim's universal validity *ex nihilo*; it discovers it through the test of the categorical imperative. That is, ethical reflection expands the validity of some of our ethical maxims by confirming those whose validity is at the same time universal. Thus, even the Kantian ethical theory is not foreclosed by the presupposition of valid norms and solidarity.[11]

It may be objected, however, that there is a certain lack of clarity in the use of the term "validity" in this discussion of Kant. It is possible to concede that ethical reflection must presuppose the existence of certain maxims; this does not necessarily mean that ethical reflection must presuppose their validity. But their validity must also be presupposed, otherwise neither the will nor reflection would have any maxims to expand into universal laws; for it is the **validity** of the maxims which is expanded. Such valid maxims supply the material to which ethical reflection adds form (i.e., universality). Furthermore, once maxims have been universalized, they must then be applied to ethical practices. Kant's universal laws require a link, a return route, as it were, to these practices. The maxims are this link. This is, I think, the practical consequence of Kant's claim that the maxims must be willed at the same time as universal laws. What we have here, rather, is the reverse: universal laws must be willed at the same time as maxims. Maxims are able to serve this role because their original validity is not negated when their scope is expanded by the categorical imperative. The issue here, again, is not the validity of the maxims, but the scope of their validity. Thus, the presupposition of the validity of ethical maxims does not entail an elimination of critical reflection; it indicates instead the starting point and conditions under which such reflection operates.

A Kantian would still object to this account of ethical reflection, claiming that it collapses two fundamental distinctions: (a) between the emergence of maxims and their justification as universal laws, and (b) between the justification and application of universal laws. Concerning the first distinction, a Kantian would argue that the ethical life from which the maxims emerge cannot provide a principle that would allow us to identify which maxims are also universal laws. He would insist that such a principle— e.g., the categorical imperative—must be based on **pure**, i.e., historically unconditioned, practical reason. But can practical reason be pure in this sense? Habermas agrees with Gadamer that practical reason is historically conditioned and that whatever principles practical reason has must originate from our historical, ethical life. Yet, against Kant, they both think that ethics can still be philosophical, that it can still have universal ethical laws, even though its principles are not derived from pure reason. Gadamer and Habermas therefore agree that the Kantian distinction between the emergence of maxims and their justification as universal moral laws is not necessary for ethics to be philosophical.

Concerning the second distinction, a Kantian would argue—this time with Habermas's support—that the task of philosophical ethics is completed when it has provided the principle that can justify certain maxims as universal laws. He recognizes that these laws must then be applied to specific moral situations, but does not consider the problem of application to be a part of philosophical ethics proper. According to Gadamer, however, this separation of the justification of moral laws from their application means that moral judgment is not a part of philosophical ethics. Yet how can philosophical ethics provide concrete moral guidance to ethical life if it remains aloof of the application of its laws? In Kant's case, this aloofness was the price of the purity of practical reason; for practical reason had to remain independent of experience on any level, and this meant that it could not take the contexts and consequences of the application of universal laws into consideration. Gadamer argues that, once it is clear that this purity is not possible because practical reason is historically conditioned, moral judgment must be understood as an integral part of philosophical ethics. Habermas acknowledges this, if only implicitly, since he includes the consideration of the consequences of the implementation of ethical laws in his "principle of universalization" (which we shall discuss below), and since he even includes the consideration of the agents'/ participants' interests; yet he defends Kant's minimalist notion of philosophical ethics. He cannot continue to defend this notion, however, if only because it entails the exclusion of moral judgment from philosophical ethics. If this exclusion cannot be maintained because of the inexorable historicity of practical reason, Habermas cannot maintain the minimalist conception of philosophical ethics as being concerned only with the justification of moral norms.[12] If this is the case, the Kantian distinction between the justification and application of moral laws is neither possible nor necessary.

michael kelly   Gadamer's conception of ethics is based on the claim that it is indeed possible for ethics to be philosophical without either one of these Kantian distinctions, that is, that philosophical ethics is possible despite the historicity of practical reason and its corollary—solidarity as the presupposition and goal of ethical reflection.

II.

The ultimate test of a hermeneutic conception of ethical theory is whether it can successfully demonstrate how critical ethical reflection is possible, in principle, even though it must begin by presupposing the validity of the norms of concrete ethical practices, and even though ethical reflection itself must remain within the hermeneutic circle of ethical tradition. Habermas argues that the hermeneutic conception is doomed to fail this test, because it is impossible to determine whether ethical reflection confined to the hermeneutic circle is critical, that is, whether ethical reflection constituted in part by solidarity is anything more than merely an ideological affirmation of a given set of ethical norms. He then develops an ethical theory that he hopes will be able to overcome the limitations of the hermeneutic conception.

The purpose of ethical theory, Habermas argues, is to provide a universal procedure with which to determine whether ethical norms and solidarity are rational, moral, and possibly universal:

A philosophical ethics not restricted to metaethical statements is possible today only if we can construct general presuppositions of communication and procedures for justifying norms and values.[13]

The "general presuppositions of communication" are the conditions of rational speech, symmetry and reciprocal recognition, which, according to Habermas, are always already there in everyday speech. They become explicit only on the level of discourse, where they form the basis of a procedure to justify the normative validity claims of truth, authenticity, moral rightness, and comprehensiveness raised in communicative action. Rational actions are those which have norms that can be consented to under these conditions of rational speech. At the same time, the criteria for rational action are also the criteria for **moral** action: an action is moral only if it is rational, which means that valid moral norms must also be consented to, in principle, under conditions of rational speech. This triumvirate of rational speech, rational action, and moral action thus forms the core of discourse ethics.

To make the procedure for justifying moral norms under the conditions of rational speech more concrete, if formal, Habermas introduces a "fundamental principle of universalization" (*Universalisierungsgrundsatz* or "U"):

Every valid norm must satisfy the condition that the consequences and side-effects which probably follow from its general compliance can, for the satisfaction of the interests of every individual, be accepted without force by all those affected.[14]

When and if this principle can be grounded in the universal presuppositions of rational speech, it assumes the form of a "fundamental principle" (*Grundsatz* or "G"):

Every valid norm must be able to be accepted by all those affected.[15]

These two principles form the heart of Habermas's minimalist notions of both morality and ethical theory:

*I prefer a relatively narrow concept of morality. Morality refers to practical questions which can be decided with reasons—to conflicts of action which can be resolved through consensus. Only those questions are moral in a strict sense which can be answered in a meaningful way from the Kantian standpoint of universalization—of what **all** could wish for. At the same time, I prefer a weak concept of moral theory...it should justify the moral point of view, and nothing more.*[16]

The sphere of **morality** is constituted by the set of norms that can be "decided with reasons," that is, discursively redeemed according to the conditions of rational speech. Moral or ethical **theory** formulates the procedure by which these norms can be rationally justified, that is, discursively redeemed. The sole task of this procedure is to justify norms that already have been enacted by individuals, embodied in social institutions, or proposed by individuals or institutions for possible future legislation. In either case, ethical theory can neither generate moral norms nor play a role in seeing that they are applied in action. Determined by the conditions of rational speech, ethical theory's sole task is to represent the "moral point of view."[17]

Habermas's "discourse ethics" thus provides a procedure to justify claims concerning the norms and solidarity of our ethical practices and tradition. In this sense, it is intended as a correction to the hermeneutic conception of ethical theory, which was limited because it remained immanent to ethical tradition and thus could not provide a basis on which to justify ethical distinctions made about this tradition. Habermas's critique and correction of hermeneutic ethics are effective, however, only if the theory of communicative action on which they are based is itself universal;

only then will it be able to identify which normative validity claims are universal and to justify them as such. The test of Habermas's discourse ethics is, thus, whether he can demonstrate that (the structure of) communicative action is universal. Otherwise, both this theory and discourse ethics will be immanent to a particular ethical tradition.

Habermas responds to this challenge by arguing that the conditions of rational speech constitute "a universal core of moral intuition in all times and in all societies":

I don't say that this intuition is spelled out the same way in all societies at all times. What I do say is that these intuitions have the same origin....[T]hey stem from the conditions of symmetry and reciprocal recognition which are unavoidable presuppositions of communicative action.[18]

The difficulty with this claim, however, is that neither of two strategies used to defend it is convincing, and it is by no means intuitively obvious.[19]

Habermas's first strategy is to argue that the conditions of rational speech are transcendental in the sense that they are the conditions of the possibility of all speech, even of speech used to deny them; they are therefore necessary and unavoidable. But he cannot rely on this strategy if it entails a transcendental argument in the strict Kantian sense, because one of the fundamental premises of his philosophy is its commitment to the shift from subject-centered reason (or self-consciousness philosophy) to communicative reason (or language philosophy), and transcendental arguments are possible only on the basis (within the structure) of a subject-centered reason.[20] There is, however, a weaker (quasi-) transcendental argument, which is similar in structure to the one traditionally used against the skeptic: one becomes entangled in a performative contradiction when denying the conditions of rational speech; for the very (speech) act of the denial presupposes the conditions of rational speech which are being denied. This argument is weaker than a transcendental argument, however, because it implies at best only the practical (i.e., performative) universality of the conditions of rational speech, but not the stronger universality which, according to Habermas himself, the theory of communicative action requires. In the absence of this stronger argument, Habermas still needs another (kind of) defense either to replace or to supplement the quasi-transcendental argument.

Habermas's second strategy for defending the universality of the theory of communicative action is more historical and Hegelian.[21] He argues that learning processes of modernization and rationalization which have developed historically since the Enlightenment are best explained in terms of a developmental theory of a species-level competence for communicative action. This argument is a combination of several different claims: (1) that the historical processes of modernity and rationality can be understood as species-level learning processes analogous to the learning processes that individuals undergo; (2) that these processes are irrevocable (logically, if not historically); (3) that they are made possible by a species-level competence for communicative action; and finally, (4) that this competence is universal and also irrevocable (again, logically, if not historically). The universality of the theory of communicative action is now explained in terms of the philosophical, if historical, discourses of modernity and rationality.[22]

But the only historical evidence that Habermas offers for the universality of the theory of communicative action is from his rational reconstructions of the history of social theory (in **The Theory of Communicative Action**) and from the history of philosophy (in **The Philosophical Discourse of Modernity: Twelve Lectures**). It still remains to be seen whether there is any concrete historical evidence for the learning processes to which he alludes, or, rather, for the relationship between these processes and the competence that he claims makes them possible. When he is challenged with this kind of objection or presented with contradictory historical evidence, Habermas tends to withdraw to a more theoretical level of argumentation, emphasizing that he is, after all, presenting a **theory** of the general competence underlying certain developments in social history. He has never claimed that he would provide an empirical account of the dynamics of concrete social developments.[23] Furthermore, since the theory of communicative action is counterfactual in general, Habermas assumes that the conditions of rational speech have never been fully realized in history, and that they do not need to be realized in order to serve their theoretical, regulative function. The problem with Habermas's response, however, is that, by withdrawing to this more theoretical level of discussion, he moves back in the direction of the quasi-transcendental arguments which he rejected earlier. Thus, Habermas's second and most recent strategy for defending the universality of the theory of communicative action is either weakly substantiated historically, for Habermas offers little conclusive, concrete historical evidence; or else it is again quasi-transcendental, in which case Habermas's own objections against such an argumentative strategy would apply to him as well.

Habermas's problem here, however, is not only that he has not provided sufficient historical evidence for the universality of michael kelly communicative action, but also that any historical argument he could offer would be circular; for his rational reconstructions of historical developments would always presuppose, and thus could not be used to justify, his claim about the universal, species-level development of communicative action. Georgia Warnke formulates the problem poignantly as follows:

The question that arises here is how we can equate the categorical distinctions we find necessary for communication with those necessary for communication in general once we admit the existence of cultures that have done without them. How can we prove our communicative competence to reflect a higher stage in a species-wide development process if all the research that we undertake in order to show it is a higher stage assumes what is to be proven? How do we escape the vicious circle in which we accept as the principle of research differentiated as opposed to undifferentiated worldviews--precisely that which is at issue: namely, the greater cognitive capacity of the latter?[24]

Habermas is seeking a philosophical defense of his theory of communicative action which establishes its non-transcendental, non-*a priori* universality. But in doing so, he is caught in a dilemma: the theory of communicative action cannot be defended by a transcendental or even quasi-transcendental argument, and any historical argument, even if one were provided, would be circular. Until Habermas can resolve this dilemma, he cannot claim that communicative action is universal; and if communicative action is not universal, he has not established the procedural theory that he promised as the basis for ethical critique. If Habermas fails on this point, he has not yet advanced beyond the hermeneutic conception of ethical reflection.[25]

III.

So far Habermas has only been able to defend the **possibility** of (i.e., a hypothesis about) the universality of communicative action, something with which he himself is not satisfied.[26] This realization has led several sympathetic critics to suggest to Habermas that he accept a weaker version of the theory of communicative action, one which does not rely on a quasi-transcendental argument and which requires only that the theory's rational desirability be coherently defended.[27] What is most puzzling about this suggestion is that it tends to push Habermas back into the hermeneutic position from which he has consistently tried to distance himself; it would mean that the Gadamer/Habermas debate would have come full circle. In this final section, I shall explore the possibility of a mediation of Gadamer's immanent ethical theory and Habermas's discourse ethics in the hopes that such a mediation may resolve the difficulties encountered in the two theories taken separately.

There is a similar paradox within both Gadamer's and Habermas's ethical theories: (1) Despite Gadamer's emphasis on the historicity and conditionedness of ethical reflection, he also argues that a historically conditioned ethical reflection can still defend the unconditionality of the moral law and the principle of freedom.[28] (2) Habermas accepts the hermeneutic ontological claim that reason is conditioned by history and embodied in language; yet he also argues that such reason, in the form of communicative action, can still justify universal ethical norms because of, in part, a universal principle of reciprocal respect between all persons. In both cases, the basic paradox is that a historically conditioned practical reason is capable of unconditional ethical principles and laws. Gadamer's and Habermas's ethical theories cannot be unified, and individually they will have internal problems, unless it is possible to resolve this paradox.

In his critique of Habermas, Albrecht Wellmer indirectly suggests one way to avoid this paradox. He argues that an unconditional ethical law (even Kant's categorical imperative) need not be thought of as a fact of **reason**, but as a fact of **a life under** conditions of reason.[29] It is a part of and has its origin in this way of life. On this interpretation, the "unconditionality" of a law refers more to the scope of its application than to its origin; to say that a law is unconditional is to say that it has no exceptions, applies to everyone, and is thus universal. It is therefore both conditioned (in terms of its origin) and unconditional and universal (in terms of its application).[30] For example, Gadamer's and Habermas's basic principles are universal in the sense that we ought to recognize the freedom of, and show respect to, **every human**; this is what we mean by an "ethical" law, that it applies equally to everyone.[31] For these principles to be unconditional and thus universal in this sense, it is not necessary that they be derived from pure reason. It is enough that they be shown to be an essential part of a historical way of life governed by reason which we cannot give up without some measure of conscious or unconscious repression. The validity of these principles would be established by their roles in this rational way of life, and would thus be historical and practical (not transcendental and theoretical). At the same time, the principles of freedom and reciprocity would be symbols of the development that has been made by the historical way of life governed by reason--which we generally refer to as the Enlightenment; that is, the fact that a historical way of life recognizes and refuses to turn its back on these principles is an indication that its reason has developed, that it is, in fact, rational to begin with. Since they are moral principles, they would also be symbols of the morality of this way of life.[32] Reason is embodied in history, but an embodied reason is still capable of attaining universal heights of rationality and morality measured by the very same principles that have traditionally been accepted as symbols (i.e., facts) of pure reason.[33]

But the historical conditionedness of these rational and moral principles would lead critics of this proposed conception of ethics to raise the charge of relativism and point to a possible circularity in the above discussion. The validity of an ethical principle is limited to the historical situation in which it originates, no matter how broad the situation is and even if the scope of the principle's validity within a given situation is universal because it is applied to everyone within its borders; hence the relativism. This problem is not resolved by saying that the general historical tradition in which the ethical principles emerge is rational and moral (as if this would then expand the validity of the principles), because the criteria for deciding whether it is rational and moral can come only from the tradition itself; hence the circularity.

There are, however, several notions in Gadamer's and Habermas's ethical theories which can mitigate, if not eliminate, the threats of relativism and circularity. The first ones are the hermeneutic conceptions of solidarity and experience. The validity of ethical principles can extend beyond a single historical situation (group, culture, society, historical period, or even ethical tradition) because of the orientation to solidarity embedded in each and every historical situation.[34] Each historical situation is constituted by its solidarity: a shared normative ground on which to conduct ethical life within its borders. This ground is not static, however, because of the structure of ethical experience--its moments of negativity and openness. That is, the solidarity that forms the basis of the validity of ethical principles will always be negated; and, at the same time, it is always open, in principle, to being combined with other forms of solidarity. When this happens, the validity of its principles is expanded. Of course, this expansion, which would break the boundaries of relativism, is not necessary or inevitable, that is, it may not happen; we can assert only its possibility. But this is all we can ever assert about historical matters. Relativism is only a threat so long as we are still hoping to discover ahistorical principles; if they are not possible because of the historicity of reason, then there is no possibility of relativism either. Another reason why relativism is not a serious threat is that the historical conditionedness of ethical norms and reflection does not mean that the particular norms and concrete solidarity formed by the norms are incommensurable with one another. Historicity does not entail incommensurability because of the moment of openness in ethical experience and in ethical tradition in general.

Another hermeneutic notion—*die Sache*—helps to eliminate the problem of circularity; for the hermeneutic circle in the context of ethics is, like the circle in a dialogue, between the participants in an ethical tradition and the *Sache* or subject matter of their tradition. The *Sache* here is the solidarity by which the tradition is constituted; for it is this solidarity, and not the participants or agents themselves, which provides the criteria for deciding about valid norms. The circle here is between the agents and the solidarity that they presuppose, because their actions are shaped by this solidarity and, at the same time, their actions alter it. The dynamic nature of solidarity itself, combined with the interaction between agents and solidarity, are what generate the circle. It is not vicious, however, because it is never closed: it forever remains broken, i.e., open, negated, transformed. Here too the moments of negativity and openness of ethical experience play a key role in defending the hermeneutic/discursive conception of ethics.

Habermas's method of rational reconstruction can also help to defend this conception against the charges of relativism and circularity. For if the hermeneutic notions just invoked seem too speculative, they can be tested through a rational reconstruction of the norms of ethical tradition embodied in the life-world. We can examine empirically and historically (1) whether ethical experience and tradition are, in fact, open and constantly negated; (2) whether the results of these negations are moral and rational in a more universal sense than what preceded them; (3) whether we can justify our judgments that the negations are more universal without presupposing that they are; (4) whether actions, practices, and traditions based on historically conditioned norms are truly commensurable and to what extent; (5) whether ethical critique is actually more possible the more ethical experience is open to negation; etc. This method of rational reconstruction makes it possible to combine discourse ethics with the hermeneutic conception of ethics, for it provides a philosophical, yet also empirical method for investigating ethical matters without denying their historicity. It will also help to eliminate the problem of relativism, because it will reveal whatever universal ethical principles there are, and the problem of circularity, because the historical and cross-cultural, empirical studies will allow us to break out of the circle of our own particular tradition (albeit only to the extent that there are, in fact, principles that we share with those outside our circle).

IV.

The combination of the hermeneutic and discursive conceptions of ethical reflection promises to resolve difficulties that each conception would likely face if it remained independent. Gadamer may resist this fusion of horizons, for he is reluctant to concede that the proceduralism entailed in Habermas's method of rational

michael kelly reconstruction is useful in ethics; and Habermas may resist it as well, for it is not clear whether he has completely given up the search for a (quasi-) transcendental basis for the counterfactual, yet non-utopian appeal to a procedural ethical theory which, he still insists, is "beyond" Gadamer's idea of tradition-bound ethical theory. Even if Gadamer and Habermas were to accept the proposed fusion of their ethical theories, a number of issues would still have to be addressed before it would yield a viable philosophical ethics. But it is a hopeful proposal which clearly deserves further reflection.

Baruch College, CUNY and Columbia University

ENDNOTES

1. The Habermas/Gadamer debate began in 1967 and culminated in 1971 with a book entitled **Hermeneutik und Ideologiekritik** (Frankfurt: Suhrkamp, 1971). For good overviews of the background, stages, and implications of the debate, see Thomas A. McCarthy, **The Critical Theory of Jürgen Habermas** (Cambridge: MIT, 1978), pp. 162-193 [hereafter **CTJH**]; Jack Mendelson, "The Habermas-Gadamer Debate," **New German Critique**, 18 (Fall 1979): 44-74; and the issues of **Cultural Hermeneutics**, 2 (February 1975), and **Continuum**, 8 (1970), devoted to the debate. Cf. Habermas's "Interpretive Social Science vs. Hermeneuticism," in **Social Science as Moral Inquiry**, N. Haan, R.N. Bellah, P. Rabinow, and W.M. Sullivan, eds. (New York: Columbia, 1983), pp. 251-263. For a more recent account of this debate, and one which is based on an interpretation of Gadamer's hermeneutics similar to the one I shall defend here, see Georgia Warnke, **Gadamer: Hermeneutics, Tradition, and Reason** (Stanford: University Press, 1987), pp. 107-138.

2. Habermas's discourse ethics is developed in the following writings: "Moral Development and Ego Identity," in **Communication and the Evolution of Society**, Thomas A. McCarthy, trans. (Boston: Beacon, 1979) [hereafter **CES**]; **The Theory of Communicative Action**, 2 volumes, Thomas A. McCarthy, trans. (Boston: Beacon, 1984/1987) [hereafter **TCA I** or **TCA II**]; "Diskursethik - Notizen zu einem Begrundungsprogramm" and "Moralbewusstsein und kommunikatives Handeln," in **Moralbewusstsein und kommunikatives Handeln** (Frankfurt: Suhrkamp, 1983), S. 53-125 and S. 127-206 [hereafter MKH]; "Über Moralität und Sittlichkeit - Was macht eine Lebensform 'rational'," in **Rationalität: Philosophische Beiträge, Hans Schnädelbach**, hrsg. (Frankfurt: Suhrkamp, 1984), S.218-235 [hereafter **RPB**]; and "Gerechtigkeit und Solidarität," in **Zur Bestimmung der Moral**, Wolfgang Edelstein und Gertrud Nunner-Winkler, hrsg. (Frankfurt: Suhrkamp, 1986), S. 291-318 [the English translation of this article is forthcoming in **The Philosophical Forum**, XXI, 1-2 (Fall 1989)]. Cf. also **Nachmetaphysisches Denken** (Frankfurt: Suhrkamp, 1988). Gadamer

has written on ethics throughout his career: **Platos dialektische Ethik** (Hamburg: Meiner, 1931); "Über die Möglichkeit einer philosophischen Ethik," in **Kleine Schriften I** (Tübingen: Mohr, 1967), pp. 179-191; but has placed more emphasis on it in the last ten years: **Die Idee des Gutens zwischen Plato und Aristoteles** (Heidelberg: Winter, 1978) [**The Idea of the Good in Platonic-Aristotelian Philosophy**, P. Christopher Smith, trans. (New Haven: Yale, 1986); "Werner Marx: Gibt es auf Erden ein Mass?", **Philosophische Rundschau**, XXXI, 3/4 (1984): 161-177; and "Heidegger und das Problem der Ethik," **Philosophische Rundschau**, XXXII, 1/2 (1985): 1-26. For a discussion of Gadamer's views on ethics, cf. my "Gadamer and Philosophical Ethics," **Man and World**, 21 (1988): 327-346; and Ronald Beiner, "Do We Need a Philosophical Ethics? Theory, Prudence, and the Primacy of Ethics," in **The Philosophical Forum**, XX, 3 (Spring 1989): 230-243. Cf. also **Nachmetaphyisches Denken** (Frankfurt: Suhrkamp, 1988).

3.   McCarthy, **CTJH**, p. 190.

4.   Norms are presupposed in action the way meanings are presupposed in speech. In both cases, the presupposition serves as a common ground without which the action or speech would be unintelligible.

5.   Gadamer uses the term *die Sache* in a consistent manner in his discussion of the structure of a dialogue and of the relationship between this structure and that of hermeneutic experience. Unfortunately, the English translators were not consistent in their translation of *die Sache*, which is why I have chosen to leave it in the original. Cf. **Wahrheit und Methode** (Tübingen: Mohr, 1960), S. 349-382 [**Truth and Method** (New York: Seabury, 1975), pp. 330-366].

6.   "Hermeneutics as a Theoretical and Practical Task," in **Reason in the Age of Science**, Frederick G. Lawrence, trans. (Cambridge: MIT, 1981), p. 135.

7.   *Ibid.*

8.   Cf. **Truth and Method**, pp. 310-325. For similar points about Gadamer's notion of experience, cf. Warnke, **Gadamer: Hermeneutics, Tradition, and Reason**, pp. 167-174; and Joel Weinsheimer, **Gadamer's Hermeneutics: A Reading of Truth and Method** (New Haven: Yale, 1985), pp. 199-212.

9.   As Warnke has pointed out [**Gadamer: Hermeneutics, Tradition, and Reason**, pp. 171-173], there are certain similarities between claims of this sort and Alasdair MacIntyre's claims about ethical theory in **After Virtue** (Notre Dame: University Press, 1981). Such similarities are even stronger, I think, in MacIntyre's most recent work: **Whose Justice? Which Rationality?** (Notre Dame: University Press, 1988), especially in chs. XI, XVII-XX, where he discusses how a tradition transforms itself through its openness to self-criticism. For a discussion of MacIntyre's and Habermas's ethical theories, my "MacIntyre, Habermas, and Philosophical Ethics," **The Philosophical Forum**, XXI, 1-2 (Fall 1989).

michael kelly

10. Aristotle would perhaps be a more likely example because, in the **Nicomachean Ethics**, he analyzes virtues as "normative notions that always stand under the presupposition of their normative validity," and because the ethical critique exercised therein was only possible "from the standpoint of their [the norms] fulfilled concretization, insofar as he [the critic] experiences himself as bound by their validity" [Gadamer, "Universality of Hermeneutic Problem," in **Philosophical Hermeneutics**, David E. Linge, trans. (Berkeley: California UP, 1976), p. 133 and p. 48]. I am focusing on Kant, however, because many of Habermas's objections to the hermeneutic conception of ethics are Kantian. For an excellent discussion of the Kantian and non-Kantian dimensions of Habermas's discourse, see Albrecht Wellmer's **Ethik und Dialog: Elemente des moralischen Urteils bei Kant und in der Diskursethik** (Frankfurt: Suhrkamp, 1986). And for an account of the Aristotelian and Kantian aspects of ethical reflection from a hermeneutic perspective, cf. my "The Dialectical/Dialogical Structure of Ethical Reflection," in **Philosophy and Rhetoric**, XXII, 3 (August 1989): 174-193.

11. As I suggested in the previous note, the hermeneutic and Kantian conceptions of ethical reflection are not incompatible. In a recent paper on Kant's **Critique of Judgment**, Rudolf Makkreel argues that hermeneutics requires certain Kantian themes in order to provide a basis for critical reflection on tradition--"Tradition and Orientation in Hermeneutics," **Research in Phenomenology**, XVI (1988): 73-85.

12. Habermas concedes to critics of his discourse ethics that the problems of application and efficacy must be resolved; but he still maintains that ethical theory proper is not the place to resolve these problems or to achieve the mediation between morality and ethical life which their resolution requires--cf. Habermas, "Questions and Counterquestions," in Richard J. Bernstein, ed., **Habermas and Modernity** (Cambridge: MIT, 1985), pp. 209-210; and **Habermas: Autonomy and Solidarity**, Peter Dews, ed. (London: Verso, 1986), p. 207. Habermas's general response to critics who argue that he has left certain "social goods" out of ethical theory is that these goods can be brought back in, but not through ethical theory; they must be brought in (i.e., be decided) by the participants of a particular ethical life-world, not by theorists. Some critics respond, however, that it is impossible for Habermas or participants to reintegrate these goods at a later point if they have been excluded at the beginning from ethical theory; see, for example, Nanette Funk, "Habermas and the Social Goods," in **Social Text**, 18 (Winter 1987/88): 19-37--the three goods she discusses are "solidarity, community, and nonalienation."

13. "Historical Materialism and the Development of Normative Structures," in **CES** p. 97; cf. also McCarthy, **CTJH**, p. 325: "What Habermas calls 'communicative ethics' is grounded in the 'fundamental norms of rational speech'."

14. **RPB**, p. 219; and **MKH**, pp. 75, 103.

15. **RPB**, p. 219. These two principles are clearly reformulations of

Kant's categorical imperative, but, as McCarthy makes clear, with the important shift of emphasis "from what each can will without contradiction to be a general law, to what all can will in agreement to be a universal norm" (**CTJH**, p. 326).

16. Dews, pp. 170-1; also, cf. pp. 160, 207.

17. Habermas consciously adopts this notion from Kurt Baier, **The Moral Point of View** (Ithaca: Cornell, 1964).

18. Dews, pp. 206-7; also, cf. p. 205.

19. Habermas suggests three possible strategies for defending the universality of the concept of communicative rationality, but he chooses only one of them: "...sociological approaches to a theory of societal rationalization"--cf. **TCA I**, pp. 138-141.

20. At times, Habermas writes as if a transcendental argument is still possible without a (transcendental) subject; at other times, he clearly distances himself from Karl-Otto Apel's efforts to develop just such an argument along Strawsonian lines. For a clear analysis of the different aspects/criteria of transcendental arguments and why Habermas cannot satisfy them (e.g., because his reconstructive science is too empirical), cf. Seyla Benhabib, **Critique, Norm, and Utopia: A Study of the Foundations of Critical Theory** (New York: Columbia, 1986), pp. 263-267).

21. "The release of a potential for reason embedded in communicative action is a world-historical process..."--cf. Dews, p. 184. On Habermas's attempt to combine Kantian and Hegelian methods and themes, cf. Thomas A. McCarthy, "Rationality and Relativism: Habermas's 'Overcoming' of Hermeneutics," in **Habermas: Critical Debates**, John B. Thompson and David Held, eds. (Cambridge: MIT, 1982), pp. 57-78.

22. According to Habermas, a denial of the theory of communicative action is tantamount to a denial of modernity and rationality; we all (including the skeptics) are equal, if unwilling, partners in the philosophical discourses of modernity and rationality. This strategy is most evident in Habermas's recent critiques of Nietzsche, Heidegger, Foucault, Derrida, and others [**The Philosophical Discourse of Modernity: Twelve Lectures**, Frederick G. Lawrence, trans. (Cambridge: MIT, 1987)]. But, as is the case with Habermas's critique of Gadamer, his critiques of these other philosophers are only persuasive if his theory of communicative action is philosophically defensible.

23. Habermas distinguishes between the logic and dynamics of historical developments; cf. **CES**, p. 98. This distinction, which is also implicit throughout **TCA**, is fundamental to his notion of rational reconstruction and is introduced to help critical theory avoid the problems stemming from the philosophy of history--cf. **TCA I**, pp. 66/7.

24. Warnke, **Gadamer: Hermeneutics, Tradition, and Reason**, pp. 133-4.

25. Habermas's more recent publication in English ["Law and Morality," in Sterling M. McMurrin, ed., **The Tanner Lectures on Human Values,** vol. VIII (Salt Lake City: University of Utah Press, 1988)] does not solve this problem; for this work seems to presuppose the strong interpretation of the theory of communicative action.

26. Earlier in his debate with Gadamer, Habermas claimed that hermeneutics could rely only on the possibility of solidarity because it could not offer an argument for its necessity. It now looks as if Habermas himself is left with a mere possibility whose necessity he cannot defend. See Benhabib's review of the modernity lectures [**Journal of Philosophy,** LXXXIV, 12 (December 1987): 752-757], where she argues that Habermas has not yet been able to, and perhaps cannot ever, defend the necessity of his conception of language and communicative action.

27. Benhabib argues that the constituents of communicative rationality are universal only in a weak sense; because reason itself is always situated, they are at best "existentially irrevocable"; cf. **Critique, Norm, and Utopia,** chs. 7-8. Wellmer criticizes Habermas for being too Kantian because of his attempts to provide a "last foundation" for discourse ethics and because of his consensus theory of truth applied to moral norms; cf. Wellmer's **Ethik und Dialog,** pp. 51-113. Finally, Agnes Heller argues that Habermas's discourse ethics is not universal in Habermas's sense because it presupposes the (meta-) norms of freedom and life, norms which cannot be redeemed via discourse; she also argues that discourse ethics is not really an ethical theory because the universalization principle can only be understood as a principle of justice, that is, of political legislation; on such an interpretation, universal laws are universal within a particular society, not between societies, cf. **Beyond Justice** (New York: Blackwell, 1987), pp. 234-242.

28. This is the main thesis of Gadamer's "Über die Möglichkeit einer philosophischen Ethik."

29. Wellmer, **Ethik und Dialog,** p. 143.

30. Cf. the discussion of Kant's notion of a universal law in section I above.

31. "In everyday life..., no one would enter into moral argumentation if he did not start from the strong presupposition that a grounded consensus could in principle be achieved among those involved. In my view, this follows with conceptual necessity from the meaning of normative validity claims. Norms of action appear in their domains of validity with the claim to express...an interest common to all those affected and thus to deserve general recognition...[We] rely on this intuitive knowledge whenever we engage in moral argument..." - **TCA** I, p. 19.

32. Habermas argues that the rationality of the modern lifeworld is a result of the differentiation of its symbolic structures (science, morality, and aesthetics) and "is expressed above all in the increasing reflexivity

of cultural traditions, in processes of individuation, in the generalization of values, in the increasing prevalence of more abstract and more universal norms..." (Dews, p. 184; and **TCA** I, esp. pp. 1-141). The issue here is how such a claim can be defended.

33. I am tempted to call the universalism implied in this last statement a form of "internal universalism," modeled perhaps on Hilary Putnam's equally paradoxical notion of "internal realism."

34. For a more Kantian reading of the notion of "orientation," cf. Makkreel, "Tradition and Orientation in Hermeneutics."

III.
practical reason and
ethical responsibility

agnes heller
what is and what is not
practical reason

The new upsurge of the Heidegger debate re-opens the question of whether certain philosophies or philosophers can be held morally or politically accountable for the gravest collective crimes of modern history. The discussants use this opportunity to explore the general issue of the relation between philosophy and morals, i.e.,theoretical and practical reason. A recent German publication titled **Destruction of Moral Self-Consciousness: Chance or Danger?**[1] addresses the above problem in a very wide framework. This is why I chose this book for the starting point of my present reflections.

Two papers by philosophical adversaries (Karl-Otto Apel and Otto Poggeler) deserve special attention. Apel's study raises the question, "Could we have learned something specific from the national catastrophe?"[2] and it promises to proceed in an autobiographical manner. It soon becomes apparent that by autobiography Apel means the description of his philosophical development from existential philosophy to transcendental pragmatics. Obviously, the personal pronoun "we" in the title does not refer to German men and women, but to German philosophers. The lesson German philosophers could, or at least should, draw from the "national catastrophe" is to accept transcendental pragmatism as the only possible modern universalistic philosophy. For Apel, philosophy is not a game confined within the walls of the academy, nor is it an exercise in mere problem-solving; it is, instead, a vocation of the highest dignity as well as of the highest moral responsibility. It is out of this conviction that he reflects all contemporary philosophies of a non-universalistic bent as morally suspect and "conservative."

Otto Poggeler[3] focuses on Heidegger's philosophy and correctly demonstrates that ethics (practical philosophy) could not have been completely fitted to the vision of Heidegger at any stage of his development. However, this theoretical reflection immediately assumes a strange practical relevance for Poggeler. Heidegger's well-known reluctance to take moral responsibility for his participation in the Nazi movement is now explained by the absence of ethics in his philosophy.

Though divided by a theoretical abyss, the papers of Apel and Poggeler are complementary in that both of them see a direct connection between personal moral stance and philosophy. Something more is involved here than the traditional injunction that a philosopher is bound to live in the spirit of his or her own philosophy. Apel insists that a philosopher should have a philosophy which offers him or her, as well as the world, a proper moral guidance; while Poggeler implicitly suggests that if one's philosophy does not offer such guidance, as in Heidegger's case, then one cannot be held responsible, as a person, for not living according to common moral principles.

The volume must have been edited by Puck, the conjurer of surprising cohabitations, for it contains, at the end, the well-known essay by Richard Rorty on the primacy of democracy over philosophy. This practical joke seems to allow the reader to make a clean sweep of almost all serious claims and counter-claims, accusations and counter-accusations, that happen to fill 272 pages. Rorty's level-headed writing comes as a wholesome antidote to the absolutist and fundamentalist philosophical ambitions; yet it rests on shaky foundations. Unlike Apel and Poggeler, who erroneously collapse practical reason into philosophy and practical philosophy into practical reason, albeit on the grounds of entirely different value-preferences, Rorty, in an haphazard and overzealous gesture, denies that there is any relevant connection between them.

According to Rorty, the ethico-political neutrality of philosophical systems, language-games and principles results from the circumstance that liberal democracy does not call for philosophical legitimation.[4] To this idea I would object that, of all forms of governance, it is only liberal democracy that has so far called for philosophical legitimation. The pre-modern forms of governance were legitimized by traditions, myths and religions, not by philosophies; whereas totalitarian societies and states claim to be legitimized by sciences, but are in fact legitimized by charisma or tradition. Active practices of legitimation are never continuous; they are mobilized in the case of acute or chronic legitimation deficiency. Since liberal democracies are constantly exposed to philosophical and ideological attacks, the absence of philosophical legitimation contributes to the demise of the ethico-political bonds of the civic commonwealth. Precisely in this regard, Hegel had a strong point. The very existence, the so-called "positivity," of institutions is an empty shell, he asserted, unless supported by the ethical practice of people committed to them. After all, in a debate on German philosophy and its responsibility, the German experience must not be dismissed so light-heartedly. Even if Rorty were right that all philosophies became politically neutral, they could not possibly remain neutral towards each other. The moment philosophers cease to detect the dangerous elements in the philosophy of others, the **genre** itself is on the wane. What remains is yet another computer-game, jigsaw or cross-word puzzle, a sheer formal mental exercise of minor relevance and interest.

II.

Works of art rarely turn to one another. They have no dispute with one another. They do not exclude one another. They are neither friendly nor unfriendly with each other. Whether classic, modern or postmodern, they stand on their own and do not care whether there are others like them. Cold stars who bring warmth to alien lives, they are but mirror images of our existential solitude. Works of philosophy are different. They constantly challenge one another; they argue, discuss, advise, denounce. They exclude some and include others. They are friendly and unfriendly. They love and hate. They are the mirror images of our "unsocial sociability." Our life experiences manifest themselves both in the world of artworks and in that of philosophy. We do a major disservice to philosophy when we treat philosophical works as if they were artworks, when we want them to coexist as do works of art. We are never in total accord with our fellow creatures; we can never entirely consent to their opinions. Philosophies which do not fight each other cannot be the mirror images of our unsocial sociability. No hierarchy between artworks and philosophical works is suggested here; no judgment is passed on any single work. Everything has been stated in the defense of the **genre** called philosophy. If one wants to have philosophies, one cannot have them as neutral entities, as beautiful flowers peacefully growing in the garden of a benevolent, but indifferent, liberal democracy. However, the plea for universal consensus fares no better. Where there is universal consensus about a universal consensus (even if this were restricted to the foundation of all our norms, including moral norms) there is no longer philosophy, for there is **nothing fundamental** to disagree and fight about.

Philosophies are always on a collision course, but philosophers need not be. The adversary is not the enemy. What my philosophy excludes, I (as a person) do not need to exclude. I may even, on many counts, like a work which has been excluded by my own. I can enjoy it aesthetically, praise it ethically, agree with it politically, or simply find it interesting. Furthermore, I can be sympathetic (or otherwise) to the authors of a work regardless of the relation between our works. The coexistence of philosophies today is **the mirror image and the legitimization of the democratic procedure.** This becomes manifest both in the philosophers' earnestness, their public spirit in raising issues and passionately arguing against other solutions, and in their tolerance toward the existence of opposing views resolutely rejected by them. This is so regardless of the eventually anti-democratic substantive position of individual philosophies.

Relativism is neither liberal nor democratic; and it is certainly aphilosophical. The attitudes toward a work and its author need not be collapsed into one. As Goethe remarked, **ideas should not be tolerant, but the attitude, the mind (Gemuth), should be.** We can go about our business in philosophy just as we do, for the most part, our everyday activities in public life. We can have allies who are not our best friends and best friends who do not share many of our opinions and judgments.

I take it to be self-evident that decent persons will not have indecent personal friends. We know from experience that a person who is committed to values we believe to be right and who, in our view, holds a few correct opinions on public matters, may still be a scoundrel and *vice versa.* Is it the ethics of the philosopher that one needs to share or to have something in common with? Or is it the ethics supposedly inherent (or lacking) in the philosophy itself?

If there is no tension (or even practical contradiction) between the message of a philosophy, on the one hand, and the character (or actions) of the philosopher, on the other, then there are no difficulties. This is the case with Rosenberg, who was sentenced to death by the standards of natural law. Although I am not a friend of the brand of utilitarianism which makes a case for the execution of innocent tourists if the "greatest happiness of the greatest numbers" so requires, I can still feel friendly toward the (personally liberal and charitable) man who made such and similar statements. The other extreme can be easily exemplified by the Heidegger case. There is definitely no Nazism "contained" in Heidegger's philosophy, though it has a strong affinity to all brands of extreme radicalism. This time, however, a great **philosopher behaved as moral scoundrel.** I do not even state that he **was** a moral scoundrel, only that he behaved like one by refusing to take responsibility for his actions (and not for his philosophy). Taking moral responsibility is tantamount to responding truthfully. Cain's answer to God's question "Where is your brother Abel?" the ominous "Am I the keeper of my brother?" is the paragon of the wrong response (for it means the refusal to take responsibility). This was also Heidegger's gesture. Instead of answering truthfully ("I was among those who murdered my brother Abel"), he repeated, both in written words and with silence, the spurious question of those determined to avoid responsibility. Has philosophy anything to do with such an **elementary** case of moral incompetence? Actually, one cannot establish any **positive**, thetic, connection between Heidegger's philosophy and his moral incompetence. The Nazis did not even use Heidegger for their own major purposes (similarly, the Bolsheviks did not need Lukács for their own major purposes). I am convinced that the perpetrators of those crimes were better judges in such matters than our contemporaries who feverishly try to pinpoint such connections. It was rather a popularized version of Nietzsche's philosophy that the Nazis exploited. My judgment of character may fail me utterly, but I still remain convinced that Nietzsche would have resolutely refused to become a Nazi. In all probability, in Heidegger's case, it was the existentialist's taboo to revoke an existential choice that was decisive. The taboo immunized him against ethical responsibility, as existential choices normally do, except when the ethic itself has been chosen existentially. It is certainly possible to remain a friend of Heidegger's philosophy while passing serious moral judgment on his action and his character; this is my inclination. It is equally possible to extend one's hostility to Heidegger's philosophy, if this is what follows from one's position in the network of unsocial sociability. But there is neither philosophical nor moral foundation for the practice of drawing overly general conclusions from this simple case, a coincidence of many heterogeneous factors, concerning a supposedly necessary connection between certain philosophies and certain kinds of public or private morals.

III.

Fundamentalist enemies have been relentlessly denouncing philosophy as a dangerous enterprise (dangerous to the state, to religion, and to morals, in particular). Yet the friends of philosophy, as well as philosophers themselves, have frequently entertained similar ideas. Plato, the first to discover that evil maxims, rather than evil impulses, tend to destroy the moral foundations of political life, made serious efforts to blame the enemies of philosophy (rhetors and sophists) for disseminating those evil maxims. Yet he still had to warn the youth about his own philosophy, for, if misunderstood, even the most sublime philosophy may have led them astray. There are two typical modern approaches to this question, the Kantian and the Hegelian. In proposing a strict dualism (between metaphysics of nature and metaphysics of morals), Kant declared the whole domain of theoretical philosophy (philosophy of nature in a broad understanding) adiaphoric, and that of practical philosophy morally relevant. In the theoretical pursuit, nothing can be forbidden and nothing should be declared dangerous, unless the theoretical pursuit contradicts the universal moral law as provided by practical philosophy. Hegel, on the other hand, cut the ties between morals and philosophy altogether. It is not that one particular philosophy is dangerous, he insisted in his lectures on **History of Philosophy**, but that philosophy as a whole is a dangerous enterprise.[5] This factor must be taken into account whenever one does philosophy; one simply has to take this factor into account.

Let us assume, together with Hegel, that philosophy is a morally and politically dangerous enterprise. Hegel made no exceptions; he assumed that every serious philosophy is, or at least can be, dangerous even if not to an equal extent, not for the same reasons, and not in a like manner. So do I.

Philosophy once stood in disrepute because those who practiced it took intellectual delight in undermining everyday knowledge and intuition, traditional beliefs and time-honored customs. This no longer seems to be our problem. In the very dynamic of modernity, the philosophical procedure comes to pass. We are constantly undermining traditional practices and moral intuitions both in our daily lives and in the political arena. The problem with philosophy is no longer **procedural**, but, **rather, substantive**. Our objections to a particular philosophy are focused not **on that** it undermines moral intuitions, but **on the kinds** of moral intuitions it undermines; not **on that** it ridicules time-honored customs but **on the kinds** of time-honored customs it ridicules. It is in the substantive aspect that we locate the source of danger. More precisely, our problem with philosophies is not that they make wrong suggestions or fail to make the right ones, but rather that philosophy makes all its suggestions look proper and right (whatever their actual merit). There is an attraction in the attitude of pure speculation that can be called demonic, for the power that can make everything look right or true is demonic indeed.

Hegel's standpoint (to which I subscribed) sounds bizarre. After all, philosophy is taught in respectable academic institutions, sometimes as a branch of learning in which excellence is measured by the number of footnotes, and sometimes as a mental exercise in which excellence is measured by the skill of discovering inconsistencies in the work of others and replacing them with consistent statements. This all sounds very respectable and completely harmless, as the legitimate continuation of some of the oldest traditions of the genre. There is nothing demonic about philosophy if it is learned and absorbed as a whole, if the results are appropriated together with the arguments which lead up to them, and if all arguments are presented in the setting in which they originally appeared, in their proper context. Elsewhere[6] I have termed the result of such a learning process the total (complete) reception of a philosophy. If one is a total recipient, one learns exactly **how** a statement assumes truth and correctness within the context of a philosophy. One also acquires the skills to refute such truth-claims by putting questions and answers into a different context. Making all this look right in the framework where it can look right is a purely speculative activity. To abandon ourselves to pure speculation is an entirely adiaphoric pastime—at least for modern men and women. Slipping into the skin of a philosophy, and dwelling therein, is neither good nor evil, neither right nor wrong from the moral point of view. But if this is true, and it would be hard to deny that it is, how could we possibly believe that conceiving a new philosophy has to be subjected to moral judgment? And if I do not censure my neighbor morally for being a Marxist, a Heideggerian or a follower of Nietzsche, what justifies me to pass moral judgments on the maîtres penseurs themselves for having conceived one of those philosophies?

The total reception of a philosophy is the philosophical reception proper. It goes on and on in the series of interpretations and reinterpretations, while all of them remain on the speculative level. But the reception of philosophy rarely remains merely speculative. Moreover, the more significant a philosophy, the less its reception remains solely on the speculative plane. All total receptions of a philosophy, in all of its subsequent interpretations, are surrounded by the partial reception of the same philosophy, like the planet Saturn by its rings. Partial reception can be aesthetic, scientific, ethical or political in nature. But whatever kind it is, partial recipients use philosophy for non-philosophical purposes, whether theoretical, pragmatic or practical. On the speculative plane, philosophies transform all statements into right (true) statements of a particular philosophy. In the process of partial reception, however, these statements are torn out of their speculative context and placed into a completely different, sometimes practical, framework, while pretending to remain as true and right in this new (practical) context as they have been in the original (speculative) one. It is at this point that philosophy can become dangerous. As a rule, this transformation does not happen without the active contribution of philosophers themselves. Philosophers have always longed for partial reception, even after the withering of the idea of a philosopher-king. And, in fact, a philosophy which can never become dangerous is worthless; it is a corpus, literally a dead body which never attracted the attention and the enthusiasm of partial recipients.

Thus we have arrived at the paradox that it is only through partial reception that philosophy can become dangerous; but without partial reception(s), a philosophy remains a kind of crossword puzzle. We have also arrived at a second paradox, that philosophy, as a mere speculative activity, is entirely adiaphoric; yet when put to pragmatic or practical use, it can become dangerous. In addition, we have added that philosophers long for the partial (dangerous) reception of their philosophy. It seems that they enjoy living dangerously while pleading innocent. However, they are rarely aware of their own paradoxical situation for at least two reasons.

The first reason is related to the qualification of being dangerous. Being dangerous for what? Being dangerous for whom?—these are the questions. Philosophers long for the practical application of their philosophies; they want to be dangerous—to the dangerous. Whoever is dangerous to the dangerous is innocent. This is not at all a false claim. Philosophy can be dangerous to ideological lies, despots and tyrants, and thus to philosophers themselves. It can also be dangerous to self-indulgency, self-righteousness, political blindness, repression, oppression and moral decay. Yet philosophy can also be dangerous to equality, human dignity, democracy, moral intuitions, practical rationality and much else. Philosophy can be dangerous to all kinds of prejudices and prejudgments, whether right or wrong.

Second, from the standpoint of philosophy, all philosophies but one are by definition untrue. It seems self-evident, then, that practices supported by those (untrue) philosophies will be morally dangerous and politically suspect. Yet, since one's own philosophy is the only right one, one cannot help longing for its partial reception. If only one's own philosophy were to be broadly accepted and followed, everything would turn right, or at least the gravest dangers would be avoided. And if they are not, other philosophers would be put to the bench of the accused.

IV.

On one hand, accusations levelled by philosophers against each other for doing mischief are entirely inappropriate. For it is not the philosopher who actually commits the mischief, but, rather, the partial recipient of the philosophy. On the other hand, the accusations are perfectly justified. Though philosophers inherit their medium, they also know, before embarking on the philosophical expedition, which statements, claims, images, visions, and intuitions need (or ought) to be made right (true) at the terminus of their speculative journey. Though the whirlwind of their own making can carry philosophers away and open before them horizons of inquiry, the very existence of which they had no premonition at the beginning of their expedition, the most decisive statements predate their philosophies. They are distilled from "life," from "practice." For example, no moral philosopher has ever invented moral norms or maxims. Rather, they distill them from life experiences, clarify them, and finally put them into the context of their philosophy. No one was more aware of this circumstance than Kant himself, who grounded the pure idea of freedom on everyday intuitions such as the existence of good persons and the voice of our conscience. This is why the well-known mutual accusations of philosophers are not entirely inappropriate moves. They know well the game they are playing. The recipients, so they argue, can pick from the bag only what the philosopher had put into it in the first place.

Actually, there is nothing morally wrong in blaming **philosophies** for some practical mischief, as well as for their speculative shortcomings, which always remain the main targets. Yet these two aspects cannot be totally disentangled from a philosophical point of view. So long as the attacks are exercises in speculation, the same must be said about them as about all kinds of philosophical speculations: they are adiaphoric. However, the moment one begins to attack the philosopher (the author) together with his or her philosophy, one exits the homogeneous medium of speculation and behaves as an actor, to whom the same moral norms apply as to every other actor. Let me enumerate only a few of these norms. One should care for the other person's sensibility; one should respect the other person's autonomy; one should pass just judgments. It is completely irrelevant, from the moral point of view, that the actors (the persons who pass value-judgment on other persons' character or action and persons whose character and actions are to be judged) happen to be partial or total recipients of different philosophies and that they have acted or are acting now in such a capacity. This qualification cuts both ways. Even if a philosopher deserves moral recrimination, the just moral judgment cannot be extended to his or her philosophy, for doing philosophy is a merely speculative, and thus adiaphoric, enterprise. And, since rejecting or criticizing a philosophy by pinpointing the dangers which have eventuated, or might eventuate, from its reception, is also a merely speculative exercise, and thus adiaphoric, one cannot claim merits in practicing a criticism of this kind. To put the moral shortcomings of others under critical scrutiny is not a virtue, unless the author exposes him/herself to negative sanctions in and because of doing so. In the latter case, it is not the right opinion that will be morally credited, but civic courage, a moral virtue. Right opinion is just *recta ratio* in theoretical reasoning, both in its philosophical and everyday usage.

Even if a morally and politically fool-proof philosophical theory were possible (which I doubt), it could not be completely shielded from dangerous reception. What follows here is meant as a qualified criticism of Kant's refutation of the celebrated common saying that what is true in theory is still irrelevant in practice. The attempt to make security fool-proof always backfires, for in real life-practice nothing is morally fool-proof, and never will be. One can find the bases of a practical guarantee on the level of speculation, but, in actual practice, the principle will still fail to offer safe guidance in our most momentous decisions. This is why even the philosophy which does its utmost to be morally fool-proof, can end up dangerous in its practical application.

Nothing exemplifies this quandary more than Kant's own philosophy. A hundred times over-secured, both morally and politically, his philosophy, too, can provide false, even evil maxims (perhaps precisely as a result of this over-protection). Let us start with the basics. The categorical imperative does not allow for any exceptions. Kant's moral philosophy could not become consistent, neither could its moral purity be protected against contamination, without such an absolute injunction. Yet Kant himself showed us how the absolute maxim of no exception can become evil if applied in practice. There is no exception to telling the truth. This is why we ought to tell the prospective murderer that his intended victim is hiding in our house. (This murderer could be the agent of the secret police.) We should never rebel against a tyrant for we cannot wish that rebellion should be a universal law. This we certainly cannot wish; and still, there are situations when we should rebel. Everyone who advises us to the contrary provides us with an argument for simply doing the wrong thing. Kant was right—in theory. His moral philosophy became subtle and conclusive because there are no exceptions to the moral law. How can there be an exception if there is a law? And still, our moral intuitions suggest that in practice, in certain situations, we should make exceptions; that we need to listen to our moral sense for the concrete, the unique, the kind of singular that cannot simply be subjected to the universal without moral offense. *Phronesis* still wields moral authority. To propose that it should not is yet another dangerous philosophical recommendation, even if given out of subtle moral intent.

I hope that none of my readers will conclude that I have joined the chorus of those who make Kant responsible for Auschwitz or the

Gulag. I am saying, rather, the opposite. Kant has protected his philosophy from the danger of being plundered in search of evil maxims as much as humanly possible. (It takes far less effort to misuse Hobbes, Nietzsche, even Hegel than to misuse Kant in this manner.) Rather, what I want to show is that no philosophy of great format can be completely sheltered from being so used. Whatever one does with one's philosophy, one cannot completely foreclose the danger of it being used for purposes unintended in the philosophical corpus itself.

Let me stress once again that philosophy, as an exercise in speculation, is adiaphoric. No one takes moral responsibility for "doing philosophy." But philosophy is also dangerous. Becoming dangerous (in some unpredictable fashion) is one of the predictable consequences which ensues from the very existence of philosophy. It is an elementary moral intuition that men and women carry moral responsibility for the foreseeable consequences of their action. Philosophy is neither a man nor a woman; it is an object. As such, it does not carry any responsibility, moral or a-moral. But the philosopher, as an author, is also a person. And as a person, he or she could, or rather should, carry (moral) responsibility for the foreseeable consequences of what s/he was doing.

V.

It is foreseeable that philosophy could be used in a dangerous way. What is not foreseeable, however, is whether or not it will actually be so used. Furthermore, it is never completely foreseeable **for whom** a particular philosophy will be dangerous, against **what** and in favor of **what** it will be (mis)used in the future. To repeat, philosophical ideas and maxims can bring havoc to tyrants and condescending ruling elites. They can prove the most formidable enemy of suicidal indifference and barbaric self-indulgence as much as they can undermine good moral intuitions and lend a hand to civilized barbarism and political corruption.

Speaking in consequentialist terms, we address the problem of **prospective**, and not of **retrospective**, responsibility. The issue here is not simply whether one is to be held responsible for certain consequences which have ensued from one's action, but whether, before embarking on an action, one is obliged to gather information about, and take account of, all foreseeable consequences of that action. And, finally, whether one should embark on actions **because** one has reason to expect the most favorable consequences. Both the strong and the weak version of consequentialism will agree on the issue of retrospective responsibility. Given that the consequence of an action could not possibly have been foreseen, the actor cannot be held morally responsible for the results of her action.

What all philosophers can foresee is **that** their language-game is open to dangerous reception. But they cannot foresee **to whom** it might or will be dangerous (in the future). To avoid the danger (in the spirit of strong consequentialism) would mean to avoid the genre. But once one gives up the practice of the genre, one resigns from the authorship of all possible consequences of a world-interpretation, including the good ones. In fact, a philosopher cannot even know what in his or her work will be considered morally and politically beneficial or harmful in the future. Plato did not foresee the collapse of his plans in Sicily, although perhaps he might have. He certainly could not have had the slightest premonition that persecuted people in the twentieth century would find solace and moral edification in his Socratic dialogues.

Representative works of philosophy are practically immortal, as are representative philosophical trends, schools and vocabularies, even if the works which carry them are not. Strong consequentialism is irrelevant here for that reason alone. One cannot compare this story to the infinite chain of events/consequences, for the chain of consequences does not provide direct access to the originating sources. In philosophy, it is precisely the originating action (the text) that is interpreted and reinterpreted in all speech-acts *ad infinitum* (for all practical purposes). Interpreters can be entirely oblivious to the circumstances of whether interpretations of the same texts became embedded in events through partial reception, and if so, when and how.

To repeat, philosophers foresee very few of the eventual consequences of a particular kind of philosophy. It follows from this that a philosopher, as author, does not carry moral responsibility for the (future) reception of his or her philosophy. But how about the **foreseeable** consequences of that philosophy? Though a philosopher is not (morally) responsible for doing philosophy and the dangers ensuing therefrom, he or she still can be responsible for certain concrete dangers which follow from certain concrete interpretations and partial receptions of his or her philosophy, which s/he could have foreseen. The theoretical quandary in this proposition, namely, that the "chain of consequences" in philosophy is unlike the "chain of events," has already been indicated. Foreseeable and direct consequences mostly coincide in discussions of an initial action which enters into the chain of events (and actions). By "direct" I mean "close," both in space and time. The foreseeable consequences are normally also the ones which directly follow from the act in question, whereas co-determining factors are sparse and well-known. In philosophy, this is otherwise. Direct consequences can ensue from the interpretation of texts two thousand years after their conception. Thus (in philosophy), direct consequences are not necessarily the foreseeable consequences, and the latter are by no means always the most momentous ones. The problem can almost be nearly, though not completely, eliminated only in Rorty's terms (philosophies are no longer dangerous because we live in a liberal democracy) provided that we are allowed to make true statements about the future (we shall live in liberal democracies *ad infinitum*), which we certainly are not.

Whenever and wherever the foreseeable consequences of an action are also the most direct consequences, one ought to take them into consideration before embarking on an action. If there is a strong likelihood that bad consequences will ensue, one should not embark on that action. It is very questionable, however, whether the same can be asserted about a language game where the foreseeable and the most formidable (or direct) do not coincide. Can I make the reproach to the philosopher, after his or her work was used for devising evil maxims, that since s/he could have, perhaps, foreseen such use, s/he ought to have foregone devising her/his own philosophy (on the analogy of the general moral reprimand: you ought not to have embarked on this particular action). This question is even more relevant for the case of Marx than that of Heidegger, and it most definitely should be answered in the negative for all the reasons indicated above.

Yet, the moral intuition concerning the accountability of philosophers for the eventual dangerous consequences of their philosophy is not entirely erratic. Where there is no prospective moral responsibility, there can still be retrospective responsibility. Philosophers qua persons can be confronted with the morally and politically dangerous consequences of their philosophy which have occurred in their **lifetimes**, if, and only if, they failed to stand up against the dangerous receptions of their own philosophy because of vested interest, whether speculative, existential, political or other. Taking responsibility, however, does not require the modification of the philosophy itself. As a tragic hero who, when confronted with the dead bodies of his friends and enemies, exclaims in despair that this is not what s/he wanted, so the philosopher is bound to exclaim if similar occasions occur. If s/he fails to do so, men and women have the reason and the right to believe that the philosopher actually wanted to be interpreted and used in the way that s/he was used. To deny the authenticity of one or another interpretation of a philosophy remains the matter of **theoretical reason**; but to deny the authenticity of a person who has failed to denounce the wrong as wrong, and the evil as evil, is a matter of **practical reason**. I have mentioned previously that the common philosophical practice to denounce the philosophy of others as morally dangerous, whether right or wrong, is not a moral merit unless civic courage is required for

175

doing so. But it is always an act of courage to stand up against the dangerous interpretations of our own philosophy, especially if they are popular, and when we and/or our position are in danger.

When, how and to what extent philosophers should intervene to disallow the legitimate use of their philosophy by social and political actors cannot be determined by a general moral norm. The threshold of moral tolerability is decided, rather, by the moral and political conviction of the philosophers (as persons). Modern consciousness is dissatisfied whenever the threshold provides a narrow room for free interpretation. For us, this seems to be a sign of fundamentalism, and indeed it is. I would recommend the following maxim at this point: **philosophers should protest against the use of their philosophy by the partial recipients if the latter forge from them legitimizing devices for genocide, mass murder and racism**. (The implication here is that if they fail to do so, they carry the moral responsibility for the consequences which ensue from the reception of their philosophy.) This is a minimalist norm which I would recommend as the single common norm of the weakest possible ethos. I hope that it can be accepted as such. The principle of the weakest possible ethos replaces, here, the principle of consequentialism. In addition, conscience suggests that the philosopher should protest on many other occasions and situations, but I would not volunteer with a stronger recommendation. Here, like almost everywhere else, the final decision rests with the author/actor himself or herself. And, as in so many other cases, one can still do wrong by doing too little or too much. Too much stands for fundamentalism, too little for moral irresponsibility and practical (though not necessarily philosophical) nihilism. The much abused *phronesis* is, thus, the moral agency upon which one needs to rely.

VI.

Practical reason suggests the right thing (for us) to do. Conscience can be described as a moral feeling, the manifestation of our involvement in the suggestions of practical reason.

What we term "practical reason" is not an empirical fact, but a philosophical construct (an idea) which encompasses, and in a few philosophies also explains, the major personal and impersonal constituents of moral practice and attitude. Both moral intuitions (moral feelings) and norms (such as customs, general guidelines, imperatives, maxims, etc.) belong to the arsenal of moral constituents. Moral feelings are both motivational and mystical *(gnostic)*. Norms are similarly both motivational and epistemic in character. In modern times, given that authorization or validation of norms became a major problem, the epistemic aspect of moral norms grew in importance.

The dispute over the moral and political responsibility of philosophy is also a dispute over practical reason. Assume that all participants in the current debates wish to **strengthen**, if not the authority of practical reason, at least the resoluteness of our resistance against genocide, mass murder and racism. Philosophers generally bet on one agency among the three major moral constituents, which they entrust with the potency of fencing off the greatest moral dangers. One philosopher bets on universal norms and universal procedures, the second on the institutions of liberal democracy, and the third puts his or her stakes on the good everyday moral intuitions. I advance my proposition that all three parties are certain losers, for the wager is the wrong one. Even betting on all three constituents of practical reason, one can still lose; but there is, at least, a fairer chance of winning. Let us cast a brief glance at the three separate constituents.

Our moral intuitions are secondary, i.e., post-cognitive, as are almost all of our intuitions. One must first be initiated into the meaning of a few moral images, concepts, attitudes, and to get into the practice of doing things according to moral expectations. Only after this can one develop moral intuitions. Thus, without moral norms, there are no moral intuitions.

However, once developed, moral intuitions prove more reliable moral guides than mere reasoning, especially in the most elementary moral situations, or if quick decisions need to be made. This is why Rousseau (among others) believed that pity is inborn and quasi-instinctual. As a matter of fact, the sheer sensual impression of the suffering of a fellow creature affects our mind (or soul) with an elementary force, so much so that we feel the impulse to bring immediate relief to the sufferer. The original power of pity (and compassion) was not unknown to the main ideologues of totalitarianism. They regarded it as one of the most serious stumbling blocks to the realization of their projects. Maxims were invented to induce people to deliberately disregard the voice of pity; this sign of human weakness was to be heroically overcome and superseded. Instead of invoking moral monsters, I prefer to exemplify this connection with an anecdote about Lenin, who, as a person, was certainly not morally inferior; if anything, he was rather superior to the human average. Lenin once remarked that he was afraid of listening to Beethoven's **Apassionata**, for the sonata strengthened in him the desire to caress people. Yet, he continued, we **should** hit their heads mercilessly. And, he concluded, our task is very difficult indeed. The story is the clearest exemplification of a norm that enjoins us to be pitiless, to overcome moral feelings.

agnes heller

The only inate moral feeling is shame; but the objects of shame (those we should be ashamed of) are learned. The elementary shame effect is very powerful whenever actions are performed within the radius of the gaze of the members of one's community. We are ashamed in front of our neighbor, but we are not particularly ashamed before unknown persons and in an unfamiliar environment. This is why, as a rule, it is easier to counterbalance the elementary effect of shame with bad or evil maxims once one leaves the boundaries of one's narrower environment, than it is to overcome the feelings of compassion and pity.

No unanimous conclusions can be drawn from the above observations. Or, rather, one can draw several conclusions, but none of them will satisfy.

Since a certain degree of conceptualization is a precondition to the development of elementary moral intuitions, and since the objects of the shame effect are also socially (conceptually) given, the universalists have a point. Whether a person's moral sense will be a good one depends, to a great degree, on the character of the norm or the concept one receives at the very beginning of moral development. If you learn, for example, that only the members of your caste feel the same pain as you, you will not extend the spontaneous feeling of pity to human beings beyond the pale of your caste—unless, of course, you go through a process of re-learning. On the other hand, if we seriously consider accepting the thesis that the only valid moral norms are those which have been established by rational discourse, we would certainly give up the sum total of our everyday moral intuitions. Since the devil argues well, moral intuitions can often put up greater resistance against evil than reasoning. It is easier to substitute evil maxims for good ones than to overcome good moral intuitions or moral feelings in full. This is one of the reasons why it is so risky to undermine everyday intuitions (which have grown out of traditions rather than from rational discourse) and to ask for moral credentials issued only by those who have already passed the examination on the universalistic grade of the Kohlberg scale.

Authors (and actors) who vest their full confidence in the institutions of liberal democracy also have a good case. They can refer to the authority of Kant, for whom the pursuit of decent politics merely requires good institutions. In such a framework, even a race of devils would behave as decent persons. Yet Kant added to his doctrine of law a doctrine of virtues. Whatever our judgment of his "doctrine," it certainly fills a place left empty by all theories of justice, in the present as much as in the past. The

institutions of liberal democracy may offer the best framework for political choices and practices; but they do not provide a framework for forms of life. Here I return to Rorty's problem. It is good that the state does not care much about our private morals, and not even about our public virtues. In the case of a total decomposition of the moral ties of a population, however, such liberal-democratic institutions would not be perpetually reproducible. One can, of course, maintain that everyday moral intuitions, if untouched, will reproduce themselves regardless. But we cannot be so sure about this. Radical cultural critics may have exaggerated the moral remissiveness and cultural decay of the (post)modern world. Yet, still, civilized barbarism cannot be easily excluded from the possibilities of contemporary history.

There are modern persons who want to do the right thing. Doing the right thing means "being guided by practical reason as conscience." The person who wants to do the right thing raises the question: "What is the right thing for me to do?" Quite often there is no completely satisfactory answer to this question. But guidelines to the answer are provided by everyday intuitions, universal norms and the political practices of liberal democracies. Everyday intuitions, for their part, rely upon traditions such as empirical universals, local customs, religious and philosophical ideas, insights and practices, or upon a mixture of them all. A person who wants to do the right thing relies upon all three moral sources, albeit to different degrees, depending on personal commitment, form of life, and also on the character of the moral problem the person actually faces.

VII.

Let me briefly summarize a few preliminary conclusions. Philosophy is adiaphoric, though it is also dangerous. Philosophers carry responsibility for the political and moral (mis)use of their philosophy during their lifetime. To face the dangerous consequences of one's own philosophy is a practice of moral relevance; whereas to write against the dangerous consequences of the philosophy of others is common philosophical practice and, as such, adiaphoric.

Philosophers can know a hundred times over that philosophy is adiaphoric, and they will still continue to denounce not only the theoretical shortcomings, but also, at least outside the walls of the academy, the possible dangerous moral and political consequences of all other philosophies. This is the game we are playing. It is why philosophy is the mirror image of our unsocial sociability. Indeed, philosophers do **have the right** to criticize, refute and denounce each other in this manner. This is so because philosophy is, in fact, a dangerous enterprise. Let me add that philosophy shares this feature with almost all other intellectual ventures. But, since philosophy pinpoints the danger in all other intellectual enterprises, it is only just and fair that it do the same when it comes to its own language game. True, philosophers expose the dangers inherent in the philosophy of others, and not in their own; but since all philosophers engage in this enterprise, all possible (foreseeable) dangers inherent in all philosophies will finally be exposed and placed at the disposal of the recipient.

The three main conditions of reasonable politics and moral decency are, in principle, of equal weight, even if each of them is of greater weight in one particular situation and of lesser weight in another. Philosophies which make a strong case for any of these three render a service. They also render a service if they point the possible dangers inherent in a philosophy which exalts only one of the three and neglects the other two. Given that partial recipients of a philosophy are mostly carried away by an "absolute," it remains wholesome, both morally and politically, to have access to alternatives—including the theoretical "destruction" of their absolutes. Finally, philosophers do a great service if they understand how to step outside their philosophy, as responsible (moral) persons and as citizens, without giving up their absolute philosophical commitments.

As responsible (honest) persons and citizens, philosophers **must** step outside their own philosophy. They then become actors, moral and political agents, who cannot be but partial recipients of philosophy, including their own. We have already briefly discussed the difference between "theory" and "practice." Moral philosophy can afford to eliminate *phronesis*, yet practice cannot. Without practicing *phronesis*, philosophers will carry their absolutes into their daily practice, and only good luck will rescue them from becoming well-meaning pawns in the service of evil powers. (Sartre, for example, had such good luck.) When Foucault became involved in movements for prison reforms, he must have been aware that this practice did not follow from his philosophy. He did it all the same, because it was the right thing to do. One can also mention the living; Habermas, for example, never spares his involvement in practical matters of formidable moral and political importance. The philosopher can be right and wrong, like everyone else in action or debate; this is precisely the exemplary. For **it is not the *philosophe engagé,* but the engaged person who also happens to be a philosopher, that we are discussing.** A *philosophe engagé* is always right (as a philosopher), since he or she made everything sound "right" in the framework of his/her philosophy. Thus s/he goes on to realize the "truth." A philosopher, who is also an engaged person patiently listening to the judgment of others, takes the situation, the time and place into consideration, and is aware of his or her dual responsibility. As a philosopher, s/he will remain absolutist (relativism is, in the framework of philosophy, yet another absolutist stance); but as a person and a citizen, s/he will learn how to absorb other people's points of view and how to do justice to their life experiences. The universalists will consider everyday intuitions and they will practice their *phronesis*; the advocates of everyday intuitions will appreciate the institutions of liberal democracy and practice civic virtues, as they will also make commitments to one universal value at least; and, finally, the lightly skeptical mouthpieces for the institutions of liberal democracy will appreciate both traditional moral intuitions and universalistic claims. Yet, back at their writing desks, they will continue to make everything right in one particular way, and will expose all other paradigms to scorn. This is neither right nor wrong; merely the only thing to do in the dense medium of philosophical speculation.

There is only one concrete **moral** rule of the game that should be heeded, and I mention it for the last time: as long as a philosopher has not done something morally reprehensible, the rejection of the dangerous implication of a philosophy should not be extended to the rejection of the person. Even **labelling** the person is unwarranted. And if the person has committed something reprehensible, the moral judgment passed on the person should not be extended to his or her philosophy as a **whole**—because theoretical and practical judgments are different in kind. Yet only fundamentalists can foreclose our right to show the possible connections between a philosophy and a morally reprehensible attitude or action of a philosopher. It is mere fundamentalism to consider as taboo the rethinking of one of the oldest philosophical doctrines or convictions. Pre-modern philosophy took it as self-evident that philosophers "live" their philosophy. Do they still do so? One can answer the question both ways, but one cannot seriously believe that it is an anti-philosophical gesture to raise this question once again and to try to answer it.

New School for Social Research

ENDNOTES

1.   **Zerstorung des moralischen Selbstbewusstseins: Chance oder Gefahrung?** Frankfurt, Suhrkamp, 1988.

2.   Karl-Otto Apel, "Zurück zur Normalität? Oder konnten wir aus der nationalen Katastrophe etwas Besonderes gelernt haben?," *ibid.*, pp. 49-66.

3.   Otto Poggeler, "Besinnung oder Ausflucht? Heideggers ursprungliches Denken," *ibid.*, pp. 238-273.

4.   Richard Rorty, "Der Vorrang der Demokratie vor der Philosophie," *ibid.*, pp. 273-290.

5.   G.W.F. Hegel, **History of Philosophy** (Volumes I and II). He writes, e.g., in his introduction to the discussion on the Sophists: "Unsere gelehrte Professoren sind unsofern viel undschuldiger als die Sophisten; um diese Unschuld gibt aber die Philosophie nichts." That Hegel saw justification in putting Socrates to death also belongs to his story, though not to mine.

6.   See in detail: Agnes Heller, **Radical Philosophy**, Oxford, Blackwell, 1984.

hauke brunkhorst
adorno, heidegger
and postmodernity

The history of the effects *[Wirkungsgeschichte]* of Heidegger, just one year before the hundredth anniversary of his birth, is as unique as it is overwhelming. It was as significant for the existentialism of the free subject as it was for post-structualist theories of discourse and power which have declared the subject and [wo]man to be a mere episode in the history of power. Without Heidegger, or so it seens, there would be no Sartre, no Foucault, no philosophical hermeneutics, no Gadamer, no Merleau-Ponty. Furthermore, Western Marxism can still draw invigorating energy from **Being and Time** and this stream of thinking, after the "turn," still feeds the deconstructionist theory of the text. The influence of Heidegger's work has long since extended beyond continental philosophy and Europe's *Zeitgeist* and, in an increasingly distinct manner, has left traces in American pragmatism and has enjoyed benevolent reception among more and more analytical philosophers. Of course, there is also, beyond the North Atlantic, a history of effects in the Far East that reaches back to the twenties.

If, however, the theory of objective spirit is not all that wrong then, under Heidegger's influence, an element of truth and reason must have been shown to be advantageous. If the thesis that the history of effects cannot be reduced to the causal history of singular

hauke
brunkhorst

effects; if even the more far-reaching thesis that in the history of effects it is not merely the formative force of great rhetoric, deepening our self-understanding and our understanding of the world and fusing horizons, that becomes operative and is already real; but rather if, beyond that, in the history of effects it is also the advance of communicative rationality, namely the forceless force of better and better arguments, that becomes operative, **then** there is every reason to believe that Heidegger has a range of good arguments, and of deep and new insights on his side. Admittedly Heidegger himself would have probably rejected such a strange suggestion since for him—at least from the "turn" onwards—all modern theories of rationality were nothing more than belated waste products of a degenerating history of metaphysics. Since Plato's image of the cave, there have been nothing but newer and flatter variations of that original "subjugation" of "humanity" to "the idea of correctness," the domination of metaphysics as the "powers of the understanding" are controlled by the will to will.[1] It was only the element of force that Heidegger perceived in the forceless force of better arguments—this element being an animal **intellect** going way beyond nature's **instinct**. After the end of the war he saw the "**ratio** of humanity" becoming "identical" with the "drive of animality" in the planning and calculating intellect.[2] For Heidegger, in his later works, rational argument was, in the strict sense of the term, "unholy"—the business of "dealers and brokers" on an earth whose "desolation" stems from "metaphysics."[3] In a unique reversal of old battle fronts, the "super-human" becomes the "exaggerated" "intellectualism" of the "sub-human."[4] In the everyday life of the occidental subject, dominated as it is by reason and science, the narrative grace of **myths** is usurped by **statements** requiring rational justification; the intact "gathering" of the **thing** into the old Germanic "thing" is usurped by the deliberating gathering of democratic public spheres.[5] "The customary life of contemporary man," wrote Heidegger in the 1946 lecture **What Are Poets For?**, "is the common life of the imposition of self on the unprotected market of the exchangers."[6] When the rescuer is supposed to come, in order to drive the exchangers/dealers out of the "temple of Being," is uncertain; but the poets tell of the origin of the holy—the truth of Being is established by the poet, admittedly under the direction of the thinker.

From this perspective, the salvation history of Being, all essential distinctions are blurred between the forceless force of better arguments and the coercive force of sanctions, between the autonomy of non-arbitrary freedom and the arbitrary freedom of the self-empowered subject, between impartial justice and the partial self-justice of the will to power. In this idealist perspective the forceless force of better arguments becomes the essence and origin of all other force—just as "armanent in the metaphysical sense," i. e. intellectualism, is the origin of all armanent industries.

In its intellectual-historical and political **consequences**, however, the perspective of the "responding and recalling" thinker *[andenkender Denker]* connects with important elements in **postmodern thinking.**[8] The universalistic validity claim of argumentation is (in Heidegger's sense) "the same" as the real general, the first and highest of ancient metaphysics; the moral universalism of the Enlightenment is "the same" as the compulsory uniformity of totalitarian regimes. Yet, at least for Lyotard, the metaphysical armament is more fundamental than the real one, the gentle weapon of critique more primordial than the martial critique of weapons. Accordingly, postmodern thinking is intellectual pacifism; the order of the day being disarm the weapons of critique which is, in Lytard's words, a "disarming" "of intelligence."[9]

Lyotard shares this idealist trait with Heidegger, but not with Richard Rorty's neo-pragmatist postmodernism. For, like Adorno and Horkheimer, Rorty believes that the freedom of the different and the plural, of the deviant and non-identical, of "abnormal discourse," is not endangered by "science or naturalistic philosophy" but by "scarcity of food and … the secret police."[10] It is not only with materialist insights of this kind that Rorty lines up with the Frankfurt School. Both Adorno and Rorty also relate a **different history** of the emergence of modernity than do, for instance, Heidegger and Lyotard. Whereas Lyotard and even Foucault conceptualize, with Heidegger, the history of occidental rationality by beginning with the **Greeks**, Rorty and Adorno favor a perspective enlightened by the sociology of religion and explain the spirit of modernity from its **Judaeo-Christian** origins. These differing histories come to a critical point in the opposition of a **neo-pagan polytheism** of heterogeneous language islands to a **moral materialism** of solidarity among life-forms.

Of course, by way of the reflexive turn to a totalizing critique of reason (Apel), both histories remain at first compatible. Both can be told in a postmodern manner when they are guided by a conceptual frame that, similarly dichotomous, falls into the unbridgeable difference of a fundamental opposition—as is the case with Heidegger's conceptual frame. Whoever opens an abyss between **truth** and **correctness** (as Heidegger does), must necessarily let all distinctions of forcelessly compelling argumentation be swallowed up in the totalitarian uniformity-compulsion. This is the case even when the guiding difference between truth and correctness remains within the framework of correspondence theories, as with Heidegger who, after all, replaces the eye (which corresponds to ideas insofar as it reflects them) with the solitary ear of the thinker, whose thought (in servile agreement) resounds the echo of the silent voice of Being. "Re-echoing is the human response to the silent voice of Being," which Heidegger also calls the "indestuctible" and which, precisely because of this, must remain deaf to the sufferings of mortals. The voice of Being responds to no one.[11]

In the dichotomously designed distinctions between truth and correctness, between imagining *[Vorstellen]* and thinking, between the will to will at one's disposal and destiny *[Geschick]* beyond one's disposal, between the "grasping" *[Zugriff]* of the concept and the "gesture" *[Gebärde]* adequate to Being, between "frantic measuring" and "moderation," between language as instrument and language as "governess"—in these and numerous other conceptual distinctions, which as a rule Heidegger merely construed as an inverted relation of instrumental domination, there are analogous differentiations in postmodern thought. Lyotard's guiding difference between meta-narrative and narrative, Rorty's alternatives of objectivity and solidarity, of realism and pragmatism, of philosophy and democracy, Foucault's (at least) implicit division between power and the counter-power of subversive knowledge, these all aim in the same direction, toward a totalizing critique of reason.

This also applies to the standard readings of Adorno: here the basic distinction seens to be that of the **non-identical** and **identifying thought**--a distinction which usurps everything else including all universal validity claims.

In place of this I will defend a different reading, for Adorno continuously relativizes the rigid dichotomy of aesthetic mimesis and instrumental reason, of the non-identical and identifying thought, at the retained vanishing-point of **rational identity**. By rational identity Adorno understands something like a non-Hegelian, de-totalized *"Aufhebung"* of the non-identical identifying thought. It is precisely this vanishing-point of a rational identity which enables Adorno to make plausible those fundamental and normatively substantive distinctions which postmodern thought from Heidegger to Rorty is forced to surrender: the difference between world-market imperialism and egalitarian freedom, between particularism and pluralism, between closed and open societies, between atomism and individualism.

I.

Heidegger's third period of influence[12] began imperceptibly in the 1960s and is only reaching its zenith now that we approach the last decade of this century. The understanding of Heidegger in the

adorno, heidegger and post-modernity

1980s is soberly pragmatic, urbanized with fashionable chic, and essentially cleansed of the exaggerated fundamentalistic expectations of the German thinker. Heidegger's emphasis on difference is now misunderstood as a radical critique of totalitarianism. Politically, the original thinker is moving to the left, towards Popper, Raymond Aron or even John Dewey. Liberal and anarchist readings of Heidegger suddenly seem possible. Philosophically, the announced "overcoming" [Verwindung] of metaphysics is being taken seriously, and philosophy is being violently removed form its throne. Once again, philosophy finds itself being confronted with a form of life which is gradually aging. But this time, the paints that philosophy uses are postmodern and colorful. One almost hears the tanks of those liberating armies that echoed across the Rhein in 1945 and put a belated end to the brown dictatorship when Richard Rorty abruptly declares an end to the waiting-for-the-rescue and expresses the assumption "that perhaps the rescue may have already taken place behind Heidegger's back—in America."[13]

Whether in moderate or radical, emphatic or serene tones, with negative or affirmative signs, Rorty, Adorno and Lyotard celebrate the innovative and creative potency of **cultural modernism**, the new and inventive, the sublime and intensive, the unconventional and the post-conventional, the abnormal discourse and the productivity of the subversive. Heidegger's farmer's guard [Hut] becomes a lively Parisien vanguard [Vor-Hut] for Lyotard. In the non-identical, Adorno informs us of a radical concept of freedom which, in its **anarchist** and **libertarian** characteristics—its left- and right-wing ones, respectively—is in accord with the anarchism of French post-structuralists and with the moderate liberalism of American neo-pragmatism. In contrast, Heidegger's history of Being resounds with the traditionalist-authoritarian counter-program, the propaganda of re-enchantment: the return of aura to culture and of the scared to art. Adorno's sharp polemic conceptualizes such attacks on the spirit of modernity of "feigned humility." Heidegger's pagan invocation of the aura of Greek temples is hopelessly bourgeois in view of the newly opened experiential horizons of aesthetic modernity: from Eisenstein's films (Benjamin) through Schönberg's music (Adorno) and Newman's paintings (Lyotard) up to Harold Bloom's critiques (Rorty).

The distance to all positive concepts of totality, the scepsis about any philosophy of origins [Ursprungsphilosopie], and the profane motives of this thinking lead Adorno away from Heidegger and, with Rorty, Lyotard and Foucault, to the front lines of a more current post-modernism. But Adorno's critique of modern subjectivity is less radical; for instance, when he talks about "consciousness of the non-identical," or even about "autonomous

hauke
brunkhorst

dissonance" in music or about the "force of the subject," when he declares cultural modernity to be the "center" and "field of force" of emancipation, he is unequivocally introducing categories of idealism and enlightenment, concepts of the conscious life, of rational freedom and individual identity. It is here that the various postmodern roads part. Rorty initially follows tracks also followed by Adorno—he is insured, however, by language analysis, a little more carefully against the pitfalls of metaphors of relection, but is also more resigned, without Adorno's utopian energy. Lyotard, in contrast, inherits Foucault's and Lacan's estate and follows the sign to Heidegger's country-path, which has since been paved. He opposes the autonomy of reason to the heteronomy of the sublime, a rational communicative community to a child-like community of feeling: heterogeneous, "popular folklore stories," the unforgettable, original "wisdom of nations," the lively scepticism of many little stories in which real life is antagonistically involved—these answer, with many voices, the imperial evil of the meta-narratives and major stories on the French Revolution, on the Declaration of Human Rights, on Bolshevism, capitalism and Nazism, on rational and racist terror.[14]

II.

What separates Rorty from most French intellectuals of the present, and also from Heidegger, is the systematic re-connecting of the pragmatist maxims of the priority of practice over theory and of democracy over philosophy to (at least) a **weak moral universalism** which prsents the de-legitimized North Atlantic life-form as a community of partisans for solidarity. Although Rorty—as Nancy Frazer has shown—repeatedly oscillates between a mere technocratic pragmatism of stability maintenance and the elitist romanticism of an ironically staged, decadent aestheticism, he nevertheless adheres to the internal reference of pragmaticism to an expanding "we"—admittedly without a truth claim. The pragmatist maxim reads: "**We** know that there must be a better way to do things than this; let us look for it together." The "we" of this maxim, however, implies "the desire to extend the reference of 'us' as far as we can."[15]

Materialist insights and moral motives separate Rorty and Adorno from Heidegger and all postmodern polytheists. For them, unlike for Heidegger, Christianity and the history of the rationalization of the world religions is much more than a mere footnote to Plato. The Protestant heritage of American pragmatism—no different than a Weberian Marxism enlightened by the sociology of religion—suggests a different reading of occidental rationalism than that of the rise and fall of Greek metaphysics as understood by the history of philosophy. It is the history of the individualizing and egalitarian forces of monotheism and Judaeo-Christian morality.

Up to Kant's non-stop polemic against passivity, the rationalism, rejected by myth, of the prophetic redemptive religions discredits the "leave things as they are" attitude: **Looking on** is replaced by the henceforth constitutive portion of human **contribution:** work, *praxis*, solidarity, subjectivity. Pagan fate, Heidegger's Greco-Germanic *"Geschicklichkeit"* (destiny), is replaced by the reconciliation-utopian universalism of the **idea of a justice for all**—a universalism denounced by Lyotard as "meta-law." This idea, unlike the more aristocratic philosophy, siezes the masses. Max Weber writes: "The annunciation and promise now, naturally enough, addresses the masses of those who are **in need of salvation.** They and their interests come to the fore."[16]

Under "the pressure of typical and ever-occurrent distress,"[17] the narcissistic particularism of the pagan **theodicy of good fortune** shatters. It becomes obvious that this theodicy was above all created for the good conscience of the rich. From the very beginning, however, in the new Judaeo-Christian **theodicy of suffering,** the **plebian motives** (Weber) of the oppressed and burdened combine with the rationality of **moral insight.** It is precisely at this point that the monotheistic religions surpass the rationality standard of Greek philosophy, which otherwise is cognitively far superior to them. It is to this reading of the history of rationality that Adorno refers when he writes: "The smallest trace of senseless suffering in the empirical world belies all the identitarian philosophy that would talk us out of that suffering."[18]

From **this** perspective of the "rational theodicy of suffering" (Weber), even the Greek ethics of the "good life" gives the impression of a cleverly rationalized theodicy of good fortune renewed on the highest of levels; an ethics, **bereft of equality,** of cleverly and well-administered privilege. Only the theodicy of suffering and misfortune is successful in breaking through to a higher rationality standard of moral consciousness. In redemptive religions, the **privileged access to moral insight** is destroyed and exposed as the ideology of the propertied male classes; in order to experience injustice, it is not necessary to have the wisdom of well-to-do, world-wise old men experienced in matters of power who, as Aristotle writes, "have an eye."[18] Only the theodicy of suffering pushes through to the true, the moral, and egalitarian concept of justice; injustice which has been experienced becomes the foundation of a moral insight accessible to **everyone.** Insight into experienced injustice is the privilege of the underprivileged. Behind the veil of ecstasy, the redemptive religions articulate the reflective force of this insight.

The moral "idea of justice" **after virtue** which grew out of the Judaeo-Christian heritage and which lives from conscious contribution, the "force of the subject," is the normative core around which Adorno's life-long polemic against Heidegger continually circles.[20]

At this point, Rorty, too, believes he has to move away from Heidegger. In order to develop an apologia (without aura) of the western world out of Heidegger's philosophy of Being, Rorty finds himself compelled to distance himself, in a revealing manner, from the latter's particularistic patriarchal morality. In order to turn the tables on Heidegger and bid farewell to Hölderlin as the founder of an immemorially farming world of shepherds and demigods, in order to declare John Dewey to be the "poet of technology" and of "human solidarity," Rorty appeals to the anchoring of American democracy in the moral substance of Christianity. Whereas Heidegger misses the meaning of the moral significance of impartiality and identifies justice with "self-righteousness" and, in the end, with the "will to power" and the "struggle for world dominance,"[21] Rorty draws a line for which he seems to have a criterion (although he never tires of explaining why there cannot be any criteria of justification for the western world and that we should accept this world as a gift of our being—accept it thankfully, though without prostrating ourselves). Rorty's formal criterion is the distinction between universalism and particularism. Along with John Dewey, Rorty recognizes that Christianity is by no means a mere footnote to Plato as Heidegger believed. Rather, a particular path is opened to escape the absolutism of metaphysics, a path which leads in a different direction from the step back into Being suggested by Heidegger. It does not lead back to the sphere of myth, nor into a de-subjectivized "destiny" [Geschicklichkeit], but forward to a justice and solidarity which are indebted to the universalizing force of subjective contributions, a force whch overcomes mere narcissism.[22] In the prophetic redemptive religions, a **moral path** out of the pitfalls of metaphysics is opened—a moral path which has been overlooked by Lyotard and Heidegger in their blind emotion against monotheism, subject autonomy, impartial justice and non-narcissistic solidarity; and this, in order to stagger back to the "Great Mother," to "Dionysius" or into the "harshness of destiny."[23]

Adorno, of course, has as little interest as Rorty in a renewal or restoration of religion and belief in salvation. For Adorno, the only path for redeeming the truth claim of religion leads through the totally profane culture of modernity. The truth claim of religion becomes fallible when, as Adorno demands, it first has to stand the test of the profane, between science, modern art and autonomous morality.

The way this functions is demonstrated by Rorty with the example of the rationalization of the Heideggerian pseudo-religion—a rationalization modelled on rational reconstruction. Rorty succeeds in a pragmatistic disenchanting of Heidegger's sacred Being by means of an approach similar to Benjamin's explication of the withering of aura in modern art. By declaring our freedom to be pure contingency, and by identifying the truth of Being with our language in its totality, in the context of our North Atlantic life-form, Rorty destroys the aura of Being. The transition from the founder-poet Hölderlin to the poet of technology has a similarly amazing modernizing effect as the transition from classical tragedy to cinema, from landscape-painting to illustrated magazines which were analyzed by Benjamin. The philosophy of Being is **aesthetically** linked to cultural modernity by Rorty.

The aesthetistic contraction in the concept of modernity in Benjamin's work, of course, already disturbed Adorno. Just as he was unwilling to trust the theologically motivated decisionism of Benjamin's explosive aesthetics of the profanely enlightened masses, he would have decisively rejected a rather weak concept of **solidarity without legitimation**. Adorno's concept of freedom has always retained an element of the non-contingent, of the **non-available**. Without recourse to the legitimating moment of a detotalized unconditional, he would scarcely have acquired an idea of egalitarian justice and anamnetic solidarity. At least something similar to a "weak messianic force" (Benjamin) must accrue to the subject from its own autonomy, and only from this, in order to be able to adopt the moral point of view beyond the standpoint of mere self-interest.

Adorno's frequent recourse to the Old Testament's **prohibition of images** ascertains the element of the non-available in the concept of freedom, i.e. its **non-instrumental meaning**. This meaning of the prohibition of images, which is built into the western history of freedom and emancipation, had to escape Heidegger's all-inclusive denouncement of Judaeo-Christian onto-theology as being, in the last analysis, an instrumental ideology of utility. It is precisely the prohibition of images that should secure that God is **not presented** as merely the highest and most general being, and thereby reified.[24]

It is this non-instrumental meaning of freedom and autonomy, as articulated in the prohibition of images, which, **after** religion, the profane Enlightenment makes accessible for modernity. But because the history of modernity, for Adorno, is not merely **any** history, as it is for Rorty, but rather one in which truth claims are articulated and operative, he is not forced to reject the question concerning the legitimation claim of modernity as being basically totalitarian. On the contrary, the legitimation claim becomes the basis for the critique of modernity's factualities.

III.

In a supplementary note (dated 31 January 1969) to **Negative Dialectics**, Adorno posed the question: How does rationality differ from mere purposive rationality? What is it really that makes our finite human reason something more and something other than a mere instrument of self-preservation?

For all his critique of independent instrumental rationality, Adorno was convinced that a rationality without an element of self-preservation was **not** rationality. He wrote, once again apodictically: "Ratio should not be **less** than self-preservation; making its way through self-preservation, ratio must transcend it."[25]

But how can the limitations of a mere **subjective reason** in the service of self-preservation be corrected? Adorno's answer: only by the **reason of the subject**. Along with the subjective reason of instrumental domination, "that which is Different from subjectivity" is also realized in **subjective reason**. And "that which is Different from subjectivity" is the **claim** of subjective reason to universal validity: "The ratio's moment of universality raises it above its subjective bearers."[26]

The strategic force of rational calculation **in the service of** self-preservation is accounted for by what Adorno calls **identifying thought.** To this extent he is in agreement with Heidegger; mere strategic rationality remains heteronomous, a useful means. However, the other, the **universal force**, which is indebted to the **autonomy** of the subject is the unconstrainedly operating power of **rational identity** which Adorno describes as having transcended identifying thought.[27]

Adorno never really clarified what he meant by rational identity or "full" and "non-violent rationality."[28] But one can find a number of remarks and examples which highlight various aspects of its meaning. In closing, I would like to mention at least a few.

"Rational identity" for Adorno is (1) **consciousness of the non-identical** in contrast to the colorlessness of the diffuse. "Consciousness of the non-identical"[29] is to be understood first (1a) as an appeal to open discourses for **all** possibly essential experiences, i.e. experiences which lie in the interest of those affected. The appeal to excluded, non-identical experiences can, for example, be ignited by the systmatically resticted universalism of supposedly universal "worldviews" as described by Heidegger in **The Age of the Worldview.** Of course the mistake of such worldviews, lacking an appropriate consciousness of the non-identical, is not their universalism, but rather the fact that they are not universalistic enough and, like scientism, exclude entire dimensions of rationality. Consciousness of the non-identical also includes (1b) **anamnetic solidarity** with those who have suffered—a suffering which can never be made good. Anamnetic solidarity is a limit concept which refers to the **irredeemable**, but **legitimate**, claims of those interests which were irreversibly violated in the past and which can no longer be articulated in practical discourses; it is now impossible to safeguard these interests. Although Heidegger analyzed the structures of temporality in a much more impressive manner than Adorno and all Marxists, he nevertheless falls completely short of the mortal dimension of the irreversibly past future. The abstraction of time to temporality misleads Heidegger to disdain the everyday suffering of mortals as "insignificant" and to develop a scarcely understandable, elitist fixation with the authentic, "creative suffering" of the thinking, poetry-writing and state-building demigods: "History is seldom."[30]

"Rational identity" for Adorno is (2) the correction of such real abstractions of identifying thought that, for example, come to expression in the reduction of freedom to "free wage labor" in modern capitalism (Weber). The exchange abstractions of the liberal idea of freedom contradict the egalitarian meaning of the modern concept of freedom. In this dimension, the concept of rational identity has a corrective function similar to John Rawls's difference principle. Adorno's formulation is just less flexible: "When we criticize the barter principle as the identifying principle of thought, we want to realize the ideal of free and just barter....If no man had part of his labor wihtheld from him any more, rational identity would be a fact, and society would have transcended the identifying mode of thinking."[31]

Adorno's concept of rational identity lies in (3) the integration of elements of instrumental and mimetic-aesthetic rationality. The central and basic concept of **Negative Dialectics**, moral freedom, is explicated by Adorno as the utmost tension between the antagonistic extremes of mimesis and self-preservation. Only the strong subject of intelligible character is free, the one identical with itself. In the integration of intelligible freedom and ego-strength, Adorno follows Kant and Freud. Autonomy, for Adorno, is the result of the compulsion to form an identity and for self-preservation. Only the strong ego is able to withstand the impulses of the empirical character that overcome the ego as if it were a piece of blind and alien nature.[32] It can open itself for a glimpse of its inner nature in order to rescue needs from their "paleosymbolic prelingisticality."[33]

Adorno's concept of the autonomous subject, which integrates Kant and Freud, makes it possible to adhere to the lasting insight

hauke
brunkhorst

of the idealist theory of action against Heidegger's exit philosophy—the insight that the planned generation of effects cannot, by means of the hypertrophy of instinct, be declared to be the intellect.[34] Rather, instrumental action has a non-instrumental autonomy as the condition of its possibility. It is only because of this that Adorno's genealogy of the intelligible character does not have the same disastrous consequences as Heidegger's and Nietzsche's. Because freedom and consciousness are genetically a late product of natural history, runs Adorno's argument, they are not simply the Other of nature; thus, because our own nature is not totally external to reason—not as opaque and absolutely alien as Kant assumed—we have an **internal** access to our needs.

Johann Wolfgang Goethe Universität Frankfurt

Translated by J. Farrell

ENDNOTES

1.   M. Heidegger, **Platons Lehre von der Wahrheit** (Bern, 1947) p. 46; **Identity and Difference**, tr. Joan Stambaugh (New York: Haper & Row, 1969) p. 62f; **An Introduction to Metaphysics**, Trans. by Ralph Manheim (New Haven: Yale University Press, 1959) p. 36ff; "The Word of Nietzsche: 'God Is Dead'," **The Question Concerning Technology and Other Essays**, tr. William Lovitt (New York: Harper & Row, 1977) p. 79f., p. 90ff.

2.   "Overcoming Metaphysics," **The End of Philosophy**, tr. Joan Stambaugh (London: Souvenir Press, 1975) p.106

3.   *Ibid.*, p.86; "What Are Poets For?" **Poetry, Language, Thought**, tr. Albert Hofstadter (New York: Harper & Row, 1971) pp. 135f.

4.   "Overcoming Metaphysics", p. 105f.

5.   "Building Dwelling Thinking," **Poetry, Language, Thought**, p. 152f; "The Thing," **Poetry, Language, Thought**, p. 173ff.

6.   "What Are Poets For?" p. 136; on the "Temple of Being," p. 132.

7.   "Overcoming Metaphysics", p. 103.

8.   Cf. J.-F. Lyotard, **The Postmodern Condition**, tr. G. Bennington and B. Massumi (Minneapolis, 1984)

9.   J.-F. Lyotard, "Das Erhabene und die Avantgarde", **Merkur**, No. 424, 1984, p. 154; cf. also "Grundlagenkrise," **neue hefte für philosophie**, No. 26, 1986, p. 10.

10.   R. Rorty, **Philosophy and the Mirror of Nature** (Princeton: Princeton University Press, 1979) p. 389.

11. M. Heidegger, **Was ist Metaphysik?** (Frankfurt, 1986) p. 50f.

12. On the second period see J. Habermas, "Martin Heidegger: The Great Influence," **Philosophical-Political Profiles**, tr. Frederick G. Lawrence (London: Heinemann, 1983) p. 53f.

13. R. Rorty, "Heidegger wider die Pragmatisten" in **neue hefte für philosophie**, No. 3, 1984, p. 22.

14. J.-F. Lyotard, **Der Widerstreit** (Munich: Fink, 1987) p. 263; see also p. 9f, p. 157f, and p. 177ff.

15. R. Rorty, "Habermas and Lyotard on Postmodernity," **Praxis International** 1, 1984, p. 40; "Solidarity of Objectivity?" J. Rajchman and C. West, eds., **Post-Analytical Philosophy** (New York, 1985) p. 5.

16. M. Weber, "The Social Psychology of the World Religions," **From Max Weber**, tr. H.H. Gerth and C. Wright Mills (London: Routledge & Kegan Paul, 1970) p. 272.

17. *Ibid.*, p. 273.

18. Theodor W. Adorno, **Negative Dialectics**, tr. E.B. Ashton (London: R. & K.P., 1973) p. 203.

19. Aristotle, **The Nicomachean Ethics**, (VI, 1143b).

20. Cf. **Negative Dialectics**, p. 130f, p. 147.

21. M. Heidegger, "The Word of Nietzsche: 'God Is Dead'," p. 90ff.

22. R. Rorty, "Heidegger wider die Pragmatisten", p. 21.

23. Cf. Lyotard, **Der Widerstreit**, p. 87, p. 197, p. 235.

24. M. Heidegger, **Identity and Difference**, p. 42ff.

25. Adorno, **Negative Dialektics** (Frankfurt: Suhrkamp, 1973) p. 530f.

26. *Ibid.*, p. 530.

27. Adorno, **Negative Dialectics**, p. 147.

28. *Ibid.*, p. 317f.

29. *Ibid.*, p. 148f.

30. M. Heidegger, "Hölderlins Hymnen 'Germanien' und 'Der Rhein'," p. 175ff; on Adorno's and Benjamin's concept of anamnetic solidarity cf. Helmut Peukert, **Wissenschaftstheorie, Handlungstheorie, fundamentala Theologie** (Frankfurt: Suhrkamp, 1978) p. 300ff.

31. **Negative Dialectics**, p. 147.

hauke
brunkhorst

32. *Ibid.*, p. 298f.

33. J. Habermas, **Communication and the Evolution of Society**, tr. Thomas McCarthy, (London: Heinemann, 1979) p. 93.

34. M. Heidegger, "Overcoming Metaphysics," p. 105f.

IV.
justification, application and history

klaus günther
impartial application of moral and legal norms: a contribution to discourse ethics[1]

With Kant's critical philosophy of morality and law, if not before, the justification expectations placed on the validity of binding norms in modern societies were put on a new foundation. Even before Kant the distinction between factual, positive validity and normative, rational validity was current in the natural law tradition. What was new, however, was the project to base normative or rational validity not on higher norms but on the autonomy of the person. Discourse ethics has continued this project by giving the moral principle of impartiality drafted by Kant a procedural formulation. A norm is valid when the consequences for the interests of each individual which arise from following this norm can be accepted by everyone.[2] The meaning of the moral principle is no longer individual self-determination **on behalf of** all others, but rather the **common** establishing of the general interest by reciprocally taking the perspective **of each individual**.

I. The Distinction Between Justification and Application

Just as for Kant, so too for the discourse ethic formulation of the moral principle of impartiality, the problem arises that the consensus about the validity of a norm must abstract from the possible situations of its application. The validity of a norm does not depend on the conditions of its application. A universalistic moral principle, as laid down by Kant's categorical imperative and klaus günther the discourse ethic principle of universal perspective taking, requires the distinction between the justification and the application of a norm.

Since a post-metaphysical criterion for the validity of a norm can only be based on the justified consent of all involved from the perspective of their respective interests, abstraction from a concrete starting point is unavoidable. Only if it were possible, at a particular point in time, to foresee every possible application situation with all its possibly relevant details, could the justification and the appropriate application of a norm be combined in one principle. This wording of a moral principle suggested in the "strong formulation" of the universalizability principle (U) would however amount to asserting that every rule contained at the same time the rules of its application for all situations in which it is possibly applicable. Instead, a weaker formulation of the universalization principle is proposed, according to which the justification of a norm concentrates on taking into consideration the effects and side-effects of norm following on the interests of each individual foreseeable at a specific point in time. It is only with the second step, with the application of the norm, that all the features of a concrete situation are taken into consideration. Only these two principles taken together, one focusing on interest generalization and the other on the specification of a concrete situation, fully exhaust the meaning of the idea of impartiality as it is laid claim to by cognitivistic ethics. The principle of taking all the features of a situation into consideration can also be implemented argumentatively in practical discourse on the application of norms. Not taking a specific feature of a situation into consideration requires justification. To this extent it is legitimate to speak of application as of a form of discourse.

Objections to the distinction between justification and application have been raised. Wellmer,[3] above all, has proposed the thesis that the moral principle is in actual fact a principle of application because—in its generally understood meaning—it refers only to the correct appraisal of a situation and to the selection of truly relevant circumstances and not so much to the situation-dependent generalization of all interests involved. Wellmer can dissolve the distinction between justification and application only because he has previously devalued the principle of universalizability to a standard which ties the acceptance of a form of action to its compatibility with a common, particular practice. Thus, a specific life form takes the place of the principle of universalizability such that, in each individual situation, there only arises the limited task of checking how this commonly shared life form can be continued here and now in an appropriate manner. In contrast to this, universalistic ethics permits the critique of a life form, paying however the price that the conditions of universalizability of a norm are detached from the respective situation as it appears to concrete, involved individuals within this life form.

II. The Problem of Application in the Development of Moral Consciousness

In addition to the systematic view, it can also be shown from the view-point of developmental theory that there are arguments for the necessity of distinguishing between justification and application. In order to do so, it is necessary to broaden the perspective and relate the changes in the relation between justification and application to the development of rule and moral consciousness in general. Norms are applied in situations, and to every situation belongs the other, whose interests and expectations are affected by the consequences of a norm application. How rules emerge in processes of social interaction and how they are followed in social situations is the classical topic of both the social sciences and the philosophy of language. As one of the first theorists, Durkheim focused attention on the conditions of the emergence and change of a collective moral consciousness and thus also introduced the essential distinguishing criteria which have set the standard for subsequent research.[4] Mechanically segmented, poorly differentiated societies have at their disposal a rigid, concretely composed rule system which, founded on sanctions, is applied in an authoritarian manner without consideration of the special circumstances of the individual case. In contradistinction to these, "organically" segmented societies organized on the division of labor are characterized by abstract norms which can be applied in a "free" manner by individualized, autonomous persons in extremely dissimilar situations. How can this concept of the "free application" of determined norms be precisely reconstructed?

The social process of the emergence of situation-independent rules was first investigated by G.H. Mead in the use of vocal gestures in primitive forms of communication.[5] According to Mead, it is decisive for this process that situation-independent meanings emerge coincidentally with a social consciousness that binds the use of identical meanings in different situations to ego's taking the perspective or role of alter ego. Only if ego can fictively put himself in the role of alter ego, is it possible for him to experience what his mode of condct means "socially." Mead abstracted the role of the other to the concept of the "generalized other" as that of a third position from where the identity of meanings used by ego and alter ego in different situations can be observed once again. If the emergence of situation-invariant rules can be explained socially in this manner, one must then ask what results from this for the application of rules in particular situations.

Wittgenstein, who interprets the intersubjective use of rules radically as a "training" to which the participants of a "chess game" are exposed, excludes from the outset the possibility of a separate analysis of situation-independent meanings. Rather, he understands rule following in situations as a particular practice which, as such, cannot be thematized; transferring this to the following of action norms, the possibility of a distinction between justification and application would thus be contested. Mead, who moves directly from the analysis of the emergence of meaning to the reconstruction of the social validity of norms, suggests a procedure of constructive hypothesis formation which obliges the participants of a discourse in every particular situation to take into consideration all the relevant value perspectives of the other person involved. However, neither does Mead thereby distinguish between questions of justification and those of application.

Nevertheless, the necessity of this distinction arises when one differentiates between linguistic rules of meaning and practical rules (norms). Habermas deepens Wittgenstein's concept of a language game in the direction of the ultimate presuppositions of linguistic understanding. The presuppositions of successful understanding oblige everyone who addresses a speech act to someone else to justify the validity claim thus raised. In cases of dispute the speaker must be able to show that the validity of his utterance can be accepted from the perspective of each individual. This moral core of consensual communication can, for the special case of normative utterances, be presented in the formulation of the universalization principle (U) with the consequence that a distinction must be drawn between validity justification and appropriate application of norms. In his Durkheim interpretation, however, Habermas does not go beyond the mere reference to the possibility of a "communicatively mediated application."[6]

A more detailed picture of the relation between justification and application presents itself when one turns to those developmental theories which distinguish various stages in the type of social relationship, in the comprehension of the validity of a norm, and in the manner in which it is followed in situations.

In anticipation of a more precise consideration of these theories, two stages in the development of the relation between justification and application can be hypothetically distinguished, stages which indirectly link up with Durkheim's distinction between mechanical and organic solidarity but integrate Mead's concept of perspective taking. Accordingly, a context-bound, situation-dependent stage of validity justification and application can be distinguished from a context-independent stage that takes all the features of a situation into consideration. What is of interest for developmental theories is, above all, a precise determination of the transition between both stages. Elucidation of this problem can be found in Piaget's and Kohlberg's somewhat neglected studies about the relation between equality and equity.[7] In empirical investigations each author, apparently independent of the other, arrived at the result that it is only at the highest— universalistic—stage of the development of moral consciousness that the ideas of equality and equity are detached from the fixation on pre-given norms which are applied without further consideration of circumstances. Thus, the rigid rule-exception scheme is overcome and potentially every feature of an individual situation becomes relevant for discourse. In contrast to this, preceding stages take their orientation from specific ideas of order which limit both the validity of a norm and the extent and manner of taking into consideration the features of a situation in an individual application context. A differentiation between justification and application cannot therefore be realized at these stages. The horizon of validity includes not only a particular group of addressees, but also a relatively small amount of conflict situations for which a norm is simultaneously valid and appropriate. Against this background one can understand how, for example, the doctrine of legal positivism could emerge, the doctrine according to which the application of a law is restricted to the examination of the features abstractly pre-given in a norm. Only because the legislator enacts, in advance, a valid (i.e., procedurally justified) and appropriate (i.e., appropriately applicable to easily graspable conflicts) norm, can the judicial application of this norm be limited to simple subsumption.

If a distinction must be drawn between justification and application at the highest stage of moral consciousness, and if, in respect of application, practical reason in the sense of taking all the features of a situation into consideration is possible, then two objections which have been raised against universalistic ethics can be refuted: First, the objection about insufficient sensitivity for the special character of interpersonal relationship conflicts which cannot be resolved according to abstract principles of justice. Here it can be shown that it is precisely the extension of perspective structures (by means of which moral consciousness is formed in its social dimension) to include all those concretely involved in each individual situation that makes possible, in the first place, the appropriate consideration of the particular aspects of a conflict. Secondly, the objection about rigorism, according to which a rigid form of application is necessarily bound up with a universalistic ethics, can be countered with the argument that an impartial application of norms in a situation precludes the very possibility of a norm, whose validity depends on the consideration of the interests of everyone involved, being applied in such a manner that the special circumstances of the individual case remain irrelevant.

With these arguments, one can oppose a very influential position still defended even today in ethics, policial science and the philosophy of law—a position which asserts that norms cannot be universalistically justified, rather, that the solution of practical problems lies in the shrewd choice, oriented by the socially given context, of appropriate means for the realization of the relatively general ends of the good life in a well-ordered political community. Aristotle presented this draft in the context of the constitution of a polis in which the validity and the appropriateness of societal norms were still intertwined with one another. When one distinguishes between justification and application, aspects of the good life in a situation can be integrated into practical deliberations without having to surrender the universalistic claim of practical reason.

III. The Logic of Appropriateness Argumentations

How can the logic of appropriateness argumentations be described? It begins by taking up the discussion about the collision problem, which has been the reference point for the discussion about the situation relatedness of norms justified in themselves. In the tradition from Ross to Baier, the distinction between *facie* norms, which are valid under unchanging circumstances, and absolute norms, which are valid under the consideration of all the circumstances of a situation, has always been equated with two implicitly different concepts of ought. Searle drew attention to the fact that, as a result, it becomes unclear in what the obligatory character of a norm actually consists. Instead, he suggests relating the distinction to the action and conversation conditions under which we argue about practical questions in a situation. This suggestion can be mobilized for the purposes of clarifying argumentations of appropriateness. When the participants of a discourse enter an appropriateness argumentation, they take up the claim of a norm to be valid under unchanging circumstances and check this claim with reference to the features of the respective situation. In this way, various features become relevant and capable of being taken into consideration. The task of appropriateness argumentations thus consists in drawing upon as many different—virtually all—normative viewpoints as possible in order to form an appropriate norm from them, one which, moreover, can sustain a universalization of its validity claim.

Of course, it has not yet been shown how a collision between different, contending normative viewpoints can be resolved in the individual case. For the solution of collision problems arising from the application of basic rights, Alexy has introduced a collision and deliberation law which allows, in the individual case, the importance of a relevant basic right to be set in relation to the importance of another. Because of their norm structure, principles refer reciprocally to one another so that they cannot be applied without an optimizing consideration of all the factual and judicial circumstances of the individual case. However, by binding the collision law to a norm-structural distinction between rules not susceptible to deliberation and principles in need of deliberation, Alexy misses the advantages offered by Searle's suggestion of a reconstruction of the action and argumentation conditions. When norms are applied under the consideration of all the circumstances of a situation, one treats them as principles. Of course, the problem of finding deliberation standards is not thus solved, but it can be posed independently of a specific, given norm structure so that appropriateness argumentations about all kinds of norms are possible.

IV. Application Discourses in Law

The reflections on the distinction between justification and application as well as on the rational reconstruction of appropriateness argumentations are burdened with the strong hypothetical presupposition that taking all the features of a situation into consideration is possible, at least in principle. Only under this demanding condition is a differentiation between justification and application possible and can the justification problem be resolved in a universalizability principle that solely concentrates on the situation-independent consideration of the interests of each individual. However, in reality, appropriateness argumentations always take place under the restricted conditions of limited time and incomplete knowledge. At this point, law fulfills a mediating function. It must, at the same time, make possible appropriateness argumentations and ensure that clear decisions are made, decisions on the basis of which stable behavior expectations can emerge. It must be flexible in varying situations and able to respond to special circumstances and, at the same time, able to generalize situations to a sufficient extent in terms of their material, temporal and social character so that not everything is thematized anew in each individual case. Systems theory describes situations in which taking all aspects into consideration is excluded and, therefore, social expectation uncertainty exists in the form of the "double contingency" of behavioral expectations, which leads to the formation of social systems. Here, the legal system assumes a prominent position since it processes the disappointment of expectations in a predictable manner and thus permits the formation of stable behavior expectations. Of course, the positivistic concept of law is thereby favored. Flexibility in varying situations can play a part

klaus günther only in the decision about the positing or "programming" of legal norms, whereas in the application of legal norms, a deliberation relating to the individual case, consideration of its consequences, etc., is precisely excluded. However, Luhmann and Teubner themselves have, in the meantime, conceded that the applicaton of legal norms, too, cannot, in the long run, avoid an appropriate consideration of the respective circumstances of the case. The increasingly observable indeterminacy of legal problems can therefore be explained by the necessity of engaging in appropriateness argumentations also when legal norms are being applied.

Johann Wolfgang Goethe Universität Frankfurt

Translated by John Farrell

ENDNOTES

1. The following paper is a summary of my book: **Der Sinn für Angemessenheit. Anwendungsdiskurse in Moral und Recht.** Frankfurt, Suhrkamp, 1988.

2. Jürgen Habermas, **Diskursethik—Notizen zu einem Begründungsprogramm**, in: *idem.*, **Moralbewußtsein und kommunikatives Handeln.** Frankfurt, Suhrkamp, 1983 (English tr. MIT Press).

3. Albrecht Wellmer, **Ethik und Dialog.** Frankfurt, Suhrkamp, 1986.

4. Emile Durkheim, **The Division of Labor in Society.** New York, The Free Press, 1964, pp. 138ff.

5. George H. Mead, **Mind, Self, and Society.** Chicago, The University of Chicago Press, 1934.

6. Jürgen Habermas, **The Theory of Communicative Action, Vol. 2, Lifeworld and System: A Critique of Functionalist Reason.** Boston, Beacon Press, 1987.

7. Jean Piaget, **The Moral Judgment of the Child.** New York, The Free Press, 1965. Lawrence Kohlberg, **Essays on Moral Development, Vol. II, The Psychology of Moral Development.** San Francisco, Harper and Row, 1984.

ethics, politics and history:
an interview with
jürgen habermas
conducted by jean-marc ferry*

FERRY: It has become clear that the "historian's dispute" *[Historikerstreit]* is no mere scholastic controversy, but much more a debate over the self-understanding of the Federal Republic of Germany. In what sense, according to your opinion, has Auschwitz so changed the conditions for the continuity of the historical life context of the Federal Republic that it is impossible today to accept that view of history which neo-historicism wants to renew?

HABERMAS: Perhaps we should briefly clarify the expression "neo-historicism." Since the 1970s, a type of reaction has grown up in the Federal Republic against the advance of social scientific methods and perspectives in the *Geisteswissenschaften*. This reaction also understands itself as a return to the important tradition of German *Geisteswissenschaften* of the nineteenth century. The key phrase here is the rehabilitation of narrative *[Erzählung]*; that is, the narrative representation of events as opposed to theoretical, explanatory claims....

During the historian's dispute, Saul Friedlander, in particular, has drawn attention to the limits and dangers of neo-historicism in relation to the historical representation of the catastrophe of Auschwitz. In this controversy, no one has opposed a

jürgen habermas "historicization"; that is, a scientifically distantiated comprehension of the Nazi period. What is questionable is only a hermeneutically unreflective way of proceeding. If one merely inserts oneself into the situation of the participants in order to understand the actors and their behavior within their own context, one runs the danger of losing sight of the disastrous connections of the epoch as a whole. In the kaleidoscope of the small, varied and gray normalities, one loses the perspective out of which alone the ambivalence *[Doppelbodigkeit]* of the seeming normality can be recognized. One cannot just consider the details from close up with the intention of empathetic understanding....As Dolf Sternberger has continually insisted: "The venerable teaching of *Verstehen* collides with a massive wall....The dreadful crime which is marked with the name Auschwitz cannot in truth be understood at all."

FERRY: Could you make these thoughts more precise?

HABERMAS: Neo-historicism bases itself upon a supposition which is represented today in practical philosophy by the neo-Aristotelians. It is supposed that a *praxis* makes itself understandable and allows itself to be judged only in relation to the life contexts and traditions in which it is embedded. That is plausible, as long as we can have confidence that practices, as they are passed on and endure from one generation to another, prove their worth only on the basis of this stability of tradition. This conviction expresses a type of anthropological basic trust *[Urvertrauen]*.

Historicism lives off this trust. Such trust is not completely unintelligible. In some way we do rely—in spite of all the spontaneous, natural bestiality in the history of the world—upon a deep-seated layer of solidarity in the face-to-face intercourse of human beings with one another. The questionless continuity of what is handed down to us also draws its sustenance from this trust. "Tradition" means just that we carry something forward as unproblematic which others began before us. We imagine normally that these "forerunners," if they were to meet us face-to-face, could not totally deceive us, could not play the role of a *deus malignus*. I believe that exactly this basis of trust was destroyed at the threshold of the gas chambers.

The complex preparation and the elaborate organization of a coolly calculated mass murder, in which hundreds of thousands, indirectly a whole people, were entangled, was carried out with an air of normality. It was straightforwardly dependent upon the normality of a highly civilized social intercourse. The monstrous occurred without interrupting the smooth breathing of everyday life. Since then a **conscious** life is no longer possible without mistrust for continuities that assert themselves without question and also want to draw their validity out of their questionlessness.

FERRY: I want to question the mode of collective identity formation available today for citizens of the Federal Republic, as well as for all Germans. On the political level of a national identity and sovereignty, "Germany" appears as an entity (problematic, at least) that corresponds to no state organization. National identity usually refers to a historical consciousness, in whose medium the self-consciousness of a nation constitutes itself. You, however, allude to a so-called "constitutional patriotismus" [Verfassungs-patriotismus] that limits itself to universalistic postulates of democratic and human rights.

Could you please clarify this universalistic option? Do you merely renounce any type of national-historical identity formation in favor of a pure, formal-practical one that basically no longer needs to make reference to its own tradition?

HABERMAS: No, the identity of a person, a group, a nation or a region is always something concrete, something particular. (It should, of course, also comply with moral standards.) We speak of our identity whenever we say who we are and who we want to be. Descriptive and evaluative elements are thus interwoven with one another. The shape that we have taken on through our life history, the history of our milieu, our people, cannot be separated out in a description from the picture that we present to ourselves and others, and according to which we want to be judged, respected and recognized by others.

Now, to the collective identity of the Germans after the Second World War. For us it is indeed nothing new, that the unity of our cultural, linguistic and historical context is not overlaid with the organizational form of a state. We were never one of the classical nation-states. Standing against the background of a thousand year history, the seventy-five year Bismarck regime constitutes a brief span. Even then the German Reich existed next to Austria, not to mention the Swiss-Germans or the German minorities in other states. In this situation, constitutional patriotism is the only possible form of patriotism for us in the Federal Republic. That in no way signifies, however, the renunciation of an identity that can never consist purely of general moral orientations and characteristics—that is to say ones shared by everyone.

For us in the Federal Republic, constitutional patriotism means, among other things, taking pride in having succeeded, in the long run, in overcoming fascism, in having established a constitutional order and in having anchored it in a halfway liberal political culture. Our patriotism, however, cannot deny the fact that in

jürgen habermas Germany democracy was able to put down roots in the motives and hearts of citizens (at least the younger generations) only after Auschwitz—and in a certain way only through the shock of this moral catastrophe. For universal principles to take root one always needs a determinate identity.

FERRY: I believe that this post-conventional and post-national identity formation that you defend also presents the claim of being able, in the more or less near future, to replace national identity as the basically valid form of life for the countries of Western Europe....Do I understand this correctly?

HABERMAS: We have to keep two things separated. Nationalism here came to a head Social-Darwinistically and culminated in a delusion of race that stood as the justification for the mass extermination of the Jews. Therefore nationalism has been drastically devalued as the basis of a collective identity. And also, therefore, the overcoming of fascism constitutes the particular historical perspective from which a post-national identity, formed around the universalistic principles of the constitutional state and democracy, is to be understood—but not just in the Federal Republic. Since the Second World War, all European countries have developed in such a way that national identity has lost weight and significance.

These countries are also on the way to post-national societies. One can mention European integration, supra-national military alliances, worldwide economic interdependencies, economically motivated waves of immigration, the growing ethnic variety of the population. Beyond these there is the thickening of the network of communication that has sharpened the perception of, and sensitivity for, abridgements of human rights, for exploitation, hunger, misery, for the concerns of national liberation movements and so forth. That leads, on the one hand, to reactions of anxiety and defense. But simultaneously a consciousness also spreads that there is no other alternative to universalistic value orientations.

What then does universalism mean? Relativizing one's own form of existence to the legitimate claims of other forms of life, according equal rights to aliens and others with all their idiosyncrasies and unintelligibility, not sticking doggedly to the universalization of one's own identity, not marginalizing that which deviates from one's own identity, allowing the sphere of tolerance to become ceaselessly larger than it is today—all this is what moral universalism means today.

210 The idea of the nation-state that arose from the French Revolution had at first a thoroughly cosmopolitan sense. Just think of the enthusiasm awakened throughout all of Europe by the Greek struggle for freedom in the early nineteenth century. This cosmopolitan element must be reawakened and further developed in the form of a multi-culturalism.

FERRY: This change in form of collective identity suggests the necessity of greater flexibility in the structures of modern forms of life....But I cannot imagine how, under your assumptions of a radically decentered life, the real need for stability and continuity of self can be met. It is a question of the force of identification and motivation provided by purely formal, universal validity claims. How can the radical universalist option or stimulus of "constitutional patriotism" provide an identity-forming force that sustains not only a moral legitimacy but also a historical plausibility?

HABERMAS: Now the attachment to principles of constitutionalism and democracy can, as said, only become a reality in different nations (those on the way to postnational identity) if these principles put down roots in different ways in the respective political cultures. In the country of the French revolution, for example, such constitutional patriotism takes another form than in a country that never generated democracy through its own force. The same universalistic content must be appropriated out of the particular life context and be anchored in the particular cultural form of life. Any collective identity, even the post-national, is much more concrete than the ensemble of basic moral, legal, and political principles around which it crystallizes.

FERRY: Insofar as you appeal to a public use of tradition whereby it must be decided "which of our traditions we want to carry forward and which not," there arises the picture of the radical-critical relation to tradition that characterized the rationalistic attitude of the Enlightenment. I would like here to bring up briefly two critiques of the Enlightenment. From the Gadamerian perspective, there arises the objection that we are not able, in principle, to transcend tradition, especially with the (supposedly) illusory intention of selectively carrying forward or totally eliminating selected strands. From the viewpoint of a Hegelian critique, I will only call attention to one issue arising from **The Philosophy of Right**: "Man has value because he is a man, not because he is a Jew, Catholic, Protestant, Italian, etc." This consciousness is supposed to be of inexhaustible significance; it only becomes marred when it crystallizes into a cosmopolitanism that stands in opposition to the concrete life of the state. In what relation does the discourse-theoretical deepening or renewal of Kantian universalism (which presumably underlies the formal-pragmatic framework of constitutional patriotism) stand to this issue?

jürgen habermas HABERMAS: Hegel lent a pejorative meaning to the word "man," because he took "mankind" to be a bad abstraction. World historical actors were for him the spirit of a people or great individuals and, above all, states. As opposed to these, that totality of all subjects capable of speech and action does not constitute a unity that can act politically. Therefore, Hegel placed morality (which refers to the susceptibility to injury of all who have a human face) **under** politics. That however is a very time-bound perspective.

Today, cosmopolitanism can no longer stand in opposition to the concrete life of the state in the same way it did in 1817, because the sovereignty of single states no longer consists of their disposal over the making of war and peace. Even the superpowers no longer have free reign here. In order to preserve themselves, all states today stand under the imperative of abolishing war as a means of solving conflicts. For Hegel the *"dulce et decorum est pro patria mori"* was still the highest ethical duty on earth. Today the duty of "service with weapons" has become rather questionable. Even the international arms business, as it is carried on today…has long since lost its innocence. The abolition of the state of nature between states is on the agenda for the first time. The conditions of a people's self-preservation thereby change. Also, the rank order between the political obligations of citizens and the moral ones of "men" does not remain untouched. General circumstances themselves thus compel a moralization of politics.

It is similar with the taking up of a critical attitude toward one's own tradition. Hegel had already incorporated into his philosophy that change in the consciousness of time which was completed around 1800, namely the experience of a peculiar acceleration of one's own history, the unifying perspective of world history, the weight and reality of the present against the horizon of a future for which we bear responsibility. The catastrophes of our century have once again changed this time consciousness.

Now our responsibility also extends to the past. This is not taken up simply as something factual and ready to hand. Walter Benjamin probably defined most precisely this claim that the dead raise for the anamnetic power of living generations. We certainly cannot make past suffering and injustice good; but we do have the weak power of an atoning remembrance *[suhnenden Erinnerung]*. It is just this sensibility for innocent victims, from whose inheritance we live, that also produces a reflexive distance toward one's own traditions, a sensitivity to the unfathomable ambivalences of that which has been passed on to us and which has formed our identity. But our identity is not only something already found, but also and simultaneously our own project. We cannot simply pick and choose our own traditions, but we can know that we must bear the burden of how we carry them forward. In this regard, Gadamer thinks too conservatively. Every carrying on of a tradition is selective, and it is just this selectivity that must be drawn through the filter of critique, of a deliberate appropriation of history—if you will, of a consciousness of sins.

Johann Wolfgang Goethe Universität Frankfurt

Translated by Stephen K. White

*This interview appeared in German in **Die Neue Gesellschaft: Frankfurter Heft** 4, April, 1989.

V.
communitarian alternatives

chantal mouffe
rawls: political philosophy
without politics

Is it possible to disentangle political liberalism from the
vocabulary that it has inherited from the rationalism of the
Enlightenment on one side and from the connotations it has
acquired by its long association with economic liberalism on the
other? This is, I believe, a crucial question for the elaboration of
a modern democratic political philosophy. Several recent
debates attest the need for such an elucidation by forcing us into
unacceptable dichotomies. It is particularly evident in the current
controversy about modernity and postmodernity and the
confrontation between the defenders of the Enlightenment and its
detractors. As Richard Rorty pointed out in "Habermas and
Lyotard on Postmodernity": "[W]e find French critics of Habermas
ready to abandon liberal politics in order to avoid universalistic
philosophy, and Habermas trying to hang on to universalistic
philosophy, with all its problems, in order to support liberal
politics."[1] A very similar confusion is happening among the
communitarian critics of liberalism, with several of them failing to
distinguish between liberal individualism as a specific doctrine
concerning the nature of the human subject, and political
liberalism as a set of institutions characteristic of the "law state":
defense of rights, recognition of pluralism, limitation of the role of
the state, separation of powers, etc. So communitarians like
Sandel and MacIntyre who refuse the atomist conception of
humans of liberal individualism, think it necessary to denounce

the "rhetoric of rights and pluralism" and end up by rejecting political liberalism. Even Rorty is guilty of illegitimate amalgamation when he makes bourgeois economic relations an intrinsic component of liberalism. Indeed, his concept of "liberalism" is extremely ambiguous; if he rightly separates—following Blumenberg—the two aspects of the Enlightenment, that of "self-assertion" (which can be identified with the political project),[2] and that of "self-foundation" (the epistemological project), he later identifies the political project of modernity with a vague concept of "liberalism" which includes both capitalism and democracy. His "postmodernist bourgeois liberalism" is therefore a pure and simple apology for the "institutions and practices of the rich North Atlantic democracies"[3] that leaves no room for democratic critique.

All those false dilemmas are the result of the conflation under the term of "liberalism" of a series of different discourses that have been articulated together in certain circumstances but that have no necessary relation. First it is important in order to understand political modernity to distinguish two traditions, liberal and democratic, which were only articulated in the nineteenth century. Then one must not confuse this "political modernity" with the process of modernization carried out under the domination of capitalist relations of production. Some liberals, of course, argue that there cannot be political liberalism without economic liberalism and a free market economy, but that is only the expression of one trend within liberalism. Finally, there are a series of philosophical discourses concerning the idea of the human being, the criteria of rationality, the nature of morality, etc.; they are sometimes referred to as "the philosophy of liberalism," but they are extremely heterogeneous and include positions as different as Kantianism and utilitarianism. It is therefore a mistake to see them as constituting a single doctrine. Many possible articulations can take place between those different "forms" of liberalism and I want to argue that the acceptance of political liberalism does not require us to endorse either individualism or economic liberalism, nor does it commit us to a defense of universalism and rationalism. I will take the case of Rawls's deontological liberalism as an example of those multiple articulations and use it as a starting point to discuss the nature and the role of political philosophy in a democratic society.

Rawls's Theory of Justice

Rawls's work is a good illustration of the point I am making. First, we have here a defense of political liberalism which establishes its autonomy from economic liberalism. As Brian Barry indicated, the significance of **A Theory of Justice** is that it is "a statement of liberalism which isolates its crucial features by making private property, in the means of production, distribution and exchange, a contingent matter rather than an essential part of the doctrine and introduces a principle of distribution which could, suitably interpreted and with certain factual assumptions, have egalitarian implications."[4] Moreover, it is an attempt to provide an alternative to utilitarian thought whose hegemony among liberal moral philosophy had been solidly established. Finally, and this is the aspect I want to examine, Rawls has been moving away from a universalistic framework and is now stressing the "situated" character of his theory of justice.

Indeed Rawls pretends that he was misunderstood and that even in his book he did not intend to pose the question of justice in an ahistorical manner. But by stating that the principles of justice as fairness "are the principles that free and rational persons concerned to further their own interests would accept in an initial position of equality as defining the fundamental terms of their association,"[5] without further historical specifications, he was leaving the door wide open for those universalistic types of interpretations. It is only later that he has specified that his aim was not to elaborate a conception of justice suitable for all types of societies regardless of their particular social or historical circumstances, but only "to settle a fundamental disagreement over the just form of social institutions within a democratic society under modern conditions."[6] He was therefore trying to find a solution to the disputed question of how basic social institutions should be arranged in order to embody the principles of equality and liberty and how those two ideals should be understood and balanced. Now, he also emphasizes that the task of articulating a public conception of justice is primarily a practical social task, not an epistemological one, and that "what justifies a conception of justice is not its being true to an order antecedent and given to us, but its congruence with a deeper understanding of ourselves and our aspirations, and our realization that, given our history and the tradition embedded in our public life, it is the most reasonable doctrine for us."[7] After having been one of the main targets of the advocates of contextualism, has Rawls become one of their champions? Has he abandoned Dworkin for Rorty? What are today the points of contention with his communitarian critics? More generally, how successful is Rawls's "historicized" version of justice as fairness?

In order to elucidate some of these problems, it is necessary to recapitulate briefly the main ideas of Rawls's theory as they are presented in a series of articles posterior to **A Theory of Justice**. There he declares that the aim of political philosophy in a constitutional democracy is to propose "a political conception of justice that can not only provide a fair public basis for the justification of political social and economic institutions but also help ensure stability from one generation to the next."[8] What is at stake is the creation of social unity. In a democratic society it cannot rest on a shared conception of the meaning, value and purpose of life; nor can it rest exclusively on a convergence of self or group interest because such a basis of justification would not be stable enough. Social unity should therefore be secured by an overlapping consensus on a reasonable political conception of justice.

Concerning the nature of such a political conception of justice, Rawls indicates that it is a moral conception worked out for political, social and economic institutions and should not be understood as an application to the political order of a general and comprehensive moral conception. This is to respect the existence of pluralism that must allow for a plurality of conflicting and incommensurable conceptions of the good. Therefore, a political conception of justice must be independent of controversial philosophical and religious doctrines and no general moral conception can provide a publicly recognized basis for a conception of justice in a modern democratic society. It can only be formulated in terms of certain fundamental intuitive ideas latent in its common sense and embedded in its institutions.[9]

For that reason, justice as fairness starts with what Rawls considers to be the central intuitive idea implicit in the public culture of a democracy: a view of society as a fair system of cooperation between free and equal persons. The fundamental question of political justice is then to find "the most appropriate principles for realizing liberty and equality once society is viewed as a system of cooperation between free and equal persons."[10] Rawls's proposal is to see those principles as the result of an agreement among the people concerned in the light of their mutual advantage. He believes that the idea of a rational self-interested choice can provide a shared idea of citizens' good appropriate for political purposes and independent of any particular doctrine. But such a choice is nevertheless subject to a series of constraints and the original position is introduced in order to specify the conditions of liberty and equality necessary for the agreement to be reached in a fair way. Its "veil of ignorance" serves to eliminate the bargaining advantages that could affect the process of decision and distort the result. Rawls affirms that once the citizens see themselves as free and equal persons they should recognize that to pursue their own different conceptions of the good they need the same primary goods, that is, the same basic rights, liberties and opportunities as well as the same all-purpose means such as income and wealth, and the same social bases of self respect. They would in consequence agree on a political conception of justice that will state that "all social primary goods—liberty and opportunity, income and wealth, and the bases of self respect—are to be distributed equally unless an unequal distribution of any or all of these goods is to the advantage of the least favored."[11] Such is precisely the general conception behind the two principles of justice specified by Justice as Fairness; the first one requires that each person is to have an equal right to the most extensive basic liberty compatible with a similar liberty for others, and the second that goods should only be distributed unequally when that unequal distribution is (a) to the greatest benefit of the least advantaged and (b) attached to offices and positions open to all under conditions of fair opportunity.[12]

The main difference with **A Theory of Justice** is the new emphasis put on the fact that the basic ideas of Justice as Fairness are regarded as implicit or latent in the public culture of a democratic society and the abandonment of the description of the theory of justice as part of the theory of rational choice. Rawls recognizes that it was a mistake and declares "What I should have said is that the conception of justice as fairness uses an account of rational choice subject to reasonable conditions to characterize the deliberations of the parties as representatives of free and equal persons....There is no thought of trying to derive the content of justice within a framework that uses an idea of the rational as the sole normative idea."[13] Rawls also stresses that the conception of the person found in the original position is a political conception, a conception of citizens concerned with our public identity, and that it does not presuppose any specific comprehensive view of the nature of the self.

Priority of the Right Over the Good

One of the characteristic features of Justice as Fairness is that it affirms the priority of the right over the good. Such a priority indicates that individual rights cannot be sacrificed for the sake of the general welfare, as is the case with utilitarianism, and that the principles of justice impose restrictions on what are the permissible conceptions of their good that individuals are allowed to pursue. This is of course why the principles of justice must be derived independently of any particular conception of the good since they need to respect the existence of a plurality of competing conceptions of the good in order to be accepted by all citizens. Rawls believes that the superiority of the deontological approach over the teleological one (which asserts the priority of the good and defines the right as what maximizes the good) is that it is the only one providing an adequate representation of the distinctness of individuals and a defense of their inalienable rights. Hence his claim that Justice as Fairness is the theory of justice best suited for a modern democracy.

chantal
mouffe

I think that Rawls is right in arguing that in a modern democracy the principles of justice must be derived independently of any moral, religious or philosophical conception and serve as a framework to determine which particular conceptions of the good are acceptable. But he is defending this thesis in a way that is inadequate and has left him vulnerable to the communitarian critique. The communitarians object that such a priority of the right cannot exist because it is only in a specific type of society, with certain institutions, that an individual with rights can exist, and that it is only through our participation in a community which defines the good in a certain way that we can acquire a sense of the right and a conception of justice. As Charles Taylor correctly points out, "[T]he basic error of atomism in all its forms is that it fails to take account of the degree to which the free individual with his own goals and aspirations, whose just rewards it is trying to protect, is himself only possible within a certain kind of civilization; that it took a long development of certain institutions and practices, of the rule of law, of rules of equal respect, of habits of common deliberation, of common association, of cultural development, and so on, to produce the modern individual."[14] Once it is recognized that the existence of rights and a conception of justice cannot exist previously and independently of specific forms of political association—which by definition imply a conception of the good—it becomes obvious that there can never be an absolute priority of the right over the good.

Does that mean that we should therefore reject Rawls's concerns with the priority of justice and the defense of individual rights and come back to a politics of the common good based on shared moral values, as Michael Sandel argues?[15] We find here a dangerous confusion which accounts for the ambiguity of the communitarian critique and which leads, in authors like Sandel, to the rejection of political liberalism and a denial of pluralism. Its origin resides in the problematic notion of the "common good" and its implications for the relationship between ethics and politics. Before the advent of modernity, the community was organized around a single idea of a substantive common good and no real distinction existed between ethics and politics, with politics being subordinated to the common good. With the emergence of the individual, the separation between Church and State, the principle of religious toleration and the development of civil society, a separation took place between politics and what became the sphere of morality. Moral and religious beliefs are now a private matter on which the state cannot legislate and pluralism is a crucial feature of modern democracy, the kind of democracy that is characterized by the absence of a substantive common good.

But if Rawls as a consequent liberal is right in wanting to defend pluralism and individual rights, he is wrong in believing that such a project requires the rejection of any possible idea of a common good. The priority of right he advocates can only exist within the context of a specific political association defined by an idea of the common good except that, in this case, it must be understood in strictly political terms as the political common good of a liberal-democratic regime, i.e., the principles of the liberal democratic regime *qua* political association: equality and liberty. There is no need, on the other side, to reject pluralism and the priority of justice in order to adopt a communitarian approach stressing the character of a person as a political and social being whose identity is created within a community of language, meanings and practices. Sandel is therefore drawing illegitimate conclusions in using the inadequacy in Rawls's formulation to criticize a politics of rights, and a communitarian defense of political liberalism is perfectly possible. Indeed, Rawls has been moving into that direction since he acknowledged that his conception of justice is a political one that concerns us *qua* citizens of a constitutional democracy whose latent ideals it tries to reflect and develop.

Nevertheless, Rawl's current position is not very consistent and he stands in an awkward position between Kant and Hegel, as Glaston has correctly pointed out. He still maintains the priority of the right, but his new emphasis on the conception of the moral person undermines such a priority since "if justice is desirable because it aims at our good as moral persons, then justice as fairness rests on a specific conception of the good, from which the 'constraints' of right and justice are ultimately derived."[16] Glaston argues that Rawls's revised theory is difficult to distinguish from the perfectionism that he continues to reject. "Clearly the ideal of the person functions as a moral goal, in two respects. Individuals choosing principles of justice will seek, first and foremost, to create circumstances in which they can realize and express their moral powers. Second, we as observers will appraise social institutions in light of their propensity to promote the realization and facilitate the expression of these powers, and this standard will take priority over our other concerns."[17]

I agree with Glaston that Rawls's position today is untenable, but I do not think that the solution would consist in assuming openly a perfectionist view; rather, as I shall try to show later, in establishing the conditions that would enable him to base his political conception of justice on strictly political grounds. That will require us to recognize that a liberal-democratic regime, if it must be agnostic in terms of morality and religion, cannot be agnostic concerning political values since by definition it asserts the principles that constitute its specificity *qua* political association, i.e., the political principles of equality and liberty.

Unfortunately, too many liberals want to identify political liberalism with the neutral state and do not understand that it is a mistaken and self-defeating strategy. Some, like Charles Larmore, even argue that the task of liberal theory is to provide a neutral justification of the neutrality of the state.[18] This can only reinforce a tendency already too much present in liberalism to transform political problems into administrative and technical ones, and it chimes with theories of neo-conservatives, like Niklas Luhmann, who want to restrict the field of democratic decisions by turning more and more areas over to the control of supposedly neutral experts.

To be sure, Rawls does not endorse those claims to neutrality and, as we have seen, his theory of justice is getting increasingly loaded with values. By subordinating the rational to the reasonable,[19] he has drastically limited the field of exercise of the rational choice approach. The original position no longer expresses a point of view of neutrality but reflects the ideals implicit in the public culture of a democratic society, and the parties, in their deliberation, are now guided by the exercise and development of their two moral powers. Moreover—against Larmore—Rawls insists that the aim of a theory of justice is not to create merely a *modus-vivendi* but an overlapping consensus on shared principles of justice that imply the realization of political values. He wants to steer a course "between the Hobbesian strand in liberalism—liberalism as a *modus vivendi* secured by a convergence of self- and group-interests as coordinated and balanced by well-designed constitutional arrangements—and a liberalism founded on a comprehensive moral doctrine such as that of Kant or Mill."[20]

Justice and the Political

Despite the fact that I sympathize with Rawls's assertion that we should start from our democratic tradition to elaborate a conception of justice instead of trying to look for a point of view exterior to our historical insertion in order to reach supposedly "true" ahistorical principles, I consider his approach to be inadequate. The reason lies, I believe, in the unsatisfactory notion of the political that we find in his work. As far as politics is present at all in Rawls, it is reduced to the "politics of interest," i.e., the pursuit of differing interests defined previously and independently of their possible articulation by competing alternative discourses. The aim of his theory of justice is to regulate that pursuit by establishing agreed-upon, neutral rules. Of course those rules have for Rawls a moral character, so his conception is not a purely instrumentalist one; there should be moral limits imposed to the search for self-interest. But between the "reasonable" and the "rational" there is no space left for something properly political, whose nature we could establish independently of morality or economics. The term might be present—and increasingly so—in his writings but only in some kind of negative way to specify a form of morality which is not based on a comprehensive doctrine and that applies only to certain areas.

We are told that "the first feature of a political conception of justice is that, while such a conception is, of course, a moral conception, it is a moral conception worked out for a specific kind of subject, namely, for political, social and economic institutions" and that "the second feature complements the first: a political conception is not to be understood as a general and comprehensive moral conception that applies to the political order."[21] Until now nothing has been said in a positive way about the specific nature of the political. Finally Rawls introduces the third feature of a political conception of justice: "[I]t is not formulated in terms of a general and comprehensive religious, philosophical or moral doctrine but rather in terms of certain fundamental intuitive ideas viewed as latent in the public political culture of a democratic society."[22] So we are left with the intuitive ideas to understand in what sense a conception of justice is political. On the other side, as we have seen before, the two main intuitive ideas from which he starts are that society is a fair system of social cooperation and that citizens are free and equal moral persons. Since for Rawls citizens are free and equal in virtue of their possession of two moral powers: (1) capacity for a sense of justice and (2) capacity for a conception of the good,[23] we are still within the discourse of morality and his conception of citizenship is hardly a political one.

After presenting his theory of justice as a contribution to moral philosophy, Rawls later declared that it should better be seen as a part of political philosophy.[24] The problem is that since the beginning Rawls has been using a mode of reasoning which is specific to moral discourse and whose effects when applied to the field of politics is to reduce it to a rational process of negotiation among private interests under the constraints of morality. So conflicts, antagonisms, relations of power, forms of subordination and repression simply disappear and we are faced with a typically liberal vision of a plurality of interests that can be regulated without need for a level superior to political decision and where the question of sovereignty is evacuated. As Carl Schmitt pointed out, "[L]iberal concepts typically move between ethics and economics. From that polarity they attempt to annihilate the political as a domain of conquering power and repression."[25] To think politics in terms of moral language, as Rawls does, necessarily leads to neglect of the role played by conflict, power and interest.

225 Analyzing the differences between moral discourse and political

discourse from a Wittgensteinian perspective, Hanna Pitkin indicates that—while both concern human action—political discourse alone concerns public action. One of the crucial questions at stake is the creation of a collective identity, a "we." In the question "What shall we do?" the "we" is not given, but constitutes a problem. Since in political discourse there is always disagreement about the possible courses of action, the identity of the "we" that is going to be created through a specific form of collective action might indeed be seen as the central question. For Pitkin, "Moral discourse is personal dialogue; political discourse concerns a public, a community, and takes place among the members generally. Thus it requires a plurality of viewpoints from which to begin; and the interaction of these varied perspectives, their reconciliation into a single public policy, though that reconciliation will always be temporary, partial and provisional."[26]

Political discourse attempts to create specific forms of unity among different interests by relating them to a common project and by establishing a frontier to define the forces to be opposed, the "enemy." Schmitt is right to affirm "the phenomenon of the political can be understood only in the context of the ever present possibility of the friend-and-enemy groupings, regardless of the aspects which this possibility implies for morality, aesthetics and economics."[27] In politics the public interest is always a matter of debate and a final agreement can never be reached; to imagine such a situation is to dream of a society without politics. One should not hope for the elimination of disagreement but for its containment within forms that respect the existence of liberal-democratic institutions. As Pitkin argues, "[W]hat characterizes political life is precisely the problem of continually creating unity, a public, in a context of diversity, rival claims and conflicting interests. In the absence of rival claims and conflicting interests, a topic never enters the political realm; no political decision needs to be made. But for the political collectivity, the 'we' to act, those continuing claims and interests must be resolved in a way that continues to preserve the collectivity."[28]

Such a view of the political is completely lacking in Rawls who takes for granted the existence of a common rational self-interest on which the citizens acting as free and equal moral persons can agree and ground principles of justice. He seems to believe that disagreements only concern religious and philosophical questions and that by avoiding those controversial issues it should be possible to reach a consensus on the way the basic institutions of society should be organized. He is so confident that there is only one solution to this problem, and that rational persons deliberating within the constraints of the reasonable and moved only by their rational advantage will choose his principles of justice that, he considers it would be enough for one person to calculate the rational self-interest of all. In that case, the process of deliberation is supererogatory.[29] Politics is not affected by the existence of pluralism which Rawls understands only as the multiplicity of the conceptions of the good that people exercise in the private sphere, separated perfectly from the public sphere where consensus based on self-interest reigns. This is the perfect liberal utopia. As current controversies about abortion clearly show, pluralism does not mean that all those conflicting conceptions of the good will coexist peacefully without trying to intervene in the public sphere, and the frontier between public and private is not given once and for all but constructed and constantly shifting. Moreover at any moment "private" affairs can witness the emergence of antagonisms and thereby become politicized. Therefore Rawls's "well-ordered society" rests on the elimination of the very idea of the political.

There is another way in which the political is absent in Rawls: it is the political understood as symbolic ordering of social relations, the aspect of "politics in the profound sense, as the ensemble of human relations in their real, social structure, in their ability to construct the world."[30] It is within such an approach, which renews with the classical type of political philosophy and enquires about the different forms of society, the "regimes" (in the Greek sense of *politeia*), that we can throw light on some problems left unresolved by Rawls. First, what he calls the "fact of pluralism" is much more than the mere consequence of the acceptance of the principle of toleration; it is the expression of a symbolic mutation: the democratic revolution understood as the end of a hierarchical type of society organized around a single substantive conception of the common good, grounded either in Nature or in God. As Claude Lefort has shown, modern democratic society is constituted "as a society in which Power, Law and Knowledge are exposed to a radical indeterminacy, a society that has become the theatre of an uncontrollable adventure."[31] The absence of power embodied in the person of the prince and tied to a transcendental instance preempts the existence of a final guarantee or source of legitimation; society can no longer be defined as a substance having an organic identity and democracy is characterized by the "dissolution of the landmarks of certainty."[32] In a modern democratic society there can no longer be a substantial unity, and division must be recognized as constitutive. Rawls is indeed right in arguing that "we must abandon the hope of a political community if by such a community we mean a political society united in affirming a general and comprehensive doctrine."[33] But this is a characteristic feature of the new ordering of social relations and not a consequence to be drawn from the "fact" of pluralism. If Rawls had possessed such an understanding of the political and been able to see the democratic tradition not as a simple collection of shared meanings, institutions and intuitive ideas but as a specific mode of institution of the social, he would have realized that there could never be, in a modern democracy, a final agreement on a single set of principles of justice.

Second, the vague notion of "intuitive ideas" can be reformulated so as to give equality and freedom a very different status. I agree with Rawls that a theory of justice in a modern democracy should be focused on how to realize liberty and equality in our institutions, but it is because those are the political principles of the liberal-democratic regime. Those principles command a certain type of ordering of the relations that people establish between themselves and their world; they give a specific form to democratic society, shape its institutions, its practices, its political culture; they make possible the constitution of a certain type of individual, create specific forms of political subjectivity and construe particular modes of identities. If equality and liberty are central signifiers for us, it is due to the fact that we have been constructed as subjects in a democratic society whose regime and tradition has put those values at the center of social life. Without such an understanding of the political as "disciplinary matrix" of the social (to borrow a term from Thomas Kuhn) it is impossible to go further than the very vague notions of "shared meanings" and "intuitive ideas" and the empirical generalizations that they imply.

Justice and Hegemony

Liberty and equality constitute the political principles of a liberal democratic regime and should be at the core of a theory of justice in a modern democracy. But there are many possible interpretations of those principles, the type of social relations where they should apply, and their mode of institutionalization. Rawls's claim that he has found the rational solution to this question has to be rejected outright, for there cannot be such a solution, providing an undisputed and "publicly recognized point of view from which all citizens can examine before one another whether or not their political and social institutions are just."[34] It is the very characteristic of modern democracy to impede such a final fixation of the social order and to preclude the possibility for a discourse to establish a definite suture. Different discourses will, indeed, attempt to dominate the field of discursivity and create nodal points through the practice of articulation, but they can only succeed in temporarily fixing meaning.

Part of the struggle characteristic of modern politics is to constitute a certain order, to fix social relations around nodal points, but successes are necessarily partial and precarious because of the permanence of antagonistic forces. Discourses about justice are part of that struggle because, by proposing competing interpretations of the principles of liberty and equality, they provide grounds of legitimation for different types of demands, create particular forms of identification, and shape political forces. In other words, they play an important role in the establishment of a specific hegemony and in construing the meaning of "citizenship" at a given moment. A successful hegemony signifies a period of relative stabilization and the creation of a widely shared "common sense," but such an overlapping consensus is to be distinguished from the Archimedian point of rational agreement that Rawls is searching. Far from providing the final, rational solution to the problem of justice—which in a modern democracy is bound to remain a permanent, unresolved question—Justice as Fairness is only one among the possible interpretations of the political principles of equality and liberty. To be sure, it is a progressive interpretation and in the context of the aggressive reassertion of neo-liberalism and its attacks against welfare rights and the widening of the field of equality, Rawls's intentions are commendable; but it must be seen as an intervention in an ongoing debate and cannot pretend to a privileged status with respect to other more or less radical interpretations. The emphasis put on the rational choice procedure might be of rhetorical value—given the current intellectual context—and it might even produce political effects, but it is no guarantee of objectivity.

Rawls has been accused of collapsing justice into equality and of presenting an equalitarian vision far from faithful to the shared meanings dominant in the United States. But that is not the point, and the problem is not how well he reflects the actual values of the Americans since what is really at stake is their transformation. As John Schaar has argued, Rawls proposes "a basic shift in our operative definition of equality and he wants to move away from our present understanding of equality of opportunity."[35] He proposes a new articulation that could—if successful—redefine the "common sense" of liberal democracies and give a new meaning to citizenship. I believe it is an important task and that we need today a political conception of justice that could provide a pole of identification for democratic forces as well as a new language of citizenship to confront the individualistic conceptions based on efficiency or individual liberty of the Hayek or Nozick type.

But if we agree to approach Rawls's theory from that angle, the real question that we should ask is how effective would it be in fulfilling such a role. The test for a discourse aiming at the establishment of new forms of articulation is its adequacy in creating a link between recognized principles and hitherto unformulated demands. Only if it manages to construct new subject positions can it have a real purchase on people's political identities. My impression is that, from that point of view, the chances of Justice as Fairness are not very good. It is a theory elaborated in the era of the "great society" and addressing a type of democratic politics which has been displaced in the following decades. New political subjects have emerged, new forms of identities and communities have been created, and a traditional type of social-democratic conception of justice exclusively centered around economic inequalities is unlikely to capture the imagination of the new social movements. A political conception of justice with little space for the new demands manifest in the women's movement, the gay movement, the ecological and anti-nuclear movements and the various anti-institutional movements, while aiming at defending and deepening ideals of liberty and equality present in our democratic culture, will not be in a position to create the overlapping consensus needed for the establishment of a new hegemony. One should also take account of the fact that a new ideological terrain has been defined by the attacks of the right against state intervention and bureaucratization and that it requires, for its deconstruction, a discursive strategy that can provide new forms of articulation for anti-state resistances. The shortcomings of Rawls on that count are all too evident since his theory of justice implies a great amount of state intervention.

In "Spheres of Justice," Michael Walzer proposes a pluralist conception of justice that I consider to be better suited to the defense of an egalitarian ideal today and more sensitive to the present political struggles. Walzer criticizes the ideal of "simple equality" because it would need continual state intervention and argues that "equality cannot be the goal of our politics unless we can describe it in a way that protects us against the modern tyranny of politics, against the domination of the party/state."[36] The solution of complex equality that he puts forward intends to avoid those problems by distinguishing different spheres of justice with their respective distributive principles. He states that the principles of justice should be pluralistic in form and that different goods should be distributed in accordance with different procedures and by different agents. Even if Walzer does not address directly the question posed by the demands of the new movements, his general approach could be useful to deal with those problems because, contrary to Rawls, he provides us with a pluralistic framework which is crucial for the formulation of an adequate theory of justice and conception of citizenship in the present stage of democratic politics.

Political Philosophy Without Foundations

Despite its shortcomings Rawls's theory of justice poses a series of very important questions for political philosophy. His very incapacity in providing a satisfactory answer to those questions

rawls: political philosophy without politics

is instructive of the limitations of the liberal approach and indicates the way towards a solution. The great merit of Rawls consists in stressing that in modern democratic societies, where there is no longer a single substantive common good and where pluralism is central, a political conception of justice cannot be derived from one particular religious, moral or philosophical conception of the good life. We should reject today the idea of a political community unified by an objective moral order for which some communitarians like Sandel are longing.

If the "priority of the right over the good" meant only that, it would be unobjectionable. The problem is that Rawls cannot accept that such a priority of the right is the consequence of the symbolic ordering of social relations characteristic of the liberal-democratic regime and is therefore derivative of an idea of the good, the political principles that define it as a political association. I think that the reasons are twofold. As I have argued, the political, properly speaking, is absent in Rawls and the very notion of regime as *politeia* is precluded; secondly his reliance on a liberal individualistic conception of the subject impedes him from thinking of the subject as discursively constructed through the multiplicity of language games in which a social agent participates. The subject in Rawls remains an origin, it exists independent of the social relations in which it is inscribed.

To be sure, he now insists that what he says about the original position only concerns us *qua* citizens and that it does not imply a full-fledged theory of the self. But the problem is that even the way he addresses our nature *qua* citizens is inadequate and does not recognize that a certain type of citizenship is the result of given practices, discourses and institutions. For Rawls, equality and liberty are properties of human beings *qua* moral persons. Against Dworkin's interpretation in terms of natural right,[37] he affirms that justice as fairness is not a "right-based" but a "conception-based" or "ideal-based" theory since it is based on intuitive ideas that reflect ideals implicit or latent in a public culture of a democratic society.[38] But, as we have seen, those intuitive ideas are never attributed any concrete status, nor are they put in relation with the principles of the regime. No explanation is ever given as to why we happen to have those ideas. Rawls seems to reject the idea of "natural rights" while being unable to accept that it is only *qua* citizens of a certain type of political community that we have rights; so his whole conception stands in a vacuum.

My guess is that he has been trying to move away from a universalistic, individualistic and natural right type of liberal discourse but has not yet succeeded in replacing it with a satisfactory alternative because of his incapacity to think of the collective aspect of human existence as constitutive. The

231

individual remains the *terminus a quo* and the *terminus ad quem* and that prevents him from conceptualizing the political. I think that it is in that context that one should understand his conflation of political discourse with moral discourse and his evasion of the central political notions of power, conflict, division, antagonism and sovereignty, as well as the values that can be realized in collective action.

As a result, what Rawls presents as political philosophy is simply a specific type of moral philosophy, a public morality to regulate the basic structure of society. Indeed, he asserts that "the distinction between political conceptions of justice and other moral conceptions is a matter of scope; that is the range of subject to which a conception applies, and the wider content a wider range requires."[39] That is exactly where the problem lies, because I believe that the distinction should be one of nature, not merely of scope. A modern political philosophy should articulate political values, the values that can be realized through collective action and through common belonging to a political association. Its subject matter is the ethics of the political which should be distinguished from morality.

But Rawls's conception precisely precludes such an understanding of political philosophy: there is no room for a notion of the political common good, no place for a really political definition of citizenship, and he can only conceive of citizens as free and equal moral persons engaged in fair terms of social cooperation. Here his communitarian critics who want to revive the ideals of civic republicanism do have a point. Such a tradition could help us to restore some dignity to political participation and go beyond the liberal conception that can only identify citizenship with the possession of rights or moral powers.

There is nevertheless a danger that needs to be avoided; we cannot go back to a premodern conception and sacrifice the individual to the citizen. A modern conception of citizenship should respect pluralism and individual liberty; every attempt to reintroduce a moral community, to go back to a *"universitas,"* is to be resisted. One task of a modern democratic political philosophy, as I see it, is to provide us with a language to articulate individual liberty with political liberty so as to construe new subject positions and create different citizens' identities. I consider that a theory of justice has an important role to play in such an endeavor because as Aristotle already noted "participation in a common understanding of justice makes a polis."[40] Nevertheless it should not be forgotten that under modern conditions the most that a theory of justice can aspire to is to cement an hegemony, to establish a frontier, to provide a pole of identification around a certain conception of citizenship but in a field necessarily crisscrossed by antagonisms where it will be confronted by opposing forces and competing definitions.

Political philosophy in a modern democratic society should not be a search for foundations but the elaboration of a language providing us with metaphoric redescriptions of our social relations. By presenting us with different interpretations of the democratic ideal of liberty and equality it will not supply metaphysical foundations for the liberal-democratic regime (they cannot exist and it does not need any) but it could help us to defend democracy by deepening and extending the range of democratic practices through the creation of new subject positions within a democratic matrix.

Rawls's theory of justice—even if he is not fully aware of it—belongs to such a struggle and despite all its limitations there is a lot in it which is of value for the advance of democracy. His defense of political liberalism should be reformulated within a discourse that would articulate it with some themes of classical political philosophy and with the valorization of politics of the civic republican tradition. To recognize the Aristotelian insight that a person is a *zoon politikon* does not commit us necessarily to a teleological and essentialist conception. Several contemporary theoretical currents converge in stressing how participation in a community of language is the *sine qua non* of the construction of human identity and allow us to formulate the social and political nature of a person in a non-essentialist way. It should therefore be possible to combine the defense of pluralism and the priority of right characteristic of modern democracy with a revalorization of the political, understood as collective participation in a public sphere where interests are confronted, conflicts sorted out, divisions exposed, confrontations staged, and in that way—as Machiavelli was the first to recognize—liberty secured.

Collège International de Philosophie

ENDNOTES

1.   Richard Rorty, "Habermas and Lyotard on Postmodernity," in **Habermas and Modernity**, ed. Richard J. Bernstein (Oxford 1985), p. 162.

2.   For this distinction see Hans Blumenberg, **The Legitimacy of the Modern Age** (MIT Press 1983).

3.   Richard Rorty, "Postmodernist Bourgeois Liberalism," **The Journal of Philosophy**, Vol. LXXX, No. 10 (October 1983), p. 585.

4.   Brian Barry, **The Liberal Theory of Justice**, (Oxford 1973), p. 166.

5. John Rawls, **A Theory of Justice**, (Oxford 1971), p. 11.

6. John Rawls, "Kantian Constructivism in Moral Theory," **Journal of Philosophy** 77, 9 (September 1980), p. 518).

7. *Ibid.*, p. 519.

8. John Rawls, "The Idea of an Overlapping Consensus," **Oxford Journal of Legal Studies**, Volume 7 No. 1, Spring 1987, p. 12.

9. John Rawls, "Justice as Fairness: Political not Metaphysical," **Philosophy and Social Affairs**, Summer 1985, Volume 14 No. 3, p. 225.

10. *Ibid.*, p. 235.

11. Rawls, **A Theory of Justice**, p. 303.

12. *Ibid.*, p. 302.

13. Rawls, "Justice as Fairness: Political not Metaphysical," p. 237, note 20.

14. Charles Taylor, **Philosophy and the Human Sciences**, Philosophical Papers 2, (Cambridge 1985), p. 309.

15. Michael Sandel, **Liberalism and the Limits of Justice**, (Cambridge 1982) and "Morality and the Liberal Ideal," **New Republic**, May 7, 1984. For a more detailed critique of Sandel see my article "Le libéralisme américain et ses critiques," **Esprit**, March 1987, Paris.

16. William A. Glaston, "Moral Personality and Liberal Theory," **Political Theory**, Vol. 10, No. 4, November 1982, p. 506.

17. *Ibid.*, p. 498.

18. Charles Larmore, **Patterns of Moral Complexity**, (Cambridge 1987).

19. This distinction is introduced by Rawls in "Kantian Constructivism in Moral Theory" to specify the two elements of any notion of social cooperation: the Reasonable refers to a conception of the fair terms of social cooperation and articulates an idea of reciprocity and mutuality; the Rational corresponds to the other element and expresses a conception of each participant's rational advantage.

20. Rawls, "The Idea of an Overlapping Consensus," p. 23.

21. *Ibid.*, p. 3.

22. *Ibid.*, p. 6.

23. Rawls, "Justice as Fairness: Political not Metaphysical," p. 226 ff.

24. *Ibid.*, p. 224, note 2.

25. Carl Schmitt, **The Concept of the Political**, (Rutgers 1976), p. 71.

26. Hanna Fenichel Pitkin, **Wittgenstein and Justice**, (Berkeley 1972), p. 216.

27. Schmitt, p. 35.

28. Pitkin, p. 215.

29. Rawls declares: "To begin with, it is clear that since the differences among the parties are unknown to them, and everyone is equally rational and similarly situated, each is convinced by the same arguments. Therefore, we can view the choice in the original position from the standpoint of one person selected at random" (**A Theory of Justice**, p. 139). As Bernard Manin has pointed out, what Rawls calls deliberation is a simple process of calculation. See B. Manin "Volonté générale ou délibération?", **Le Débat**, No. 33, January 1985, Paris.

30. Roland Barthes, **Mythologies**, (Paris 1957), p. 230.

31. Claude Lefort, **The Political Forms of Modern Society** (Oxford 1986), p. 305.

32. Claude Lefort, **Essais sur le Politique** (Paris 1986), p. 29.

33. John Rawls, "The Idea of an Overlapping Consensus," p. 10.

34. John Rawls, "Justice as Fairness: Political not Metaphysical," p. 229.

35. John Schaar, **Legitimacy in the Modern State** (Transaction Books, 1981), p. 214.

36. Michael Walzer, **Spheres of Justice**, (New York 1983), p. 316.

37. Ronald Dworkin, **Taking Rights Seriously**, (Harvard 1977), chapter 6.

38. John Rawls, "Justice as Fairness: Political not Metaphysical," p. 236.

39. John Rawls, "The priority of Right and Idea of the Good in Justice as Fairness" mimeographed paper given to the conference in Paris on **A Theory of Justice** on March 21, 1987, p. 2.

40. Aristotle, **Politics**, book I, chapter II, 1253a15.

235

hubert l. dreyfus
stuart e. dreyfus
what is morality?
a phenomenological
account of the development
of ethical expertise[1]

This paper will seek to show that phenomenology has much to contribute to contemporary discussion concerning which has priority, a detached critical morality based on principles that tells us what is **right** or an ethics based on involvement in a tradition that determines what is **good**. This new confrontation between Kant and Hegel, between *Moralität* and *Sittlichkeit*,[2] has produced two camps which can be identified with Jürgen Habermas and John Rawls, on the one hand, and Bernard Williams and Charles Taylor, on the other. The same polarity appears in feminism where the Kohlberg scale, which defines the highest stage of moral maturity as the ability to stand outside the situation and justify one's actions in terms of universal moral principles, is attacked by Carol Gilligan in the name of an intuitive response to the concrete situation.

What one chooses to investigate as the relevant phenomena will prejudice from the start where one stands on these important issues. If one adopts the traditional approach one will focus on moral **judgments** and their **validity**. Thus, on the first page of his classic text, **The Moral Judgment of the Child**, Jean Piaget explicitly restricts ethics to judgments. "It is moral judgment that we propose to investigate, not moral behavior ...,"[3] and comes to the extreme cognitivist conclusion: "Logic is the morality of

hubert l.
dreyfus,
stuart e.
dreyfus

thought just as morality is the logic of action.... Pure reason [is] the arbiter both of theoretical reflection and daily practice."[4] Jürgen Habermas identifies himself with this tradition when he endorses the Kohlberg/Piagetian claim that "moral consciousness expresses itself chiefly in judgments."[5]

This approach was linked with phenomenology by Maurice Mandelbaum in his book, **The Phenomenology of Moral Experience**:

The phenomenological approach's ... essential methodological conviction is that a solution to any of the problems of ethics must be reduced from, and verified by, a careful and direct examination of individual moral judgments.[6]

But Mandelbaum, like Piaget and Habermas, does not seem to realize that he has already made a fateful exclusionary move. He claims that: "Such an approach ... aims to discover the generic characteristics of **all** moral experience."[7]

Why equate moral experience with judgment, rather than with ethical comportment? Mandelbaum's answer to this question is symptomatic of the intellectualist prejudice embodied in this approach. He first gives a perceptive nod to the spontaneous ethical comportment:

I sense the embarrassment of a person, and turn the conversation aside; I see a child in danger and catch hold of its hand; I hear a crash and become alert to help.[8]

He then notes:

Actions such as these (of which our daily lives are in no small measure composed) do not ... seem to spring from the self: in such cases I am reacting directly and spontaneously to what confronts me.... [I]t is appropriate to speak of "reactions" and "responses," for in them no sense of initiative or feeling of responsibility is present.... [W]e can only say that we acted as we did because the situation extorted that action from us.[9]

Mandelbaum next contrasts this unthinking and egoless[10] response to the situation with deliberate action in which one experiences the causal power of the "I."

In "willed" action, on the other hand, the source of action is the self. I act in a specific manner because I wish, or will, to do so.... The "I" is experienced as a being responsible for willed action.[11]

238   He continues:

moral maturity   *To give a phenomenological account of this sense of responsibility is not difficult. It is grounded in the fact that every willed action aims at and espouses an envisioned goal.*[12]

And focusing on willed or deliberate action and its goal, we arrive at rationality.

*In willed actions ... we can give a **reason**: we acted as we did because we aimed to achieve a particular goal. [W]hen asked to explain our action, we feel no hesitation in attributing it to the value of the goal which we aimed to achieve.*[13]

Thus the phenomenology of moral experience comes to focus on judgment and justification. Granted that one aspect of the moral life and most of moral philosophy has been concerned with choice, responsibility, and justification of validity claims, we should, nonetheless, take seriously what Mandelbaum sees and immediately dismisses, viz., that our moral consciousness expresses itself chiefly in everyday ethical comportment which consists in unreflective, egoless responses to the current interpersonal situation. Why not begin our investigation of ethical experience on the level of this spontaneous coping?

Several methodological precautions must then be born in mind in attempting a phenomenology of the ethical life.

1.   We should begin by describing our everyday, ongoing ethical coping.

2.   We should determine under which conditions deliberation and choice appear.

3.   We should beware of making the typical philosophical mistake of reading the structure of deliberation and choice back into our account of everyday coping.

Since our everyday ethical skills seem to have been passed over and even covered up by moral philosophy, we had best begin with some morally neutral area of expertise and delineate its structure. To this end we will lay out a phenomenological description of five stages in the development of expertise, using driving and chess as examples. Only then will we turn to the much more difficult questions of the nature of ethical expertise, the place and character of moral judgments, and the stages of moral maturity.

* * *

239

hubert l.
dreyfus,
stuart e.
dreyfus

I. A Phenomenology of Skill Acquisition

Stage 1: Novice

Normally, the instruction process begins with the instructor decomposing the task environment into context-free features which the beginner can recognize without benefit of experience. The beginner is then given rules for determining actions on the basis of these features, like a computer following a program.

The student automobile driver learns to recognize such interpretation-free features as speed (indicated by the speedometer). Timing of gear shifts is specified in terms of speed.

The novice chess player learns a numerical value for each type of piece regardless of its position, and the rule: "Always exchange if the total value of pieces captured exceeds the value of pieces lost." But such rigid rules often fail to work. A loaded car stalls on a hill; a beginner in chess falls for every sacrifice.

Stage 2: Advanced beginner

As the novice gains experience actually coping with real situations, she begins to note, or an instructor points out, perspicuous examples of meaningful additional components of the situation. After seeing a sufficient number of examples, the student learns to recognize them. Instructional **maxims** now can refer to these new **situational aspects**. We use the terms **maxims** and **aspects** here to differentiate this form of instruction from the first, where strict **rules** were given as to how to respond to context-free **features**. Since maxims are phrased in terms of aspects they already presuppose experience in the skill domain.

The advanced beginner driver uses (situational) engine sounds as well as (non-situational) speed. He/she learns the maxim: shift up when the motor sounds like it is racing and down when it sounds like it is straining. No number of words can take the place of a few choice examples of racing and straining sounds.

Similarly, with experience, the chess student begins to recognize such situational aspects of positions as a weakened king's side or a strong pawn structure, despite the lack of precise definitional rules. She is then given maxims to follow, such as attack a weakened king's side.

Stage 3: Competence

With increasing experience, the number of features and aspects to be taken into account becomes overwhelming. To cope with this information explosion, the performer learns to adopt a hierarchical view of decision-making. By first choosing a plan, goal or perspective which organizes the situation and by then examining only the small set of features and aspects that she has learned are relevant given that plan, the performer can simplify and improve her performance.

A competent driver leaving the freeway on a curved off-ramp may, after taking into account speed, surface condition, criticality of time, etc., decide she is going too fast. She then has to decide whether to let up on the accelerator, remove her foot altogether, or step on the brake. She is relieved when she gets through the curve without a mishap and shaken if she begins to go into a skid.

The class A chess player, here classed as competent, may decide after studying a position that her opponent has weakened her king's defenses so that an attack against the king is a viable goal. If the attack is chosen, features involving weaknesses in her own position created by the attack are ignored as are losses of pieces inessential to the attack. Removing pieces defending the enemy king becomes salient. Successful plans induce euphoria and mistakes are felt in the pit of the stomach.

In both of these cases, we find a common pattern: detached planning, conscious assessment of elements that are salient with respect to the plan, and analytical rule-guided choice of action, followed by an emotionally involved experience of the outcome. The experience is emotional because choosing a plan, goal or perspective is no simple matter for the competent performer. Nobody gives her any rules for how to choose a perspective, so she has to make up various rules which she adopts or discards in various situations depending on how they work out. This procedure is frustrating, however, since each rule works on some occasions and fails on others, and no set of objective features and aspects correlates strongly with these successes and failures. Nonetheless the choice is unavoidable. Familiar situations begin to be accompanied by emotions such as hope, fear, etc., but the competent performer strives to suppress these feelings during her detached choice of perspective.

One of us, Stuart, knows all too well what it is to think like a competent chess player, as he is stuck at that level. He recalls:

I was always good at mathematics and took up chess as an outlet for that analytic talent. At college, where I captained the chess team, my players were mostly mathematicians and mostly, like me, at the competent level. At this point, a few of my teammates who were not mathematicians began to play fast chess at the rate of five or ten minutes a game, and also eagerly to play over the

hubert l.
dreyfus,
stuart e.
dreyfus

*great games of the grandmasters. I resisted. Fast chess was no fun for me, because it didn't give me time to **figure out** what to do. I found grandmaster games inscrutable, and since the record of the game seldom if ever gave principles explaining the moves, I felt there was nothing I could learn from the games. Some of my teammates, who through fast chess and game studying acquired a great deal of concrete experience, have gone on to become masters.*

Stage 4: Proficiency

As soon as the competent performer stops reflecting on problematic situations as a detached observer, and stops looking for principles to guide her actions, the gripping, holistic experiences from the competent stage become the basis of the next advance in her skill. Having experienced many emotion-laden situations, chosen plans in each, and having obtained vivid, emotional demonstrations of the adequacy or inadequacy of the plan, the performer involved in the world of the skill "notices," or "is struck by" a certain plan, goal or perspective. No longer is the spell of involvement broken by detached conscious planning.

Since there are generally far fewer "ways of seeing" than "ways of acting," after understanding without conscious effort what is going on, the proficient performer will still have to think about what to do. During this thinking, elements that present themselves as salient are assessed and combined by rule and maxim to produce decisions.

On the basis of prior experience, a proficient driver fearfully approaching a curve on a rainy day may sense that she is traveling too fast. Then, on the basis of such salient elements as visibility, angle of road bank, criticalness of time, etc., she decides whether to let up on the gas, take her foot off the gas or to step on the brake. (These factors were used by the **competent** driver to **decide that** she is speeding.)

The proficient chess player, who is classed a master, can discriminate a large repertoire of types of positions. Experiencing a situation as a field of conflicting forces and seeing almost immediately the sense of a position, she sets about calculating the move that best achieves her goal. She may, for example, know that she should attack, but she must deliberate about how best to do so.

Stage 5: Expertise

The proficient performer, immersed in the world of skillful activity, **sees** what needs to be done, but must **decide** how to do it. With enough experience with a variety of situations, all seen from the same perspective but requiring different tactical decisions, the proficient performer seems gradually to decompose this class of situations into subclasses, each of which share the same decision, single action, or tactic. This allows an immediate intuitive response to each situation.

The expert driver, generally without any awareness, not only knows by feel and familiarity when an action such as slowing down is required; she knows how to perform the action without calculating and comparing alternatives. She shifts gears when appropriate with no awareness of her acts. On the off ramp her foot simply lifts off the accelerator. What must be done, simply is done.

The expert chess player, classed as an international master or grandmaster, in most situations experiences a compelling sense of the issue and the best move. Excellent chess players can play at the rate of 5-10 seconds a move and even faster without any serious degradation in performance. At this speed they must depend almost entirely on intuition and hardly at all on analysis and comparison of alternatives. We recently performed an experiment in which an international master, Julio Kaplan, was required rapidly to add numbers presented to him audibly at the rate of about one number per second, while at the same time playing five-second-a-move chess against a slightly weaker, but master level, player. Even with his analytical mind completely occupied by adding numbers, Kaplan more than held his own against the master in a series of games. Deprived of the time necessary to solve problems or construct plans, Kaplan still produced fluid and strategic play.

It seems that beginners make judgments using strict rules and features, but that with talent and a great deal of involved experience the beginner develops into an expert who sees intuitively what to do without applying rules and making judgments at all. The intellectualist tradition has given an accurate description of the beginner and of the expert facing an unfamiliar situation, but normally an expert does not **deliberate**. She does not reason. She does not even act **deliberately**. She simply spontaneously does what has normally worked and, naturally, it normally works.

We are all experts at many tasks and our everyday coping skills function smoothly and transparently so as to free us to be aware of other aspects of our lives where we are not so skillful. That is why philosophers (with the exception of Aristotle) overlooked them for 2500 years, until pragmatism and existential phenomenology came along.

hubert l.
dreyfus,
stuart e.
dreyfus

John Dewey introduced the distinction between knowing-how and knowing-that to call attention to just such thoughtless mastery of the everyday:

*We may ... be said to **know how** by means of our habits.... We walk and read aloud, we get off and on street cars, we dress and undress, and do a thousand useful acts without thinking of them. We know something, namely, how to do them.... [I]f we choose to call [this] knowledge ... then other things also called knowledge, knowledge **of** and **about** things, knowledge **that** things are thus and so, knowledge that involves reflection and conscious appreciation, remains of a different sort ...* [14]

Heidegger calls our transparent dealing with ready-to-hand equipment, circumspection, and considers it our basic way of being-in-the-world.[15] We should try to impress on ourselves what a huge amount of our lives—working, getting around, talking, eating, driving, and responding to the needs of others—manifest know-how, and what a small part is spent in the deliberate, effortful, subject/object mode of activity which requires knowing-that. Yet deliberate action and its extreme form, deliberation, are the ways of acting we tend to notice, and so are the only ones that have been studied in detail by philosophers.

II. Implications of the Phenomenology of Expertise for Ethical Experience

The rest of this paper is based on a double conditional: If the skill model we have proposed is correct and if everyday ethical comportment is a form of expertise, we should expect ethical expertise to exhibit a developmental structure similar to that which we have described above. On analogy with chess and driving it would seem that the budding ethical expert would learn at least some of the ethics of her community by following strict rules, would then go on to apply contextualized maxims, and, in the highest stage, would leave rules and principles behind and develop more and more refined spontaneous ethical responses.

To take a greatly oversimplified and dramatic example, a child at some point might learn the rule: never lie. Faced with the dilemma posed by Kant—an avowed killer asking the whereabouts of the child's friend—the child might tell the truth. After experiencing regret and guilt over the death of the friend, however, the child would move toward the realization that the rule, "Never lie," like the rule "Shift at ten miles per hour," needs to be contextualized, and would seek maxims to turn to in different typical situations. Such a maxim might be, "Never lie except when someone might be seriously hurt by telling the truth." Of course, this maxim too will, under some circumstances, lead to regret. Finally, with enough experience, the ethical expert would learn to tell the truth or lie, depending upon the situation, without appeal to rules and maxims.

Since we are assuming that such a spontaneous response exhibits ethical expertise, the parallel with chess and driving expertise raises two difficult questions: (1) What is **ethical** expertise? and (2) How does one learn it? In driving and chess there is a clear criterion of expertise. In chess one either wins or loses, in driving one makes it around a curve or skids off the road. But what, one may well ask, counts as success or failure in ethics? It seems that in ethics what counts as expert performance is doing what those who already are accepted as ethical experts do and approve. Aristotle tells us: "What is best is not evident except to the good man" (VI.12). This is circular but not viciously so.[16]

Learning exhibits the same circularity. To become an expert in any area of expertise one has to be able to respond to the same types of situations as similar as do those who are already expert. For example, to play master level chess one has to respond to the same similarities as masters. This basic ability is what one calls having talent in a given domain. In addition, the learner must experience the appropriate satisfaction or regret at the outcome of her response. To become an expert driver one should feel fear not elation as one skids around a curve. Likewise, to acquire ethical expertise one must have the talent to respond to those ethical situations as similar that ethical experts respond to as similar, and one must have the sensibility to experience the socially appropriate sense of satisfaction or regret at the outcome of one's action.[17]

There is one further problem. In activities such as driving or chess one gets immediate feedback as to the adequacy or inadequacy of one's actions. This presumably acts directly, i.e., without reflection, to cause the synaptic charges in the brain which constitute learning. But this raises the further questions: How does one learn from successes and failures in ethical situations where outcomes are observed only much later? Does one engage in **detached reflection** on one's feelings of satisfaction or regret? If our account of skill acquisition is correct, there are two reasons why an expert cannot improve future performance by **abstract** reflection on previous situations, actions and outcomes.

(1) If one reflected in a detached way, one's brain presumably would not modify the way the already experienced type of situation was paired with an action. The past situation has presumably been responded to in terms of the emotionally charged way it presented itself to an involved agent, so to modify a past response the agent has to **feel** satisfaction or regret, not

just **judge** a past action was praiseworthy or condemnable. Thus the ability to remember with involvement the original situation while emotionally experiencing one's success or failure is required if one is to learn to be an ethical expert.

(2) Detached reflection typically asks the philosophical question: What was it about the previous action that made it satisfying or regrettable? This is like the competent chess player trying to figure out what principles of chess theory explain why a master made a particular move, or why her own failed. One might discover, for example, that in an ethical situation one had treated a person as a means rather than as an end, and conjecture that violating the principle, never treat a person as a means, accounted for one's regret. But, as we have seen in the case of chess, in the next situation when one applies the principle one may well lose the game, or, in the case of ethical action, still feel regret. This is not because it is difficult to determine which features define membership in the right similarity set, nor because it is hard to find the principles which lead to expert action. Rather, as far as anyone knows, there just aren't any such features and principles. It is an unsubstantiated assumption of philosophers since Socrates that there must be a theory underlying every skill domain. The failure of expert systems based on the assumption that expertise is produced by principles and inferences, suggests that there is no such theory.[18] As we have seen in the case of chess, the search for principles is not only fruitless, it blocks further development.

Once he has abandoned principles and acquired experience, we would expect the ethical expert to respond instinctively and appropriately to each ethical situation. Like a good phenomenologist dedicated to "saving the phenomena," Aristotle stays close to normal everyday experience and sees the immediate, intuitive response, precisely as characteristic of an expert. "Know-how *[techné]* does not deliberate" he says in the **Physics** (Bk. II, Ch. 8). Dewey repeats his insight when he brings his distinction between knowing-how and knowing-that to bear on ethical issues:

*As Aristotle pointed out ... it takes a fine and well-grounded character to **react immediately** with the right approvals and condemnations.*[19]

Yet even Aristotle seems, in this area, to be corrupted by intellectualism. When it comes to ethics, he seems to make the philosophical mistake of reading the structure of deliberation, in which one does indeed choose and pursue a goal, back into skillful coping. In **The Nichomachean Ethics**, he tells us that to act justly or temperately the agent "must choose the acts, and choose them **for their own sakes.**"[20] "Choice" here could be given a non-intellectualist reading as meaning responding to the situation by doing one thing rather than another. But that still leaves the troubling claim that the action must be done for its own sake. It seems that according to Aristotle there must be something the agent is attempting to achieve. This is like saying that good chess players and drivers should be praised or blamed not for their brilliant intuitive responses, but only for what they were **trying** to do. But as we have seen there may be no intentional content which determines under what aspect we are to judge an action. We can tell if a person is courageous, for example, not by inspecting his or her intentions, but only by seeing his or her spontaneous response in many situations.

In most contexts Aristotle can be interpreted as having understood this, but many commentators seem to go out of their way to emphasize Aristotle's intellectualism. Alasdair MacIntyre, for example, who is willing to correct Aristotle where necessary, tells us that according to Aristotle: "The genuinely virtuous agent … acts on the basis of a true and rational judgment."[21] Indeed, in MacIntyre's account of the virtuous life, the moral agent is reduced to a competent performer deliberately choosing among maxims.

In practical **reasoning** the possession of [an adequate sense of the tradition to which one belongs] … appears in the kind of capacity for **judgment** which the agent possesses in knowing how to **select** among the relevant stack of **maxims** and how to **apply them** in particular situations. [22]

Perhaps MacIntyre accepts this view, which would seem to undermine his own neo-Aristotelian position, because he has not understood the nature of intuitive skills. It may be no coincidence that his description of chess expertise sees it as "a certain highly particular kind of analytical skill."[23]

We have shown so far that everyday intuitive ethical expertise, which Aristotle saw was formed by the sort of daily practice that produces good character, has been, from Aristotle himself to Mandelbaum and MacIntyre, passed over by philosophers, or, if recognized, distorted by reading back into it the mental content found in deliberation. It would be a mistake, however, to become so carried away by the success of spontaneous coping as to deny an important place to deliberative judgment. Getting deliberation right is half of what phenomenology has to contribute to the study of ethical expertise. One should not conclude from the pervasiveness of egoless, situation-governed comportment, that reflection is always disruptive and always produces inferior practices.

**hubert l.
dreyfus,
stuart e.
dreyfus**

Expert deliberation is not inferior to intuition, but neither is it a self-sufficient mental activity that can dispense with intuition.

The intellectualist account of self-sufficient cognition fails to distinguish the **involved** deliberation of an intuitive expert facing a **familiar** but problematic situation from the **detached** deliberation of an expert facing a **novel** situation in which she has no intuition and can at best resort to abstract principles. A chess master confronted with a chess problem, constructed precisely so as not to resemble a position that would show up in a normal game, is reduced to using analysis. Likewise, an ethical expert when confronted with cases of "life-boat morality" may have to fall back on ethical principles. But since **principles** were unable to produce expert behavior for the competent performer, it should be no surprise if falling back on them produces inferior responses. The resulting decisions are necessarily crude since they have not been refined by the experience of the results of a variety of intuitive responses to emotion-laden situations and the learning that comes from subsequent satisfaction and regret. Therefore, in familiar but problematic situations, rather than standing back and applying abstract principles, the expert deliberates about the appropriateness of her **intuitions**. As common as this form of deliberation is, little has been written about such buttressing of intuitive understanding, probably because detached, principle-based, deliberation is often incorrectly seen as the only alternative to intuition. Let us turn again to the phenomenon.

Sometimes, but not often, an intuitive decision-maker finds herself torn between two equally compelling decisions. Presumably this occurs when the current situation lies near the boundary between two discriminable types of situations, each with its own associated action. Occasionally one can compromise between these two actions, but often they are incompatible. Only a modified understanding of the current situation can break the tie, so the decision-maker will delay if possible and seek more information. If a decision-maker can afford the time, the decision will be put off until something is learned that leaves only one action intuitively compelling. As Dewey puts it:

[T]he only way out [of perplexity] is through examination, inquiry, turning things over in [the] mind till something presents itself, perhaps after prolonged mental fermentation, to which [the good person] can directly react. [24]

Even when an intuitive decision seems obvious, it may not be the best. Dewey cautions:

[An expert] is set in his [sic] ways, and his immediate appreciations travel in the grooves laid down by his

moral maturity

unconsciously formed habits. Hence the spontaneous "intuitions" of value have to be entertained subject to correction, to confirmation and revision, by personal observation of consequences and cross-questioning of their quality and scope.[25]

When deeply involved, one views a situation from one perspective. One sees certain elements as salient and entertains certain expectations. As the situation develops, elements may gain or lose prominence; as these prominences evolve, the perceived situation changes. Finally the decision-maker clearly grasps the problem and sees what must be done. Her clear-sightedness is the result of a long chain of events, each gradually modifying her understanding. If any event in the chain had presented itself differently, even slightly, subsequent events would have been viewed differently, and a different chain of interpretation, culminating in an entirely different "obvious" decision, might have resulted. For that reason two experts, even though they share a common background, can, due to some seemingly trivial different experiences, come to very different conclusions. And, although on our model agreement is by no means a necessary result of expert deliberation, disagreement does suggest that further discussion may be in order.

Aware that her current clear perception may well be the result of a chain of perspectives with one or more questionable links and so might harbor the dangers of tunnel vision, the wise intuitive decision-maker will attempt to dislodge her current understanding. She will do so by attempting to re-experience the chain of events that led her to see things the way she does, and at each stage she will intentionally focus upon elements not originally seen as important to see if there is an alternative intuitive interpretation. If current understanding cannot be dislodged in this way, the wise decision-maker will enter into dialogue with those who have reached different conclusions. Each will recount a narrative that leads to seeing the current situation in her way and so demanding her response. Each will try to see things the other's way. This may result in one or the other changing her mind and, therefore, in final agreement. But, since various experts have different past experiences, there is no reason why they should finally agree. The most that can be claimed for universalization is that, given the shared *Sittlichkeit* underlying their expertise, two experts, even when they do not agree, should be able to understand and appreciate each other's decisions. This is as near as expert ethical judgments can or need come to impartiality and universality.

III. Current Relevance

249

But, one might ask, so what? Transparent, spontaneous, ethical

hubert l.
dreyfus,
stuart e.
dreyfus

coping might, indeed, occur, but why not begin our philosophical analysis where the tradition has always begun—where there is something interesting to describe, viz., moral judgments, validity claims, and justification? Still, before passing over everyday coping as philosophically irrelevant, we should remember that getting the story right about action and mind had huge consequences for the pretensions of a new discipline that calls itself cognitive science. Concentrating on representations, rules, reasoning and problem solving, cognitivists passed over but presupposed a more basic level of coping, and this blindness is now resulting in what more and more researchers are coming to recognize as the degeneration of their research program.[26] So it behooves us to ask: Does the passing over of ethical expertise have equally important practical implications?

We believe it does. The phenomenology of expertise allows us to sharpen up and take sides in an important contemporary debate. The debate centers on the ethical implications of Lawrence Kohlberg's cognitivist model of moral development. Kohlberg holds that the development of the capacity for moral judgment follows an invariant pattern. He distinguishes three levels. A Preconventional Level on which the agent tries to satisfy her needs and avoid punishment; a Conventional Level, during the first stage of which the agent conforms to stereotypical images of majority behavior; and a Postconventional and Principles Level. The highest stage of this highest level is characterized as follows:

Regarding what is right, Stage 6 is guided by universal ethical principles....These are not merely values that are recognized, but are also principles used to generate particular decisions. [27]

Jürgen Habermas has taken up Kohlberg's findings and modified them on the basis of his own discourse ethics, adding a seventh stage—acting upon universal procedural principles that make possible arriving at rational agreement through dialogue.

Charles Taylor has remarked that for Habermas, " 'Moral' defines a certain kind of reasoning, which in some unexplained way has in principle priority."[28] Kohlberg's developmental stages are supposed to explain the priority; they serve to give empirical support to Habermas's claim that detached moral reasoning develops out of and is superior to ethical intuition. As Habermas explains: "The stages of moral judgment form a hierarchy in that the cognitive structures of a higher stage dialectically 'sublate' those of the lower one."[29]

Habermas sees Kohlberg's work as evidence that moral consciousness begins with involved ethical comportment, but that the highest stages of moral consciousness require the moral maturity willingness and the ability to "consider moral questions from the hypothetical and disinterested perspective."[30] Thus, according to Habermas, Kohlberg's research lends empirical support to his modified, but still recognizable, Kantian view that the highest level of moral maturity consists in judging actions according to abstract, universal principles. He tells us that "The normative reference point of the developmental path that Kohlberg analyzes empirically is a principled morality in which we can recognize the main features of discourse ethics."[31]

It follows for Habermas that our Western European morality of abstract justice is developmentally superior to the ethics of any culture lacking universal principles. Furthermore, when the Kohlberg developmental scale is tested in empirical studies of the moral judgments of young men and women, it turns out that men are generally more mature than women.

In her book, **In a Different Voice**, Carol Gilligan contests this second result, claiming that the data on which it is based incorporates a male bias. She rests her objection on her analyses of responses to a moral dilemma used in Kohlberg's studies. She explains as follows:

The dilemma...was one in the series devised by Kohlberg to measure moral development in adolescence by presenting a conflict between moral norms and exploring the logic of its resolution....[A] man named Heinz considers whether or not to steal a drug which he cannot afford to buy, in order to save the life of his wife....[T]he description of the dilemma...is followed by the question, "Should Heinz steal the drug?" [32]

Kohlberg found that morally mature men, i.e., those who have reached stage 6, tended to answer that Heinz should steal the drug because the right to life is more basic than the right to private property. Women, however, seemed unable to deal with the dilemma in a mature, logical way. I quote from Gilligan's analysis of a typical case:

Seeing in the dilemma not a math problem...but a narrative of relationships that extends over time, Amy envisions the wife's continuing need for her husband and the husband's continuing concern for his wife and seeks to respond to the druggist's need in a way that would sustain rather than sever connection....

Seen in this light, her understanding of morality as arising from the **recognition** *of relationship, her* **belief** *in communication as the mode of conflict resolution, and her* **conviction** *that the solution to the dilemma will follow from its compelling* **representation** *seem far from naive or* **cognitively** *immature.* [33]

hubert l.
dreyfus,
stuart e.
dreyfus

The first point to note in responding to these interesting observations is that many women are "unable to verbalize or explain the rationale"[34] for their moral responses; they stay involved in the situation and trust their intuition. Many men, on the other hand, when faced with a moral problem, attempt to step back and articulate their principles as a way of deciding what to do. Yet as we have seen, principles can never capture the know-how an expert acquires by dealing with, and seeing the outcome of, a large number of concrete situations. Thus, when faced with a dilemma, the expert does not seek principles but, rather, reflects on and tries to sharpen his or her spontaneous intuitions by getting more information until one decision emerges as obvious. Gilligan finds the same phenomenon in her subjects' deliberations:

*The proclivity of women to reconstruct hypothetical dilemmas in terms of the real, **to request or to supply missing information** about the nature of the people and the places where they live, shifts their judgment away from the hierarchical ordering of principles and the formal procedures of decision making.* [35]

Gilligan, however, undermines what is radical and fascinating in her discoveries when she seeks her subjects **solutions** to **problems**, and tries to help them articulate the **principles** underlying these solutions. "Amy's moral **judgment** is **grounded** in the belief that, 'if somebody has something that would keep somebody alive, then it's not right not to give it to them',"[36] she tells us. Yet, if the phenomenology of skillful coping we have presented is right, principles and theories serve only for early stages of learning; no principle or theory "grounds" an expert ethical response, any more than in chess there is a theory or rule that explains a master-level move. As we have seen in the case of chess, recognizing that there is no way to ground one's intuitions in an explanation is an important step on the way to acquiring expertise.

As we would expect, Gilligan's intuitive subjects respond to philosophical questions concerning the principles justifying their actions with tautologies and banalities, e.g., that they try to act in such a way as to make the world a better place in which to live. They might as well say that their highest moral principle is "do something good." If Gilligan had not tried to get her intuitive subjects to formulate their principles for dealing with problems, but had rather investigated how frequently they **had** problems and how they deliberated about their spontaneous ethical comportment when they did, she might well have found evidence that moral maturity results in having fewer problems, and, when problems do arise, being able to act without detaching oneself from the concrete situation, thereby retaining one's ethical intuitions.

The second, and most important, point to consider is that Gilligan correctly detects in Amy's responses to the Heinz dilemma an entirely different approach to the ethical life than acting on universal principles. This is the different voice she is concerned to hear and to elaborate in her book. In answering her critics she makes clear that it is not the central point of her work that these two voices are gendered.

*The title of my book was deliberate, it reads, "in a **different** voice," not "in a **woman's** voice." ... I caution the reader that "this association is not absolute, and the contrasts between male and female voices are presented here to highlight a distinction between two modes of thought...rather than to represent a generalization about either sex."* [37]

She calls the two voices "the justice and care perspectives." [38] Under one description to be good is to be **principled**, on the other, it is to be **unprincipled**, i.e., without principles.

Although Gilligan does not make the point, it should be obvious to philosophers that we inherit the justice tradition from the Greeks, especially Socrates and Plato. It presupposes that two situations can be the same in the relevant moral respects, and requires principles which treat the same type of situation in the same way. The principle of universalizability thus becomes, with Kant, definitive of the moral. All of us feel the pull of this philosophical position when we seek to be fair, and when we are called upon to justify what we do as right, rather than merely what one happens to do in our society. Moreover, we seek universal principles guaranteeing justice and fairness as the basis of our social and political decisions.

The other voice carries the early Christian message that, as Saint Paul put it, "the law is fulfilled," so that henceforth to each situation we should respond with love. Proponents of this view sense that no two situations, and no two people, are ever exactly alike. Even a single individual is constantly changing, for, as one acquires experience, one's responses become constantly more refined. Thus there is no final answer as to what the appropriate response in a particular situation should be. Since two abstractly identical situations will elicit different responses, caring comportment will look like injustice to the philosopher but will look like compassion or mercy to the Christian. We feel the pull of these Christian caring practices when we respond intuitively to the needs of those around us.

It is important to be clear, however, as Gilligan is not, that the care perspective does not entail any particular way of action—for example, that one should promote intimate human relationships. The Christian command to love one's neighbor does not dictate how long that love should be expressed. Caring in its purest form is not ordinary loving; it is doing spontaneously whatever the situation demands. As we have seen, even if two situations were identical in every respect, two ethical experts with different histories would not necessarily respond in the same way. Each person must simply respond as well as he or she can to each unique situation with nothing but experience-based intuition as guide. Heidegger captures this ethical skill in his notion of **authentic care** as a response to the **unique**, as opposed to the **general**, situation.[39]

Responding to the general situation occurs when one follows ethical maxims and gives the standard acceptable response. This would correspond to the last stage of Kohlberg's Conventional Level. For Kohlberg and Habermas, on the next Level the learner seeks principles justification. On our model, however, reaching the Postconventional Level would amount to acting with authentic care. When an individual becomes a master of the *Sittlichkeit* he or she no longer tries to do what one normally does, but rather responds out of a fund of experience in the culture. This requires having enough experience to give up following the rules and maxims dictating what **anyone** should do, and instead acting upon the intuition that results from a life in which talent and sensibility have allowed learning from the experience of satisfaction and regret in similar situations. Authentic caring in this sense is common to *agape* and *phronesis*.

This gets us back to the debate over which is more mature, acting upon rational judgments of rightness, or intuitively doing what the culture deems good. On the other hand, we have Kohlberg's Stage 6 and Habermas's Stage 7, both of which define moral maturity in terms of the ability to detach oneself from the concrete ethical situation and to act on abstract, universal, moral principles. On the other hand, we have John Murphy and Gilligan who, following W.B. Perry, view the "transition to maturity as a shift from 'the moral environment to the ethical, from the formal to the existential'."[40] According to this view the mature subject accepts "contextual relativism."[41] Murphy and Gilligan state the issue as follows:

There are...people who are fully formal in their logical thinking and fully principled in their moral judgments; and yet...are not fully mature in their moral understanding. Conversely, those people whose thinking becomes more relativistic in the sense of being more open to the contextual properties of moral judgments and moral dilemmas frequently fail to be scored at the highest stages of Kohlberg's sequence. Instead, the relativising of their thinking over time is construed as regression or moral equivocation, rather than as a developmental advance. [42]

Habermas recognizes that "the controversy [raised by Gilligan] has drawn attention to problems which, in the language of the philosophical tradition, pertain to the relation of **morality** to ethical life *(Sittlichkeit)*."[43] He, of course, continues to contend that rational morality is developmentally superior to *Sittlichkeit*. His argument has two stages: (1) He attempts to describe the move from the Conventional Level to the Postconventional Level in a way which will show the move to contextual relativism to be a **regression**, and (2) he tries to incorporate what he finds to be valid in Gilligan's contextualism into his modified Kohlbergian framework. It is illuminating to look at both these moves in the light of our phenomenology of skill acquisition.

Habermas asserts that as the adolescent outgrows acting on conventional stereotypes his or her "task is to come to terms with the dissonance between his [sic] moral intuitions, which continue to determine his unreflective everyday knowledge and actions, and his (presumed) insight into the illusory nature of this conventional moral consciousness, which reflection has discredited but which has not ceased to function in daily life."[44] As the adolescent outgrows rigid and limited ethical rules and maxims, he/she is led to search for moral principles to replace the rules he/she has internalized as a beginner.

According to Habermas the new principles the developing moral agent discovers were already implicit in everyday ethics:

*Principled moral judgments are described theoretically as no longer representing merely the prereflective expression or reproduction of an intuitively applied **know-how**; rather, they already represent the beginnings of an **explication of this knowing**, the rudiments, so to speak, of a moral theory.* [45]

There are then two possibilities open to the adolescent. Either she makes explicit the principles of rational justification implicit in the *Sittlichkeit*, or if she fails to find such principles, "[s]he views the collapse of the world of conventions as a debunking of false cognitive claims with which conventional norms and prescriptive statements have hitherto been linked."[46] That is, she either goes on to Stages 5, 6 and 7 of rational morality or else regresses to an earlier stage of self-centered ethical relativism.

255 Our account of the acquisition of expertise parallels Kohlberg's and Habermas's account as to the need to be beyond

hubert l.
dreyfus,
stuart e.
dreyfus

automatically doing what the conventional rules and maxims dictate, but offers an alternative account of the next stage. We have seen in the case of chess how Stuart was led at this intermediary stage to question the rules and maxims he had acquired as a beginner and to try to figure out the sophisticated theory of the domain he supposed the masters must be using. But, as we have also seen, it is precisely this clinging to the demand for rational justification, rather than accepting the nonrationalizability of appropriate intuitive responses, that blocks the development of expertise. Given our account, we would expect that the transition from the Conventional to the Postconventional would be precisely where both those who accept ethical relativism and those who try to rationalize the *Sittlichkeit* get stuck and are separated from those who go on to develop an ethics of care.

Habermas needs to supply an argument why the development of ethical expertise should follow a different course than the development of expertise in other domains. Otherwise, it looks like we should follow Murphy and Gilligan in recognizing that at the Postconventional Level the learner accepts her intuitive responses, thus reaching a stage of maturity that leaves behind the rules of Conventional morality for a new contextualism that is clearly distinguishable from a regression to ethical relativism. We are not denying that the ability to ask what is right reveals a kind of maturity, but we see no reason to claim it is the *telos* of ethical comportment. Indeed, if ethical intuition and moral development (understood as acting on universal principles) **is regarded as one single developing skill**, the skill development model we are proposing reverses the regression argument and demotes rational, post-conventional moral activity to the status of a regression to a pre-expert stage of ethical development.

Thus when one measures Gilligan's two types of morality—her two voices—against a phenomenology of expertise, the traditional Western and male belief in the maturity and superiority of critical detachment is reversed. The highest form of ethical comportment is seen to consist in being able to stay involved and to refine one's intuitions. If, in the name of a cognitivist account of development, one puts ethics and morality on one single developmental scale, the claims of justice, in which one needs to judge that two situations are equivalent so as to be able to apply one's universal principles, looks like regression to a competent understanding of the ethical domain, while the caring response to the unique situations stands out as practical wisdom.[47]

To incorporate what is valid in Gilligan's findings, stage (2) of his argument, Habermas distinguishes **justification** from **application**.

moral maturity *The question of the context-specific application of universal norms should not be confused with the question of their justification. Since moral norms do not contain their own rules of application, acting on the basis of moral insight requires the additional competence of hermeneutic prudence or, in Kantian terminology, reflective judgment. But this in no way results in the prior decision in favor of a universalistic position being put into question.* [48]

Perhaps Gilligan's attempt to find principles underlying her subjects' solutions to moral problems misleads Habermas into thinking that Gilligan is concerned with the problem of how to apply universal principles to particular cases, for he continues:

*[C]onnections between cognition, empathy, and **agape** can be shown to hold for the hermeneutic activity of applying universal norms in a context-sensitive manner. This kind of integration of cognitive operations and emotional dispositions and attitudes in justifying and applying norms characterizes the **mature** capacity for moral judgment....This concept of maturity, however, should not be applied **externally** to postconventional thought in the form of an opposition between an ethics of love and an ethics of law and justice; rather, it should flow from an adequate description of the highest stage of morality itself.* [49]

But it is far from clear how the ability to apply universal norms to the particular case is supposed to flow from a description of the mature commitment to abstract universal principles, and Habermas's example does not help.

It is in the light of concrete circumstances and particular constellations of interests that valid principles must be weighed against one another, and exceptions to accepted rules justified. There is no other way to satisfy the principle that like is to be treated in like manner and unlike in unlike manner. [50]

This leaves what counts as like situations up to ethical tact. But, as Wittgenstein pointed out so tellingly, if one has to stop the regress of rules for applying rules by, at some point, simply knowing how to apply a principle, why not just admit that skilled people know how to act justly in specific situations and drop the appeal to rules or principles to guide action in the first place. The ethical expert responds intuitively, and when appropriate, fairly, to everyday ethical situations such as dividing her time between her work and her family, doing what needs to be done at home or at work, or, to take a more Aristotelian case, fighting for causes with courage and steadfastness, so that precisely the sort of problems that require reflection, judgment and decision normally do not arise. Even when they do, she deliberates over her

257

hubert l.
dreyfus,
stuart e.
dreyfus

intuitions, not her principles. To see Gilligan as offering a solution to the problem of **the application of principles** completely misses the radically anti-cognitivist implications of her work and of a phenomenology of skilled comportment in general.[51]

Furthermore, if knowing what is good is **required** in order to apply principles of rightness, this again seems to call into question the idea that the ethical and moral are on a single developmental scale in which judgments of rightness **replace** judgments of goodness. If there is any question of priority, expertise in everyday practices would have to be seen to be prior to acting on principle, since even though one could call any everyday action into question by asking if it is right, ethical practices can function perfectly well without abstract universal principles of rightness being invoked, while principles of rightness are totally dependent upon the everyday practices for their application.

None of the above is meant to deny that an ethical situation could occur so unlike any previous situation that no one would have an expert intuitive response to it. Then no amount of involved deliberation would serve to sharpen the expert's intuitions. In the face of such a total breakdown, and in that case alone, the ethical expert would have to turn to detached reflection. But the need to appeal to principles in cases of total breakdown does not support the claim that ethical comportment normally involves implicit validity claims nor that grasping rational principles of morality is the *telos* of ethical practice. We need to distinguish such breakdown cases from the cases of everyday intuitive ethical comportment and deliberation **internal** to our *Sittlichkeit*. If we fail to distinguish these two sorts of cases and read the breakdown case back into the normal one, then ethical comportment looks like an incipient form of practical reason and ethical expertise is "rationally constructed" as a cognitive capacity which shows the same development as other cognitive capacities—from disequilibrium and perspectivity to reciprocity and reversibility. Thus Habermas summarizes and endorses Kohlberg's claim:

*[T]he notion of a path of development which can be described in terms of a **hierarchy ordered sequence of structures** is absolutely crucial to Kohlberg's model of developmental stages....[T]he lower stage is replaced while at the same time being preserved in a reorganized, more differentiated form."*[52]

But Merleau-Ponty has argued against Piaget's intellectualism in the case of perception that there is no reason to think that the sensory-motor skills required in learning to perceive are ever **replaced** by cognitive rules. Likewise, there is no evidence that intuitive ethical expertise can be **replaced** by rational principles. Even if the principles of justice show the sort of equilibrium and

moral maturity reversibility that cognitivists like Piaget hold are characteristic of cognitive maturity, and situated ethical comportment lacks reversibility and universality, this does not show that acting on abstract, universal moral principles is developmentally superior to an untuitive contextual response. The cognitivist move looks plausible only because the tradition has overlooked intuitive deliberation and has read the structure of detached deliberation back into normal ethical comportment.

Kohlberg claims, and Habermas concurs, that "Science...can test whether a philosopher's conception of morality phenomenologically fits the psychological facts."[53] Our phenomenology of expertise, however, suggests that Kohlberg's empirical investigations or moral maturity are founded on a traditional but mistaken phenomenology, and the attempt to use his results to defend the superiority of abstract, universal, critical moral consciousness demonstrates the danger of picking up congenial but phenomenologically unfiltered pronouncements from allegedly objective social science.

It is important to see that the above in no way shows that questioning the justice or rightness of aspects of our *Sittlichkeit* is illegitimate or immature. We can agree with Habermas that

the formation of the moral point of view goes hand in hand with a differentiation within the sphere of the practical: **moral questions,** *which can in principle be decided rationally in terms of criteria of* **justice** *or the universalizability of interests [can be] distinguished from* **evaluative questions,** *which fall into the general discussion only* **within** *the horizon of a concrete historical form of life.* [54]

But this "differentiation" does not show that the ethical and the moral can be ranked on a single developmental scale, let alone which mode of response is superior. The demand for fairness and justice in social decision making and for a rational critique of ethical judgments has to exhibit its own developmental stages and requires an independent source of justification. Our skill model is meant neither to contribute to finding grounds for such rightness claims nor to call into question Habermas's important contribution to this area. What we are arguing here is that even if there are claims on us as rational moral agents, acting on such claims cannot be shown to be superior to involved ethical comportment by asserting that such claims are the outcome of a development that makes explicit the abstract rationality implicit in context-dependent ethical comportment. Like any skill, ethical comportment has its *telos* in involved intuitive expertise.

259

hubert l.
dreyfus,
stuart e.
dreyfus

ENDNOTES

1. An earlier version of this paper was delivered as the Aron Gurwitsch Memorial Lecture, at the 1989 meeting of the Society for Phenomenology and Existential Philosophy. We want to thank Drew Cross, David Greenbaum, Wayne Martins, Charles Spinosa, Charles Taylor and Kailey Vernallis for their helpful comments.

2. *Sittlichkeit* as we are using the term refers to everyday customs and practices. In using the term we do not accept the Hegelian claim that these practices can be understood as embodying one unifying principle, nor that these skills can be made exhaustively explicit. *Sittlichkeit* can be equated with Husserl's **lifeworld**, as Habermas has done, but again, in accepting this identification, we do not accept the idea that the lifeworld corresponds to an implicit belief system that can be made explicit to whatever extent is necessary to deal with problematic situations. When we have laid out our skill model it will be clear that we hold that background practices, like all skills, cannot be captured in rules and principles.

3. Jean Piaget, **The Moral Judgment of the Child**, 1935, p. vii.

4. Piaget, p. 404.

5. Jürgen Habermas, "Moral Development and Ego Identity," **Telos**, Summer, 1975, Number 24, p. 47.

6. Maurice Mandelbaum, **The Phenomenology of Moral Experience**, The Free Press, 1955, p. 31.

7. Mandelbaum, p. 36. (Our italics.)

8. Mandelbaum, p. 48.

9. Mandelbaum, pp. 48-49.

10. "Egoless," as we are using the term, means free of mental content. It does not imply selflessness, self-sacrifice and the like.

11. Mandelbaum, p. 48.

12. Mandelbaum, p. 48.

13. Mandelbaum, p. 49.

14. John Dewey, **Human Nature and Conduct. An Introduction to Social Psychology**. London: George Allen and Unwin, 1922, pp. 177-178.

15. Heidegger's phenomenology of everyday skill is discussed in detail in Hubert L. Dreyfus, **Being in the World: A Commentary on Heidegger's Being and Time**, M.I.T. Press, forthcoming.

16. In our modern pluralistic society it is much harder than it was in Aristotle's time to pick out the one good life and thus to recognize the good individuals. One must relativize one's admiration and imitation to one's sub-culture. One may well wonder to what extent this is possible, but this is not an issue between us and the cognitivists, since, as we shall see, any cognitivist needs to assume there remains a coherent view (or views) of the good life in order to account for the **application** of universal principles of justice. As long as there is enough uniformity in the *Sittlichkeit* to make application of principles possible, there is enough to make practical wisdom *(phronesis)* possible too.

17. It is easy to see that if one enjoyed skidding one could never become an accepted member of the everyday driving community (although one might well become an expert stunt driver). Similarly, without a shared ethical sensibility to what is laudable and what condemnable one would go on doing what the experts in the community found inappropriate, develop bad habits, and become what Aristotle calls an unjust person.

18. The attempt to build expert systems depends on treating expert responses as judgments, soliciting the principles underlying these judgments and running them on a computer acting as an inference machine. This approach has been called into question by the exceptionless failure of expert systems based on experts' proffered heuristics to achieve expertise. See H. Dreyfus and S. Dreyfus, **Mind Over Machine**, Free Press, 1988.

19. John Dewey, **Theory of the Moral Life**. Holt, Rinehart and Winston, 1960, p. 131. (Our italics.)

20. Aristotle, **The Nichomachean Ethics**, Book II, 4, Ross translation. (Our italics.)

21. Alasdair MacIntyre, **After Virtue**, University of Notre Dame Press, 1981, p. 140.

22. MacIntyre, pp. 207-208. (Our italics.)

23. MacIntyre, pp. 175-176.

24. John Dewey, **Theory of the Moral Life**, p. 131.

25. Dewey, p. 132.

26. See H. Dreyfus and S. Dreyfus, "Making a Mind vs. Modeling the Brain: AI Back at a Branchpoint," **The Artificial Intelligence Debate**, M.I.T. Press, 1988.

27. Dreyfus and Dreyfus, "Making a Mind," p. 412.

28. Charles Taylor, **The Sources of the Self**, Harvard University Press, 1989, p. 88.

**hubert l.
dreyfus,
stuart e.
dreyfus**

29. Jürgen Habermas, **Moral Consciousness and Communicative Action**, M.I.T. Press, forthcoming. Draft p. 162.

30. Jürgen Habermas, "A Reply to My Critics," **Habermas Critical Debates**, M.I.T. Press, 1982, p. 253.

31. Jürgen Habermas, **Moral Consciousness and Communicative Action**, p. 150.

32. Carol Gilligan, **In a Different Voice: Psychological Theory and Women's Development**, Harvard University Press, 1982, p. 27.

33. Gilligan, pp. 27-30. The cognitivist vocabulary we have italicized should warn us that, in spite of her critique, Gilligan may well have uncritically taken over the cognitivist assumptions underlying Kohlberg's research.

34. Gilligan, p. 49.

35. Gilligan, pp. 100-101. (Our italics.)

36. Gilligan, p. 28. (Our italics.)

37. Gilligan, "On **In a Different Voice**: An Interdisciplinary Forum," **Signs: Journal of Women in Culture and Society**, 1986, Vol. 11, no. 2, p. 327.

38. Gilligan, "On **In A Different Voice**," p. 330. For an early intuition that the two voices are, indeed, gendered, at least in our culture, see Nietzsche in **Human all too Human**:

Can women be just at all if they are so used to loving, to feeling immediately pro or con? For this reason they are also less often partial to causes, more often to people; but if to a cause, they immediately become partisan, therefore ruining its pure innocent effect.... What would be more rare than a woman who really knew what science is? The best even nourish in their hearts a secret disdain for it, as if they were somehow superior. (# 416)

39. Martin Heidegger, **Being and Time**, Harper & Row, 1962, p. 346.

40. W.B. Perry, **Forms of Intellectual and Ethical Development in the College Years: A Scheme**. Holt, Rinehart and Winston, 1968, p. 205, as quoted in John M. Murphy and Carol Gilligan, "Moral Development in Late Adolescence and Adulthood: A Critique and Reconstruction of Kohlberg's Theory," **Human Development**, 1980, p. 79.

41. John M. Murphy and Carol Gilligan, p. 79.

42. Murphy and Gilligan, p. 80. (Again note the cognitivist vocabulary: thinking, judgment, dilemmas.)

43. Jürgen Habermas, **Moral Consciousness and Communicative Action**, p. 223.

44. Habermas, pp. 236 and 237. For Habermas, intuitive, unreflective behavior based on know-how seems to mean automatic responses based on rules derived from accepted behavior, rather than reflectively reasoned out actions. Such "intuition" should not be confused with the intuitive unreflective behavior of experts as described in Stage 5 of our skill-acquisition model.

45. Jürgen Habermas, "Justice and Solidarity: On the Discussion Concerning 'Stage 6'," **The Philosophical Forum**, Vol. XXI, Nos. 1-2, Fall-Winter, 1989-90, p. 34. (Our italics.) This seems to beg the question at issue by assuming that ethical expertise involves an implicit m oral theory. Seyla Benhabib bluntly states this cognitivist claim:

By "ethical cognitivism," I understand the view that **ethical judgments and principles have a cognitively articulable kernel, that they are neither mere statements of preference nor mere statements of taste, and that they imply validity claims** of the following sort: "X is right," where by "X" is meant a principle of action or a moral judgment, which means "I can justify to you with good grounds why one ought to respect, uphold, agree with X." (Seyla Benhabib, "In the Shadow of Aristotle and Hegel: Communicative Ethics and Current Controversies in Practical Philosophy," **The Philosophical Forum**, Vol. XXI, Nos. 1-2, Fall-Winter, 1989-90, p. 20.)

46. Jürgen Habermas, **Moral Consciousness and Communicative Action**, p. 237.

47. If one accepts the view of expertise presented here, one must accept the superiority of the involved caring self. But our skill model does not support Gilligan's Piagetian claim that the **development** of the self requires crises. Skill learning, and that would seem to be **any** skill learning, requires learning from **mistakes** but not necessarily from **crises**. A crisis would occur when one had to alter one's criterion for what counted as success. Aristotle surely thought that in his culture, the men at least, could develop character without going through crises. The idea of the necessity of moral crises for development goes with an intellectualist view of theory change that may well be true for science but which has nothing to do with selves. This is not to deny that in our pluralistic culture, and especially for those who are given contradictory and distorting roles to play, crises may be necessary. It may well be that women are led into traps concerning success and need crises to get out of them. Thus Gilligan may well be right that crises **in fact** play a crucial role in modern Western women's moral development, even if they are not **necessary**.

48. Habermas, **Moral Consciousness and Communicative Action**, p. 228.

49. Habermas, **Moral Consciousness and Communicative Action**, p. 231.

hubert l.
dreyfus,
stuart e.
dreyfus

50. Jürgen Habermas, "Justice and Solidarity," p. 44.

51. If this account of Gilligan's position is correct, Seyla Benhabib misses Gilligan's point completely when she construes her contribution as a supplement to Habermas's Stage 7 in which the moral agent, **in the interest of fairness and universality,** takes into account the needs not just of the generalized other but of the concrete other. See Seyla Benhabib, "The Generalized and the Concrete Other: The Kohlberg-Gilligan Controversy and Feminist Theory," **Feminism as Critique,** Benhabib and Cornell, ed., University of Minnesota Press, 1987.

52. Jürgen Habermas, **Moral Consciousness and Communicative Action,** p. 162.

53. Lawrence Kohlberg, quoted in **Habermas Critical Debates,** p. 259.

54. Jürgen Habermas, **Moral Consciousness and Communicative Action,** p. 226.

VI.
bibliography

michael zilles
universalism and communitarianism: a bibliography

The following bibliography is intended to provide a comprehensive guide to literature central to the question of universalism and communitarianism in modern ethical theories. Obviously, claiming comprehensiveness is a tricky matter. Work which has been published as a direct or explicit contribution to contemporary scholarship provides less of a problem. Here I was able to rely heavily upon indexes and other bibliographical sources. It has been in determining what is relevant to the debate that I have necessarily had to be more selective. I certainly have not included all contributions to liberal ethical and political theory of the last century. Instead, I have focused on those sources which have recently come under scrutiny, citing those more or less classic 20th century sources of liberal theory and of liberalism's critics, which are now drawing the attention of contemporary scholars. For the most part I have refrained from listing classical sources written prior to the 20th century.

The publication in which this bibliography appears, to a great extent, is exemplary of scholarship in the Continental tradition. One of the obvious intentions of this volume is to promote dialogue between Anglo-American and Continental philosophy, with a focus on ethics. This bibliography reflects that intention.

In order to facilitate its use, I have divided citations into six

michael zilles   categories: general; continental; feminist studies; historical studies; law; and language, mind and method. At the beginning of each section I have provided section by section cross-referencing to sources which also contain pertinent material.

I would like to thank Emily Zakin, who began work on this bibliography by compiling the citations of individual contributors to this volume.

1. General

Ackerman, Bruce 1980. **Social Justice in the Liberal State**. New Haven: Yale University Press.

Ackerman, Bruce 1983. "What is Neutral about Neutrality?" From "A Symposium on Social Justice in the Liberal State," including contributions by Benjamin Barber, James Fishkin, Richard Flathman and Bernard Williams, in **Ethics** 93:372-390.

Ackerman, Bruce 1989. "Why Dialogue?" **Journal of Philosophy** 86:5-23.

Arendt, Hannah 1951, 1972a. **The Origins of Totalitarianism**. New York: Harcourt Brace Jovanovich.

Arendt, Hannah 1958. **The Human Condition**. Chicago: University of Chicago Press.

Arendt, Hannah 1970. **On Violence**. New York: Harcourt, Brace and World.

Arendt, Hannah 1972b. **Crises of the Republic**. New York: Harcourt Brace Jovanovich.

Arendt, Hannah 1977a (enlarged edition). **Between Past and Future: Eight Exercises in Political Thought**. New York: Penguin.

Arendt, Hannah 1977b. **On Revolution**. New York: Penguin.

Arendt, Hannah 1978a. **The Jew as Pariah: Jewish Identity and Politics in the Modern Age**, edited by Ron H. Feldman. New York: Grove Press.

Arendt, Hannah 1978b. **The Life of the Mind**. New York: Harcourt Brace Jovanovich.

Arendt, Hannah 1982. **Lectures on Kant's Political Philosophy**, edited, with an interpretive essay, by Ronald Beiner. Chicago: University of Chicago Press.

bibliography   Armour, Leslie 1985. "Liberty, Community and the Social Good."
Cogito 3:27-38.

Baier, Kurt 1989. "Justice and the Aims of Political Philosophy."
From "A Symposium on Rawls's Theory of Justice: Recent
Developments," including contributions by G.A. Cohen, Thomas
Hill, Joshua Cohen, William A. Galston, Allen Buchanan, Jean
Hampton, Gerald Doppelt, and Will Kymlicka. **Ethics** 99:771-
790.

Barber, Benjamin R. 1983. "Unconstrained Conversations: A
Play on Words, Neutral and Otherwise." From "A Symposium on
Social Justice in the Liberal State," including contributions by
Bruce Ackerman, James Fishkin, Richard Flathman and Bernard
Williams, in **Ethics** 93:330-356.

Barber, Benjamin 1984. **Strong Democracy. Participatory
Politics for a New Age**. Berkeley: University of California Press.

Barber, Benjamin 1988a. "Spirit's Phoenix and History's Owl *or*
The Incoherence of Dialectics in Hegel's Account of Women."
Political Theory 16:5-28.

Barber, Benjamin 1988b. **The Conquest of Politics: Liberal
Philosophy in Democratic Times**. Princeton: Princeton
University Press.

Beiner, Ronald 1983. **Political Judgment**. Chicago: University of
Chicago Press.

Bell, Daniel 1976. **Cultural Contradictions of Capitalism**. New
York: Basic Books.

Bellah, Robert Neelly, *et al.* 1985. **Habits of the Heart.
Individualism and Commitment in American Life**. Berkeley:
University of California Press.

Berlin, Isiah 1969. **Four Essay on Liberty**. London: Oxford
University Press.

Bernstein, Richard 1984. "Nietzsche or Aristotle?: Reflections on
Alasdair MacIntyre's **After Virtue**." With a reply by Alasdair
MacIntyre in **Soundings** 37:6-29.

Bernstein, Richard 1987. "One Step Forward, Two Steps
Backward. Richard Rorty on Liberal Democracy and Philosophy."
Political Theory 15:538-563.

269   Bobbio, Norberto 1987. **The Future of Democracy: A Defense**

michael zilles   **of the Rules of the Game**. Minneapolis: University of Minnesota Press.

Brink, David O. 1987. "Rawlsian Constructivism in Moral Theory." **Canadian Journal of Philosophy** 17:71-90.

Buchanan, Allen E. 1989. "Assessing the Communitarian Critique of Liberalism." From "A Symposium on Rawls's Theory of Justice: Recent Developments," including contributions by G.A. Cohen, Thomas Hill, Kurt Baier, William A. Galston, Joshua Cohen, Jean Hampton, Gerald Doppelt, and Will Kymlicka. **Ethics** 99:852-882.

Buchanan, Allen E. 1982. **Marx and Justice: The Radical Critique of Liberalism**. Totowa: Rowman and Littlefield.

Carter, W.R. 1982. "On the Scope of Justice and the Community of Persons." **Tulane Studies in Philosophy** 31:155-168.

Cohen, Gerald Allen 1986. "Self-Ownership, World-Ownership and Equality: Part 2." **Social Philosophy and Policy** 3:77-96.

Cohen, Gerald Allen 1989. "Equality of What? On Welfare, Resources, and Capabilities." From "A Symposium on Rawls's Theory of Justice: Recent Developments," including contributions by Joshua Cohen, Thomas Hill, Kurt Baier, William A. Galston, Allen Buchanan, Jean Hampton, Gerald Doppelt, and Will Kymlicka. **Ethics** 99:906-944.

Cohen, Joshua 1986. "Review of **Spheres of Justice**." **Journal of Philosophy** 83:457-468.

Cohen, Joshua 1989. "Democratic Equality." From "A Symposium on Rawls's Theory of Justice: Recent Developments," including contributions by G.A. Cohen, Thomas Hill, Kurt Baier, William A. Galston, Allen Buchanan, Jean Hampton, Gerald Doppelt, and Will Kymlicka. **Ethics** 99:727-751.

Cragg, Wesley 1986. "Two Concepts of Community or Moral Theory and Canadian Culture." **Dialogue** (Canada) 25:31-52.

Daniels, Norman 1974 (editor). **Reading Rawls**. New York: Basic.

Davis, Charles 1983. "Reason, Tradition, Community: The Search for Ethical Foundations." In **Foundations of Ethics**, edited by Leroy S. Rouner. Notre Dame: Notre Dame University Press.

bibliography

Doppelt, Gerald 1981. "Rawls's System of Justice: A Critique from the Left." **Nous** 15:259-307.

Doppelt, Gerald 1984. "Conflicting Social Paradigms of Human Freedom and the Problem of Justification." **Inquiry** 27:51-86.

Doppelt, Gerald 1985. "Modernity and Conflict." **Analysis and Critique** (West Germany) 2:206-233.

Doppelt, Gerald 1989. "Is Rawls's Kantian Liberalism Coherent and Defensible?" From "A Symposium on Rawls's Theory of Justice: Recent Developments," including contributions by G.A. Cohen, Thomas Hill, Kurt Baier, William A. Galston, Allen Buchanan, Jean Hampton, Joshua Cohen, and Will Kymlicka. **Ethics** 99:815-851.

Edwin, R.E. 1987. **Liberty, Community, and Justice**. Totowa: Rowman and Littlefield.

Feinberg, Joel 1988. "Liberalism, Community, and Tradition." Drafted excerpt from **Harmless Wrongdoing**, Volume 4 of **The Moral Limits of the Criminal Law**. Oxford: Oxford University Press.

Fischer, John Martin 1986 (editor). **Moral Responsibility**. Ithaca: Cornell University Press.

Fishkin, James S. 1983. "Can There Be a Neutral Theory of Justice?" From "A Symposium on Social Justice in the Liberal State," including contributions by Bruce Ackerman, Benjamin Barber, Richard Flathman and Bernard Williams, in **Ethics** 93:348-356.

Fishkin, James S. 1984. **Beyond Subjective Morality: Ethical Reasoning and Political Philosophy**. New Haven: Yale University Press.

Flathman, Richard E. 1983. "Egalitarian Blood and Skeptical Turnips." From "A Symposium on Social Justice in the Liberal State," including contributions by Bruce Ackerman, James Fishkin, Benjamin Barber, and Bernard Williams, in **Ethics** 93:357-366.

Fried, Charles 1983. "Liberalism, Community, and the Objectivity of Values." **Harvard Law Review** 96:960-68.

Galston, William 1980. **Justice and the Human Good**. Chicago: University of Chicago Press.

271

michael zilles   Galston, William 1982. "Moral Personality and Liberal Theory: John Rawls's 'Dewey Lectures'." **Political Theory** 10:492-519.

Galston, William A. 1989a. "Community, Democracy, Philosophy: The Political Thought of Michael Walzer." **Political Theory** 17:119-130.

Galston, William A. 1989b. "Pluralism and Social Unity." From "A Symposium on Rawls's Theory of Justice: Recent Developments," including contributions by G.A. Cohen, Thomas Hill, Kurt Baier, Joshua Cohen, Allen Buchanan, Jean Hampton, Gerald Doppelt, and Will Kymlicka. **Ethics** 99:711-726.

Gauthier, David 1986. **Morals by Agreement**. Oxford: Clarendon Press.

Gewirth, Alan 1978. **Reason and Morality**. Chicago: University of Chicago Press.

Gewirth, Alan 1985. "Rights and Virtues." **Review of Metaphysics** 38:739-762.

Goldman, Alvin I. and Kim, Jaegwon 1978 (editors). **Values and Morals: Essays in Honor of William Frankena, Charles Stevenson and Richard Brandt**. Dordrecht: Reidel.

Gutmann, Amy 1980. **Liberal Equality**. Cambridge: Cambridge University Press.

Gutmann, Amy 1985. "Communitarian Critics of Liberalism." **Philosophy and Public Affairs** 14:308-322.

Hampton, Jean 1989. "Should Political Philosophy be Done Without Metaphysics?" From "A Symposium on Rawls's Theory of Justice: Recent Developments," including contributions by G.A. Cohen, Thomas Hill, Kurt Baier, William A. Galston, Allen Buchanan, Joshua Cohen, Gerald Doppelt, and Will Kymlicka. **Ethics** 99:791-814.

Hill,Thomas Jr. 1989. "Kantian Constructivism in Ethics." From "A Symposium on Rawls's Theory of Justice: Recent Developments," including contributions by G.A. Cohen, Joshua Cohen, Kurt Baier, William A. Galston, Allen Buchanan, Jean Hampton, Gerald Doppelt, and Will Kymlicka. **Ethics** 99:752-770.

Isaac, Jeffrey C. 1988. "Republicanism Versus Liberalism: A Reconsideration." **History of Political Thought** 9:349-377.

bibliography   Jones, L. Gregory 1987. "On Narrative, Community, and the Moral Life." **Modern Theology** 4:53-69.

Keane, John 1984. **Public Life in Late Capitalism**. Cambridge, MA: MIT Press.

Kohlberg, Lawrence 1981 and 1984. **Essays in Moral Development**, Volumes 1 and 2. New York: Harper and Row.

Kymlicka, Will 1988a. "Liberalism and Communitarianism." **Canadian Journal of Philosophy**. 18:181-204.

Kymlicka, Will 1988b. "Rawls on Teleology and Deontology." **Philosophy and Public Affairs** 17:173-190.

Kymlicka, Will 1989a. "Liberal Individualism and Liberal Neutrality." From "A Symposium on Rawls's Theory of Justice: Recent Developments," including contributions by G.A. Cohen, Thomas Hill, Kurt Baier, William A. Galston, Allen Buchanan, Jean Hampton, Gerald Doppelt, and Joshua Cohen. **Ethics** 99:883-905.

Kymlicka, Will 1989b. **Liberalism, Community and Culture**. London: Oxford University Press. (In Press.)

Larmore, Charles 1987. **Patterns of Moral Complexity**. Cambridge: Cambridge University Press.

Laski, Harold Joseph 1917. **Studies in the Problem of Sovereignty**. New Haven: Yale University Press.

Laski, Harold Joseph 1919. **Authority in the Modern State**. New Haven: Yale University Press.

Laski, Harold Joseph 1921. **The Foundations of Sovereignty and Other Essays**. New York: Harcourt Brace and Co.

Lowi, Theodore 1969. **The End of Liberalism**. New York: Norton.

Lukes, Steven 1973, 1984. **Individualism**. New York: Basil Blackwell.

Lukes, Steven 1974. **Power: A Radical View**. New York: Macmillan.

MacIntyre, Alasdair 1981. **After Virtue: A Study in Moral Theory**. Notre Dame: University of Notre Dame Press.

michael zilles

MacIntyre, Alasdair 1982. "How Moral Agents Have Become Ghosts." **Synthese** 53:295-312.

MacIntyre, Alasdair 1984a. "Is Patriotism a Virtue?" **The Lindley Lecture.** University of Kansas: Department of Philosophy.

MacIntyre, Alasdair 1984b. "Bernstein's Distorting Mirrors: A Rejoinder." A response to Richard Bernstein's review of **After Virtue** in the same issue of **Soundings** 37:30-41.

MacIntyre, Alasdair 1988. **Whose Justice? Which Rationality?** Notre Dame: University of Notre Dame Press.

Mansbridge, Jane 1980. **Beyond Adversary Democracy.** Chicago: University of Chicago Press.

Marshall, T.H. 1950. **Citizenship and Social Class and Other Essays.** Cambridge: Cambridge University Press.

Nagel, Thomas 1986. **The View from Nowhere.** New York: Oxford University Press.

Nagel, Thomas 1987. "Moral Conflict and Political Legitimacy." **Philosophy and Public Affairs** 16:215-240.

Neal, Patrick 1987. "A Liberal Theory of the Good?" **Canadian Journal of Philosophy** 17:567-581.

Nozick, Robert 1974. **Anarchy, State and Utopia.** New York: Basic Books.

Pinkard, Terry 1987. **Democratic Liberalism and Social Union.** Philadelphia: Temple University Press.

Rasmussen, David M. 1982. "The Enlightenment Project: After Virtue." **Philosophy and Social Criticism** 3/4:381-394.

Rawls, John 1955. "Two Concepts of Rules." **Philosophical Review** 64:3-32.

Rawls, John 1971. **A Theory of Justice.** Cambridge: Harvard University Press.

Rawls, John 1975a. "Fairness to Goodness." **Philosophical Review** 84:536-554.

Rawls, John 1975b. "The Independence of Moral Theory." **The Proceedings and Addresses of the American Philosophical Association** 48:5-22.

bibliography

Rawls, John 1977. "The Basic Structure as Subject." **American Philosophical Quarterly** 14:159-165.

Rawls, John 1980. "Kantian Constructivism in Moral Theory: The Dewey Lectures." **Journal of Philosophy** 77:515-572.

Rawls, John 1982. "The Basic Liberties and Their Priority." In **The Tanner Lectures on Human Values**, Volume 3, edited by S. McMurrin. Salt Lake City: University of Utah Press.

Rawls, John 1985a. "A Kantian Conception of Equality." In **Post-Analytic Philosophy** edited, with an introductory essay, by John Raijchman and Cornelius West. New York: Columbia University Press.

Rawls, John 1985b. "Justice as Fairness: Political Not Metaphysical." **Philosophy and Public Affairs** 14:223-252.

Rawls, John 1987. "The Idea of an Overlapping Consensus." **The Oxford Journal of Legal Studies** 7:1-25.

Rawls, John 1988. "The Priority of Right and Ideas of the Good." **Philosophy and Public Affairs** 17:251-276.

Ripstein, Arthur 1987. "Foundationalism in Political Theory." **Philosophy and Public Affairs** 16:115-137.

Rodewald, Richard A.1985 "Does Liberalism Rest on a Mistake?" **Canadian Journal of Philosophy** 15:231-51.

Rorty, Richard 1985. "Post-modernist Bourgeois Liberalism." In **Hermeneutics and Praxis**, edited by R. Hollinger. Notre Dame: University of Notre Dame Press.

Rorty, Richard 1986. "The Contingency of Community." **London Review of Books** 24 (July) 10-14.

Rorty, Richard 1987a. "The Priority of Democracy to Philosophy." In **The Virginia Statute of Religious Freedom** edited by M. D. Peterson and R. C. Vaughan. Cambridge: Cambridge University Press.

Rorty, Richard 1987b. "Thugs and Theorists. A Reply to Bernstein." **Political Theory** 15:564-580.

Rosenblum, Nancy 1983. "Moral Membership in a Post-liberal State." **World Politics** (August) 581-596.

michael zilles

Rosenblum, Nancy 1987. **Another Liberalism**. Cambridge: Harvard University Press.

Sandel, Michael 1982. **Liberalism and the Limits of Justice**. Cambridge: Cambridge University Press.

Sandel, Michael 1984a (editor). **Liberalism and its Critics.** New York: New York University Press.

Sandel, Michael 1984b. "Morality and the Liberal Ideal." **The New Republic,** May 7, 1984.

Sandel, Michael 1984c. "The Procedural Republic and the Unencumbered Self." **Political Theory** 12:81-96.

Sandel, Michael 1988. "The Political Theory of the Procedural Republic." **Revue de Métaphysique et de Morale** 93:57-68.

Scanlon, Thomas 1982. "Contractualism and Utilitarianism." In **Utilitarianism and Beyond,** edited by Amartya Sen and Bernard Williams. Cambridge: Cambridge University Press.

Scheffler, Samuel 1981a. "Ethics, Personal Identity, and the Ideals of the Person." **Canadian Journal of Philosophy** 12:229-246.

Scheffler, Samuel 1981b. "Moral Skepticism and the Ideals of the Person." **The Monist** 62:288-303.

Scheffler, Samuel 1987. "Morality Through Thick and Thin. A Critical Notice of **Ethics and the Limits of Justice.**" **The Philosophical Review** 96:411-434.

Schwartz, Adina 1981. "Against Universality." **The Journal of Philosophy** 78:127-143.

Shklar, Judith 1984. **Ordinary Vices**. Cambridge MA: Harvard University Press.

Taylor, Charles 1975. **Hegel**. Cambridge: Cambridge University Press.

Taylor, Charles 1979. **Hegel and Modern Society**. Cambridge: Cambridge University Press.

Taylor, Charles 1985. **Philosophical Papers. Volume 1: Human Agency and Language; Volume 2: Philosophy and the Human Sciences**. Cambridge: Cambridge University Press.

bibliography

Taylor, Michael 1982. **Community, Anarchy and Liberty.** Cambridge: Cambridge University Press.

Teitleman, Michael 1972. "The Limits of Individualism." **The Journal of Philosophy** 69:545-556.

Thalberg, Irving Jr. 1979. "Socialization and Autonomous Behavior." **Tulane Studies in Philosophy** 28:21-37.

Thigpen, Robert B. and Downing, Lyle A. 1986. "Beyond Shared Understandings." **Political Theory** 14:451-472.

Thigpen Robert B., and Downing, Lyle A. 1987. "Liberalism and the Communitarian Critique." **American Journal of Political Science** 31:637-655.

Waldron, J. 1984. **Theories of Rights.** London: Oxford University Press.

Wallach, John R. 1987. "Liberals, Communitarians, and the Tasks of Political Theory." **Political Theory** 15:581-611.

Walzer, Michael 1965. **The Revolution of the Saints. A Study in the Origins of Radical Politics.** Cambridge, MA: Harvard University Press.

Walzer, Michael 1970. **Obligations: Essays on Disobedience, War, and Citizenship.** Cambridge, MA: Harvard University Press.

Walzer, Michael 1977. **Just and Unjust Wars.** New York: Basic Books.

Walzer, Michael 1980. **Radical Principles: Reflections of an Unreconstructed Democrat.** New York: Basic Books.

Walzer, Michael 1981. "Philosophy and Democracy." **Political Theory** 9:379-399.

Walzer, Michael 1983a. **Spheres of Justice: A Defense of Pluralism and Equality.** New York: Basic Books.

Walzer, Michael 1983b. **"Spheres of Justice:** An Exchange." **New York Review of Books,** July 21:43-44.

Walzer, Michael 1984. "Liberalism and the Art of Separation." **Political Theory** 12:315-330.

Walzer, Michael 1985. **Exodus and Revolution**. New York: Basic Books.

Walzer, Michael 1986. "Justice Here and Now." In **Justice and Equality Here and Now**, edited by Frank Lucash. Ithica: Cornell University Press.

Walzer, Michael 1987. **Interpretation and Social Criticism**. Cambridge, MA: Harvard University Press.

White, John and White, Patricia 1986. "Education, Liberalism and Human Good." In **Education, Values and Mind**, edited by David E. Cooper. London: Routledge and Kegan Paul.

Williams, Bernard 1973. **Problems of the Self**. Cambridge: Cambridge University Press.

Williams, Bernard 1976. "Persons, Character, and Morality." In **Identities of Persons**, edited by Amélie Oksenberg Rorty. Berkeley: University of California Press.

Williams, Bernard 1981. **Moral Luck**. Cambridge: Cambridge University Press.

Williams, Bernard 1983. "Space Talk: The Conversation Continued." From "A Symposium on Social Justice in the Liberal State," including contributions by Bruce Ackerman, James Fishkin, Richard Flathman and Benjamin Barber, in **Ethics** 93:367-371.

Williams, Bernard 1985. **Ethics and the Limits of Philosophy**. London: Fontana Press.

Wolin, Sheldon 1960. **Politics and Vision**. Boston: Little, Brown.

2. Continental

(See also: Section 1: Arendt , Beiner, Eldridge [1983], Larmore, Taylor; Section 3: Blum [1982], Kittay, Fraser, P. Williams; Section 5: Cornell, Dworkin [1986], Luhmann, Pusíc, Rasmussen, Unger, Section 6: Cavell, Rorty, Tugendhat.)

Apel, Karl-Otto 1980. **Towards the Transformation of Philosophy**. London: Routledge and Kegan Paul. A translation, with revisions, by Glyn Adey and David Frisby, of selected essays published under the title **Transformation der Philosophie**. Frankfurt: Suhrkamp 1973.

bibliography

Apel, Karl-Otto 1982. "Normative Ethics and Strategic Rationality: The Philosophic Problem of a Political Ethic." **The Graduate Faculty Philosophy Journal** 9:81-107.

Apel, Karl-Otto 1983. "Kant, Hegel und das asktuelle Problem der normativen Grundlagen von Recht und Moral." In Dieter Henrich, editor, **Kant oder Hegel: Über Formen der Begründung in der Philosophie.** Stuttgart: Klett-Cotta.

Apel, Karl-Otto 1984. **Understanding and Explanation. A Transcendental-Pragmatic Perspective.** A translation, with introductory essay, by Georgia Warnke, of **Die Erklären-Verstehen-Kontroverse in Transzendental-Pragmatischer Sicht.** Frankfurt: Suhrkamp 1979.

Baxter, Hugh 1987. "System and Life-World in Habermas's **Theory of Communicative Action.**" **Theory and Society** 16:39-86.

Benhabib, Seyla 1981. "Modernity and the Aporias of Critical Theory." **Telos** 49:38-59.

Benhabib, Seyla 1982a. "The Logic of Civil Society: A Reconsideration of Hegel and Marx." **Philosophy and Social Criticism** 8:149-167.

Benhabib, Seyla 1982b. "The Methodological Illusions of Modern Political Theory: The Case of Rawls and Habermas." **Neue Hefte Für Philosophie** 21:47-74.

Benhabib, Seyla 1984. "Obligation, Contract, Exchange: On the Significance of Hegel's Abstract Right." In Z.A. Pelczynski, editor, **The State and Civil Society** 2:159-178. Cambridge: Cambridge University Press.

Benhabib, Seyla 1986. **Critique, Norm, and Utopia.** New York: Columbia University Press.

Benhabib, Seyla 1987a. "Autonomy, Modernity and Community. An Exchange Between Communitarianism and Critical Social Theory." Paper read at the Annual Meeting of the American Political Science Association.

Benhabib, Seyla 1987b. "The Generalized and the Concrete Other." In **Feminism as Critique: On the Politics of Gender,** edited by Seyla Benhabib and Drucilla Cornell. Minneapolis: University of Minnesota Press.

Benhabib, Seyla 1988. "Judgment and the Moral Foundations of Politics in Arendt's Thought." **Political Theory** 16:29-51.

michael zilles

Bernstein, Richard 1983. **Beyond Objectivism and Relativism: Science, Hermeneutics, and Praxis.** Oxford: Blackwell.

Cohen, Jean 1979. "Why More Political Theory?" **Telos** 40:70-94.

Cohen, Jean and Arato, Andrew (forthcoming). **Civil Society and Social Theory.** Cambridge: MIT Press.

Ferrara, Alessandro 1985. "A Critique Of Habermas's *Diskursethik.*" **Telos** 6:45-74.

Ferrara, Alessandro 1987. "A Critique of Habermas's Consensus Theory of Truth." **Philosophy and Social Criticism** 13:39-67.

Gadamer, Hans-Georg 1971a (*et al.,* editors). **Hermeneutik und Ideologiekritik.** Frankfurt: Suhrkamp. (Contains principle texts of Habermas-Gadamer debate.)

Gadamer, Hans-Georg 1971b. "Replik." In **Hermeneutik und Ideologiekritik,** edited by Gadamer, *et. al.* Frankfurt: Suhrkamp.

Gadamer, Hans-Georg 1971c. "Rhetorik, Hermeneutik und Ideologiekritik." In **Hermeneutik und Idealogiekritik,** edited by Gadamer *et. al.* Frankfurt: Suhrkamp.

Gadamer, Hans-Georg 1975. **Truth and Method.** Garrett Barden and John Cumming, translators. New York: Seabury Press.

Gadamer, Hans-Georg 1980. "The Universality of the Hermeneutical Problem." In **Contemporary Hermeneutics,** edited by Josef Bleicher. Boston: Routledge and Kegan Paul.

Habermas, Jürgen 1971. **Knowledge and Human Interests.** A translation, by Jeremy Shapiro, of **Erkenntnis und Interesse.** Boston: Beacon Press.

Habermas, Jürgen 1973a **Theory and Practice.** Boston: Beacon Press. A translation by John Viertel, of **Theorie und Praxis: Sozial-philosophische Studien.** Frankfurt: Suhrkamp 1978.

Habermas, Jürgen 1973b. "A Postscript to **Knowledge and Human Interests.**" **Philosophy of the Social Sciences** 3:157-189.

Habermas, Jürgen 1973c. "Wahrheitstheorien." In **Wirklichkeit und Reflexion,** edited by H. Fahrenbach. Pfüllingen: Neske.

Habermas, Jürgen 1974. **Strukturwandel der Öffentlichkeit.** Frankfurt: Suhrkamp.

Habermas, Jürgen 1975. **Legitimation Crisis**. Boston: Beacon Press. A translation, with introductory essay, by Thomas McCarthy, of **Legitimationsprobleme im Spätkapitalismus**. Frankfurt: Suhrkamp 1973.

Habermas, Jürgen 1976. **Zur Rekonstruktion des historischen Materialismus**. Frankfurt: Suhrkamp.

Habermas, Jürgen 1977. "A Review of **Truth and Method**." In **Understanding and Social Inquiry**, edited by F. Dallmayr and T. McCarthy. Notre Dame: Notre Dame University Press.

Habermas, Jürgen 1979. **Communication and the Evolution of Society**. Translated, with an introductory essay, by Thomas McCarthy. Boston: Beacon Press.

Habermas, Jürgen 1980. "The Hermeneutic Claim to Universality." In **Contemporary Hermeneutics**, edited by Josef Bleicher. Boston: Routledge and Kegan Paul.

Habermas, Jürgen 1983a. **Moralbewusstsein und kommunikatives Handeln**. Frankfurt: Suhrkamp.

Habermas, Jürgen 1983b. "Neo-Conservative Cultural Critique in the United States and West Germany." **Telos** 56:75-89.

Habermas, Jürgen 1984a, 1988a. **The Theory of Communicative Action. Volume 1: Reason and the Rationalization of Society. Volume 2: Lifeworld and System: A Critique of Functionalist Reason**. Boston: Beacon Press. A translation, with introductory essay, by Thomas McCarthy, of **Theorie des kommunikativen Handelns**. Frankfurt: Suhrkamp 1981.

Habermas, Jürgen 1984b. "Über Moralität und Sittlichkeit: Was macht eine Lebensform 'Rational'?" In **Rationalität**, edited by Herbert Schnädelbach. Frankfurt: Suhrkamp.

Habermas, Jürgen 1986. "The New Obscurity: The Crisis of the Welfare State and the Exhaustion of Utopian Energies." Translated by Phil Jacobs. **Philosophy and Social Criticism** 11:1-18.

Habermas, Jürgen 1987a. "Law and Morality." In **The Tanner Lectures on Human Values VIII**, edited by Sterling M. McMurrin. Salt Lake City: University of Utah Press.

Habermas, Jürgen 1987b. **The Philosophical Discourse of Modernity: Twelve Lectures**. Cambridge, MA: MIT Press. A

michael zilles

translation, by Frederick Lawrence, with an introductory essay by Thomas McCarthy, of **Der philosophische Diskurs der Moderne: Zwölf Vorlesungen**. Frankfurt: Suhrkamp 1985.

Habermas, Jürgen 1988b. **Nachmetaphysisiches Denken: Philosophische Aufsätze**. Frankfurt: Suhrkamp.

Held, David, and Thompson, John B. 1982 (editors). **Habermas: Critical Debates**. Cambridge, MA: MIT Press.

Heller, Agnes 1985. **Power of Shame: A Rational Perspective**. Boston: Routledge and Kegan Paul.

Heller, Agnes 1987. **Beyond Justice**. New York: Basil Blackwell.

Heller, Agnes 1988. **General Ethics**. New York: Basil Blackwell.

Henrich, Dieter 1983 (editor). **Kant oder Hegel: Über Formen der Begründung in der Philosophie**. Stuttgart: Klett-Cotta.

Honneth, Axel and Jaeggi, U. 1980 (editors). **Arbeit, Handlung, Normativität**. Frankfurt: Suhrkamp.

Honneth, Axel 1985. **Kritik der Macht: Reflexionsstufen einer kritischen Gesellschaftstheorie**. Frankfurt: Suhrkamp.

Kelly, Michael 1988. "Gadamer and Philosophical Ethics." **Man and World** 21:327-346.

Kelly, Michael 1989. "The Gadamer/Habermas Debate Revisited: The Question of Ethics." **Philosophy and Social Criticism** 14: (In Press)

Kirchheimer, Otto 1961. **Political Justice: The Use of Legal Procedure for Political Ends**. Princeton: Princeton University Press.

Kirchheimer, Otto 1964. **Politik und Verfassung**. Frankfurt: Suhrkamp.

Kirchheimer, Otto 1972. **Funktionen des Staates und der Verfassung: Zehn Analysen**. Frankfurt: Suhrkamp.

Lefort, Claude 1986. "Politics and Human Rights." In **The Political Forms of Modern Society: Bureaucracy, Democracy, Totalitarianism**. Edited and introduced by John B. Thompson. Cambridge: MIT Press.

Lukes, Steven 1982. "Of Gods and Demons: Habermas and

bibliography

Practical Reason." In **Habermas: Critical Debates,** edited by David Held and John B. Thompson. Cambridge, MA: MIT Press.

Lyotard, Jean-François 1984. **The Post-Modern Condition: A Report on Knowledge.** Minneapolis: University of Minnesota Press. A translation, by G. Bennington and B. Manumi, with a foreword by Fredric Jameson, of **La condition postmoderne: rapport sur le savoir.** Les Editiones Minuit.

McCarthy, Thomas 1973. "A Theory of Communicative Competence." **Philosophy and the Social Sciences** 3:135-156.

McCarthy, Thomas 1978. **The Critical Theory of Jürgen Habermas.** Cambridge: MIT Press.

McCarthy, Thomas 1982. "Rationality and Relativism: Habermas's 'Overcoming' of Hermeneutics." In **Habermas: Critical Debates,** edited by David Held and John B. Thompson. Cambridge, MA: MIT Press.

McCarthy, Thomas 1984. "Reflections on Rationalization in the Theory of Communicative Action." **Praxis International** 4:177-191.

McCarthy, Thomas 1987. "The Relationship of Philosophy to History: Postscript to the Second Edition of **After Virtue.**" In **After Philosophy,** edited by Kenneth Baynes, James Bohman, and Thomas McCarthy. Cambridge: MIT Press.

Mendelson, J. 1979. "The Habermas-Gadamer Debate," in **New German Critique** 18:44-73.

Mouffe, Chantal 1987. "Rawls: Political Philosophy Without Politics." **Philosophy and Social Criticism** 13:105-124.

Mouffe, Chantal 1988. "American Liberalism and Its Critics: Rawls, Taylor, Sandel and Walzer." **Praxis International** 8:193-206.

Offe, Claus 1984. **Contradictions of the Welfare State.** Edited by John Keane. Cambridge MA: MIT Press.

Offe, Claus 1985. **Disorganized Capitalism: Contemporary Transformations of Work and Politics,** edited by John Keane. Cambridge: MIT Press.

Rasmussen, David 1982. "Communicative Action and Philosophy: Reflections on Habermas's **Theorie des kommunikativen Handelns.**" **Philosophy and Social Criticism** 9:1-29.

283

michael zilles

Riedel, Manfred 1970a (editor). **Studien zu Hegels Rechtsphilosophie**. Frankfurt: Suhrkamp.

Riedel, Manfred 1970b. "Hegels Kritik des Naturrechts." In **Studien zu Hegels Rechtsphilosophie**, edited by Riedel. Frankfurt: Suhrkamp.

Riedel, Manfred 1970c. "Objektiver Geist und praktische Philosophie." In **Studien zu Hegels Rechtsphilosophie**, edited by Riedel. Frankfurt: Suhrkamp.

Riedel, Manfred 1972 (editor, with Foreward). **Rehabilitierung der praktischen Philosophie. Volume 1.** Freiberg: Rombach.

Riedel, Manfred 1975a. "Hegel's Begriff der 'bürgerlichen Gesellschaft' und das Problem seines geschlichtlichen Ursprungs." In **Materialien zu Hegels Rechtsphilosophie**, edited by Reidel. Frankfurt: Suhrkamp.

Reidel, Manfred 1975b (editor). **Materialien zu Hegels Rechtsphilosophie**. Frankfurt: Suhrkamp.

Riedel, Manfred 1976. **Theorie und Praxis im Denken Hegels**. Stuttgart: Ullstein.

Riedel, Manfred 1984. **Between Tradition and Revolution: The Hegelian Transformation of Political Philosophy.** Cambridge: Cambridge University Press. A translation, by Walter Wright, of **Zwischen Tradition und Revolution: Studien zu Hegels Rechtsphilosophie**. Stuttgart: Klett-Cotta.

Riedel, Manfred 1985. "In Search of a Civic Union: The Political Theme of European Democracy and its Primordial Foundation in Greek Philosophy." **Graduate Faculty Philosophy Journal** 10:101-111.

Ritter, Joachim 1982. **Hegel and the French Revolution: Essays on the** *Philosophy of Right*. A partial translation, by Richard D. Winfield, of **Metaphysik und Politik: Studien zu Aristoteles und Hegel.** Cambridge, MA: MIT Press.

Ritter, Joachim.1975. "Moralität und Sittlichkeit: Zu Hegels Auseinandersetzung mit der Kantischen Ethik." In **Materialien zu Hegels Rechtsphilosophie**, edited by Manfred Reidel. Frankfurt: Suhrkamp.

Rorty, Richard 1985a. "Cosmopolitanisme sans Emancipation: Réponse á Jean-François Lyotard." **Critique**.

bibliography

Rorty, Richard 1985b. "Habermas and Lyotard on Post-Modernity." In **Habermas and Post-Modernity**, edited by Richard J. Bernstein. Cambridge: Cambridge University Press.

Schmidt, James. "Recent Hegel Literature." Part I, **Telos** 46:113-48. Part II, **Telos** 48:114-41.

Schmitt, Carl 1931. The Necessity of Politics: An Essay on the Representative Idea in the Church and Modern Europe. London: Sheed and Ward.

Schmitt, Carl 1976. The Concept of the Political. New Brunswick, NJ: Rutgers University Press. A translation of **Der Begriff des Politischer**. Berlin: Duneker and Humblot 1932 (second edition).

Schmitt, Carl 1979. Political Theology. Cambridge, MA: MIT Press. A translation, with an introductory essay, by George Schwab, of **Politische Theologie**. Berlin: Duneker and Humblot, 1922, 1934.

Schmitt, Carl 1982 (second edition). **Der Leviathon in der Staatslehre des Thomas Hobbes: Sinn und Fehlschlag eines politischen Symbols**. Köln: Hohenheim Verlag.

Schmitt, Carl 1985. The Crisis of Parliamentary Democracy. A translation, with an introductory essay, by Ellen Kennedy, of **Die Geistesgeschictlicke Lage des Heutigen Parlamentarismus**. Berlin: Duneker and Humblot, 1923, 1926.

Schmitt, Carl 1986. Political Romanticism: Four Chapters on the Concept of Sovereignty. Cambridge, MA: MIT Press. A translation, with an introductory essay, by Guy Oakes, of **Politische Romantik: Vier Kapitel zur Lehre von der Souveränität**. Berlin: Duneker and Humblot, 1919, 1925.

Theunissen, Michael 1978. **Sein und Schein: Die kritische Funktion der Hegelschen Logik**. Frankfurt: Suhrkamp.

Theunissen, Michael 1982. "Die verdrängte Intersubjektivität in Hegels **Philosophie des Rechts**." In **Hegels "Philosophie des Rechts": die Theorie der Rechsformen und ihre Logik**, edited by K. Henrich and R.P. Horstmann. Stuttgart: Klett-Cotta.

Theunissen, Michael 1984. **The Other: Studies in Social Ontology of Husserl, Heidegger, Sartre and Buber**. Cambridge, MA: MIT Press. A translation, with introductory essay, by Christopher Macann, of **Der Andere: Studien zur**

michael zilles

Socialontologie der Gegenwart. Berlin: Walter Gruyter and Co. 1972, second edition, 1965, first edition.

Tugendhat, Ernst 1985. "Habermas on Communicative Action." In **Social Action**, edited by Gottfried Seebass and Raim Tuomela. Dordrecht: Reidel.

Warnke, Georgia 1987. **Gadamer: Hermeneutics, Tradition, and Reason**. Stanford, CA: Stanford University Press.

Wellmer, Albrecht 1979. **Praktische Philosophie und Theorie der Gesellschaft: Zum Problem der normativen Grundlagen einer kritischen Sozialwissenschaft**. Konstanz: Universität Konstanz Universitätsverlag.

Wellmer, Albrecht 1986. **Ethik und Dialog**. Frankfurt: Suhrkamp.

White, Stephen K. 1988. **The Recent Work of Jürgen Habermas. Reason, Justice and Modernity**. Cambridge: Cambridge University Press.

Wimmer, R. 1980. **Universalisierung in der Ethik**. Frankfurt: Suhrkamp.

Zimmermann, Rolf 1984. "Emancipation and Rationality." **Ratio** 26:143-165.

Zimmermann, Rolf 1985. **Utopie - Rationalität - Politik. Zu Kritik, Rekonstruktion und Systematik einer emanzipatorischen Gesellschaftstheorie bei Marx und Habermas,** part 2. Freiburg-Munich: Karl Alber.

3. Feminist Studies

(See also: Section 1: Barber [1988], Nussbaum [1989], Thalberg; Section 2: Benhabib [1987,1988]; Section 4: Nussbaum [1986, 1985]; Section 6: Baier, Diamond, Pitkin) (and check Mansbridge, section 1, and Shklar, section 1 and 6).

Baier, Annette C. 1987. "Hume, the Women's Moral Theorist." In **Women and Moral Theory,** edited by Eva Feder Kittay and Diana T. Meyers. Totowa, NJ: Rowman and Littlefield.

Benhabib Seyla, and Cornell, Drucilla 1987 (editors). **Feminism as Critique: On the Politics of Gender**. Minneapolis: University of Minnesota Press.

bibliography   Blum, Lawrence 1982. "Kant's and Hegel's Moral Rationalism: A
Feminist Perspective." **Canadian Journal of Philosophy**
12:296-97.

Blum, Lawrence 1988. "Gilligan and Kohlberg: Implications for
Moral Theory." **Ethics** 98:472-491.

Clark, Lorenne M. G., and Lange, Lynda 1979. **The Sexism of
Social and Political Thought**. Toronto: University of Toronto
Press.

Dietz, Mary 1985. "Citizenship with a Feminist Face: The Problem
with Maternal Thinking." **Political Theory** 13:19-37.

Eisenstein, Zillah 1981. **The Radical Future of Liberal
Feminism**. New York: Longman.

Elshtain, Jean Bethke 1981. **Public Man, Private Woman:
Women in Social and Political Thought**. Princeton, NJ:
Princeton University Press.

Feder Kittay, Eva, and Meyers, Diana T. 1987 (editors). **Women
and Moral Theory**. Totowa, NJ: Rowman & Littlefield.

Flanagan, Owen, and Jackson, Kathryn 1987. "Justice, Care and
Gender: The Kohlberg-Gilligan Debate Revisited." **Ethics**
97:622-637.

Fraser, Nancy 1985. "What's Critical about Critical Theory? The
Case of Habermas and Gender." **New German Critique** 35:97-
131.

Fraser, Nancy 1987. "Women, Welfare, and the Politics of Need
Interpretation." **Hypatia: A Journal of Feminist Philosophy**
2:103-121.

Fraser, Nancy 1989a. "Talking About Needs: Interpretive
Contests as Political Conflicts in Welfare-State Societies." From
a "Symposium on Feminism and Political Theory," including
contributions by Cass R. Sunstein, Iris Marion Young, Marilyn
Friedman, Susan Moller Okin, and others. **Ethics** 99:291-314.

Fraser, Nancy 1989b. **Unruly Practices: Power, Discourse and
Gender in Late-Capitalist Social Theory**. Minneapolis:
University of Minnesota Press. (In Press.)

Friedman, Marilyn 1989. "Autonomy in Social Context." In
Freedom, Equality and Social Change: Problems in Social

michael zilles

Philosophy Today, edited by James Sterba and Creighton Peden. Lewiston, NY: Edwin Mellen Press. (In Press.)

Friedman, Marilyn 1989. "Feminism and Modern Friendship: Dislocating the Community." From a "Symposium on Feminism and Political Theory," including contributions by Cass R. Sunstein, Iris Marion Young, Susan Moller Okin, Nancy Fraser, and others. **Ethics** 99:275-290.

Gilligan, Carol 1982. **In a Different Voice**. Cambridge, MA: Harvard University Press.

Grimshaw, Jean 1986. **Philosophy and Feminist Thinking**. Minneapolis: University of Minnesota Press.

Hartstock, Nancy C.M. 1983. **Money, Sex, and Power**. Boston: Northeastern University Press.

Held, Virginia 1987. "Non-Contractual Society." In **Science, Morality and Feminist Theory**, edited by Marsha Hanen and Kai Nielsen, **Canadian Journal of Philosophy** 13, suppl.:111-38.

Jagger, Allison 1984. **Feminist Politics and Human Nature**. Totawa, NJ: Rowman and Allenheld.

Kearns, Deborah 1983. "A Theory of Justice — and Love; Rawls on the Family." **Politics** 18:36-42.

Minow, Martha 1987. "Interpreting Rights: An Essay for Robert Cover." **Yale Law Journal** 96:1860-1915.

Moller Okin, Susan 1979. **Women in Western Political Thought**. Princeton, NJ: Princeton University Press.

Moller Okin, Susan 1982. "Women and the Making of the Sentimental Family." **Philosophy and Public Affairs** 11:65-88.

Moller Okin, Susan 1987. "Justice and Gender." **Philosophy and Public Affairs** 16:41-72.

Moller Okin, Susan 1989a. "Reason and Feeling in Thinking About Justice." From a "Symposium on Feminism and Political Theory," including contributions by Cass R. Sunstein, Iris Marion Young, Marilyn Friedman, Nancy Fraser, and others. **Ethics** 99:229-249.

Moller Okin, Susan 1989b. "Thinking Like a Woman." In **Theoretical Perspectives on Sexual Difference**, edited by Deborah Rhode. New Haven: Yale University Press.

bibliography

Nicholson, Linda 1986. **Gender and History: The Limits of Social Theory in the Age of the Family**. New York: Columbia University Press.

Noddings, Nel 1984. **Caring: A Feminist Approach to Ethics and Moral Education**. Berkeley and Los Angeles: University of California Press.

Nunner-Winkler, Gertrud 1984. "Two Moralities? A Critical Discussion of an Ethic of Care and Responsibility verus an Ethic of Rights and Justice." In **Morality, Moral Behavior, and Moral Development**, edited by W. Kurtines and J. Gewirtz. New York: Wiley.

O'Brien, Mary 1981. **The Politics of Reproduction**. London: Routledge and Kegan Paul.

Pateman, Carole 1970. **Participation and Democratic Theory**. Cambridge: Cambridge University Press.

Pateman, Carole 1979. **The Problem of Political Obligation: A Critical Analysis of Liberal Theory**. New York: Wiley.

Pateman, Carole 1980. "'The Disorder of Women'; Women, Love and the Sense of Justice." **Ethics** 81:20-34.

Pateman, Carole, and Brennan, Theresa 1979. "'Mere Auxiliaries to the Commonwealth': Women and the Origins of Liberalism." **Political Studies** 27:183-200.

Pateman, Carole and Gross, Elizabeth 1987 (editors). **Feminist Challenges: Social and Political Theory**. Boston: Northeastern University Press.

Pateman, Carole 1988. **The Social Contract**. Stanford, CA: Stanford University Press.

Pitkin, Hannah Fenichel 1984. **Fortune is a Woman**. Berkeley: University of California Press.

Rhode, Deborah 1989 (editor). **Theoretical Perspectives on Sexual Difference**. New Haven: Yale University Press.

Riley, E.M.D. 1989. **"Am I that Name?" Feminism and the Category of 'Women' in History**. London: Macmillan. (In press.)

Schneider, Elizabeth M. 1986. "The Dialectic of Rights and Politics: Perspectives from the Women's Movement." **New York University Law Review** 61:589-652.

michael zilles

Stiehm, Judith 1984 (editor). **Women's Views of the Political World of Men**. Dobbs Ferry, NY: Transnational Publishers.

Sunstein, Cass 1989. "Introduction [to Symposium]: Notes on Feminist Political Thought." From a "Symposium on Feminism and Political Theory," including contributions by Susan Moller Okin, Iris Marion Young, Marilyn Friedman, Nancy Fraser, and others. **Ethics** 99:219-228.

Tronto, Joan 1987. " 'Women's Morality': Beyond Gender Difference to a Theory of Care." **Signs: Journal of Women in Culture and Society**. 12:644-663.

Williams, Patricia J. 1987. "Alchemical Notes: Reconstructed Ideals from Deconstructed Rights." **Harvard Civil Rights Civil Liberties Law Review**. 22:401-433.

Young, Iris Marion 1981. "Toward a Critical Theory of Justice." **Social Theory and Practice** 7:279-301.

Young, Iris Marion 1986. "The Ideal of Community and the Politics of Difference." **Social Theory and Practice** 12:1-26

Young, Iris Marion 1987. "Impartiality and the Civic Public: Some Implications of Feminist Critiques of Moral and Political Theory." In **Feminism as Critique**, edited by Seyla Benhabib and Drucilla Cornell. Minneapolis: University of Minnesota Press.

Young, Iris Marion 1989a. "Five Faces of Oppression." **Philosophical Forum**. (In Press).

Young, Iris Marion 1989b. "Polity and Group Difference: A Critique of the Ideal of Universal Citizenship." From a "Symposium on Feminism and Political Theory," including contributions by Cass R. Sunstein, Susan Moller Okin, Marilyn Friedman, Nancy Fraser, and others. **Ethics** 99:250-274.

Young, Iris Marion 1989c. **Stretching Out: Essays in Feminist Social Theory and Female Body Experience**. Indianapolis: Indiana University Press. (In Press.)

4. Historical Studies

(See also: Section 1: Arendt , Barber [1988], Bell, Bellah, Buchanan, Isaac , Laski, MacIntyre [1982, 1988], Nussbaum, Rasmussen, Rosenblum [1987], C. Taylor, Walzer, Wolin; Section 2: Apel [1983], Benhabib [1982, 1984, 1986], Gadamer

bibliography

1975, Habermas, Henrich, Riedel, Ritter, Schmidt, Theunissen; Section 3: Baier, Blum [1982], Clark, Elshtain, Jagger, Moller Okin [1979], Nicholson, Pateman [1979, 1988], Pitkin, Riley, Stiehm; Section 5: Unger; Section 6: Cavell, Heller, Pitkin.)

Bellamy, Richard 1987. "Hegel and Liberalism." **History of European Ideas** 8:693-708.

Cole, G. D. H. 1980. **Guild Socialism Restated**. New Brunswick: Transaction Books.

Cranston, Maurice W. and Peters, R. S., (editors) 1972. **Hobbes and Rousseau**. New York: Anchor Books.

Hill, Christopher 1969. **Puritanism and Revolution**. London: Panther Edition.

Hill, Christopher 1972. **The World Turned Upside Down**. Harmondsworth: Penguin Books.

Karka, Gregory S. 1986. **Hobbesian Moral and Political Theory**. Princeton: Princeton University Press.

MacPherson, C.B. 1962. **The Political Theory of Possessive Individualism**. Oxford: Oxford University Press.

MacPherson, C.B., **The Life and Times of Liberal Democracy**. Oxford: Oxford University Press.

Madigan, Arthur 1983. "Plato, Aristotle and Professor MacIntyre." **Ancient Philosophy** 3:171-183.

Miller, James 1984. **Rousseau: Dreamer of Democracy**. New Haven: Yale University Press.

Nussbaum, Martha 1985. "The Discernment of Perception: An Aristotelian Conception of Private and Public Rationality." **Proceedings of the Boston Area Colloquium in Ancient Philosophy** 1:151-201.

Nussbaum, Martha 1986. **The Fragility of Goodness: Luck and Ethics in Greek Tragedy**. Cambridge: Cambridge University Press.

Oakeshott, Michael 1933, 1978. **Experience and its Modes**. New York: Cambridge University Press.

Oakeshott, Michael Joseph 1939. **The Social and Political**

Doctrines of Contemporary Europe. Cambridge: Cambridge University Press.

Oakeshott, Michael Joseph 1962. **Rationalism and Politics, and Other Essays.** New York: Basic Books.

Oakeshott, Michael Joseph 1975. **Hobbes on Civil Association.** Berkeley: University of California Press.

Oakeshott, Michael Joseph 1983. **On History and Other Essays.** Totawa, NJ: Barnes and Noble.

Pinkard, Terry 1988. **Hegel's Dialectic. The Explanation of Possibility.** Philadelphia: Temple University Press.

Riley, Patrick 1982. **Will and Political Legitimacy: A Critical Exposition of Social Contract Theory in Hobbes, Locke, Rousseau, Kant and Hegel.** Cambridge: Harvard University Press.

Samples, John 1987. "Kant, Toennies, and the Liberal Idea of Community in Early German Sociology." **History of Political Thought** 8:245-262.

Skinner, Quentin 1965. "History and Ideology in the English Revolution." **The Historical Journal** 8:151-178.

Skinner, Quentin 1966. "The Ideological Context of Hobbes's Political Thought." **The Historical Journal** 9:286-317.

Smith, Steven B. 1989. **Hegel's Critique of Liberalism.** Chicago: University of Chicago Press.

Watkins, J.W.N. 1965. **Hobbes's System of Ideas.** London: Hutchinson.

Zagorin, Perez. 1954. **A History of Political Thought in the English Revolution.** London: Routledge and Kegan Paul.

5. Law

(See also: Section 1: Feinberg, Laski; Section 2: Habermas 1987a, Reidel [1970b, 1975a, 1984], Ritter, Schmitt [1985]; Section 3: Minow, Schneider, P. Williams.)

Auerbach, Jerold 1983. **Justice Without Law.** New York: Oxford University Press.

bibliography

Cornell, Drucilla 1985. "Toward a Modern/Postmodern Reconstruction of Ethics." **University of Pennsylvania Law Review** 133:291-380.

Cornell, Drucilla 1987a. "Beyond Tragedy and Complacency." **Northwestern University Law Review** 81:693-717.

Cornell, Drucilla 1987b. "The Poststructuralist Challenge to the Ideal of Community." **Cardoza Law Review** 8:989-1022.

Cornell, Drucilla 1987c. "Two Lectures on the Normative Dimensions of Community in the Law." **Tennessee Law Review** 54:327-343.

Dworkin, Ronald 1981a. **Taking Rights Seriously**. London: Duckworth.

Dworkin, Ronald 1981b. "What is Equality? Part 1: Equality of Welfare," and "Part 2: Equality of Resources." **Philosophy and Public Affairs** 10:185-246, 283-345.

Dworkin, Ronald 1983. "In Defense of Equality." **Social Philosophy and Policy** 1:24-40.

Dworkin, Ronald 1985. **A Matter of Principle**. Cambridge: Harvard University Press.

Dworkin, Ronald 1986. **Law's Empire**. Cambridge: Harvard University Press.

Green, Leslie and Hutchinson, Alan (editors). 1989. **Law and Community**. Toronto: Carswell, in press.

Hirsch, H.N. 1986. "The Threnody of Liberalism." **Political Theory** 14:423-449.

Luhmann, Niklas 1985. **The Sociological Theory of Law**. London: Routledge and Kegan Paul. A translation, by Elizabeth King and Martin Abrow, of **Rechtssoziologe**. Reinbek: Rowohlt 1972.

Macedo, Stephen 1988. "The New Right and Constitutional Self-Government in America." **Praxis International** 8:171-182.

O'Hagan, Timothy 1988. "Four Images of Community." **Praxis International** 8:183-192.

293 Postema, G. 1987. "Collective Evils, Harms, and the Law," review

of **The Moral Limits of the Criminal Law**, Vols. 1 and 2 by J. Feinberg, **Ethics** 999:418-423.

Pusíc, Eugen 1988. "Law as Exclusion and Under Inclusion." **Praxis International** 8:207-221.

Rasmussen, David 1988. "Communication Theory and the Critique of the Law: Habermas and Unger on the Law." **Praxis International** 8:155-170.

Raz, Joseph 1975. **Practical Reason and Norms**. London: Hutchinson.

Raz, Joseph 1978. **Practical Reasoning**. New York: Oxford University Press.

Raz, Joseph 1979. **The Authority of Law: Essays on Law and Morality**. New York: Oxford University Press.

Raz, Joseph 1986. **The Morality of Freedom**. Oxford: Oxford University Press.

Raz, Joseph, and Hacker, P.M.S 1977 (editors). **Law, Morality and Society: Essays in Honor of H.L.A. Hart**. Oxford: Clarendon Press.

Selznick, Philip. 1987. "The Idea of Communitarian Morality," **California Law Review** 75:445-63.

Shklar, Judith 1964. **Legalism**. Cambridge, MA: Harvard University Press.

Tribe, Laurence 1973. "Foreword: Toward a Model of Roles in the Due Process of Life and Law." **Harvard Law Review** 87:1-53.

Tribe, Laurence 1975. "Structural Due Process." **Harvard Civil Rights - Civil Liberties Law Review** 10:269-321.

Tribe, Laurence 1978. **American Constitutional Law**. Mineola: Foundation Press.

Unger, Roberto M. 1975. **Knowledge and Politics**. New York: Free Press.

Unger, Roberto 1976. **Law and Modern Society**. New York: Free Press.

Unger, Roberto M. 1984. **Passion. An Essay on Personality**. New York: Free Press.

bibliography

Unger, Roberto M. 1988. **Politics: A Work in Constructive Social Theory**. 3 Volumes. Cambridge: Cambridge University Press.

6. Language, Mind and Method

(See also: Section 1: Arendt [1958, 1978, 1982], Barber [1988], Beiner [1983], Eldridge, Gregory, MacIntyre [1981, 1988], Nagel [1986], Rawls [1955, 1980, 1985], Sandel [1982, 1984], C. Taylor [1985], Thalberg, Walzer [1987], Williams; Section 2: Apel, Baxter, Benhabib [1982, 1986, 1987, 1988], Ferraro, Gadamer, Habermas, Held, Honneth, Lyotard, McCarthy, Tugendhat, Warnke, Wellmer, White, Wimmer, Zimmermann; Section 3: Kittay, Fraser, Gilligan, Pitkin; Section 4: Nussbaum; Section 5: Dworkin [1986], Luhmann, Rasmussen, Unger.)

Baier, Annette 1984. **Postures of the Mind: Essays on Mind and Morals**. Minneapolis: University of Minnesota Press.

Baier, Annette C.1986. "Trust and Antitrust." **Ethics** 96:231-60.

Cavell, Stanley 1969. **Must We Mean What We Say?** Cambridge: Cambridge University Press.

Cavell, Stanley 1979. **The Claim of Reason**. Oxford: Oxford University Press.

Cavell, Stanley 1989a. **In Quest of the Ordinary: Themes in Skepticism and Romanticism**. Chicago; University of Chicago Press.

Cavell, Stanley 1989b. **This New Yet Unapproachable America:** Chicago: University of Chicago Press.

Daniels, Norman 1979a. "Moral Theory and the Plasticity of Persons." **The Monist** 62:265-287.

Daniels, Norman 1979b. "Wide Reflective Equilibrium and Theory Acceptance in Ethics." **Journal of Philosophy** 76:256-282.

Daniels, Norman 1980. "Reflective Equilibrium and Archimedean Points." **Canadian Journal of Philosophy** 10:83-103.

Davidson, Donald 1984. "On the Very Notion of a Conceptual Scheme." In his **Inquiries into Truth and Interpretation**. Oxford: Clarendon Press.

michael zilles

Diamond, Cora 1988. "Losing Your Concepts." **Ethics** 98:255-277.

Eldridge, Richard 1983. "Philosophy and the Achievement of Community: Rorty, Cavell, and Criticism." **Metaphilosophy** 14:107-125.

Eldridge, Richard 1986a. "Self-Understanding and Community in Wordsworth's Poetry." **Philosophy and Literature** 10:273-294.

Eldridge, Richard 1986b. "The Normal and the Normative: Wittgenstein's Legacy, Kripke and Cavell." **Philosophy and Phenomenological Research** 46:555-575.

Green, Leslie and Hutchinson, Alan (editors) 1989. **Law and Community**. Toronto: Carswell (in press).

Hanson, Karen 1986. **The Self Imagined. Philosophical Reflections on the Social Character of Psyche.** London: Routledge and Kegan Paul.

Heller, Thomas C; Sosna, Morton; and Wellberg, David E. 1986 (editors). **Reconstructing Individualism: Autonomy, Individuality, and the Self in Western Thought.** Stanford: Stanford University Press.

Montefiore, Alan 1973 (editor). **Philosophy and Personal Relations.** London: Routledge and Kegan Paul.

Nozick, Robert 1981. **Philosophical Explanations.** Cambridge, MA: Harvard University Press.

Nussbaum, Martha 1989. **Love's Knowledge: Essays on Philosophy and Literature.** Oxford: Oxford University Press. (In Press.)

Parfit, Derek 1984. **Reasons and Persons.** Oxford: Clarendon Press.

Perry, John 1975 (editor). **Personal Identity.** Berkeley: University of California Press.

Pitkin, Hanna Fenichel 1972. **Wittgenstein and Justice.** Berkeley: University of Caifornia Press.

Pitkin, Hannah Fenichel 1981. "Justice: On Relating Public and Private." **Political Theory** 9:327-352.

bibliography

Pitkin, Hannah Fenichel 1989. "Are Freedom and Liberty Twins?" **Political Theory** 16:523-552.

Rorty, Amélie Oksenberg 1976 (editor). **Identities of Persons**. Berkeley: University of California Press.

Rorty, Richard 1979. **Philosophy and the Mirror of Nature**. Princeton: Princeton University Press.

Rorty, Richard 1982. **Consequences of Pragmatism**. Minneapolis: University of Minnesota Press.

Rorty, Richard 1985. "Solidarity or Objectivity?" In **Post-Analytic Philosophy**, edited by John Rajchman and Cornel West. New York: Columbia University Press.

Rorty, Richard 1986. "Freud and Moral Reflection." In **The Pragmatists' Freud**, edited by Joseph Smith and William Kerrigan. Baltimore: Johns Hopkins University Press.

Rorty, Richard 1986. "From Logic to Languages to Play." **Proceedings and Addresses of the American Philosophical Association** 59:747-53.

Rorty, Richard 1986. "The Contingency of Selfhood." **London Review of Books** #8, May.

Tugendhat, Ernst 1981. "Language et Ethique." **Critique** October.

Tugendhat, Ernst 1984. **Probleme der Ethik**. Stuttgart: Reclam.

Tugendhat, Ernst 1986. **Self-Consciousness and Self-Determination**. A translation, with introductory essay, by Paul Stern, of **Selbstbewusstsein und Selbstbestimmung. Sprachanalystische Interpretationen**. Frankfurt: Suhrkamp 1979.

acknowledgement

The editor wishes to thank Deanne Harper and Tracey Stark, whose work on this volume was indispensable.